HOUSING ISSUES, LAWS AND PROGRAMS

REVERSE MORTGAGES

ELEMENTS, CONSIDERATIONS AND MARKET DEVELOPMENTS

HOUSING ISSUES, LAWS AND PROGRAMS

Additional books in this series can be found on Nova's website under the Series tab.

Additional e-books in this series can be found on Nova's website under the e-books tab.

ECONOMIC ISSUES, PROBLEMS AND PERSPECTIVES

Additional books in this series can be found on Nova's website under the Series tab.

Additional e-books in this series can be found on Nova's website under the e-books tab.

HOUSING ISSUES, LAWS AND PROGRAMS

REVERSE MORTGAGES

ELEMENTS, CONSIDERATIONS AND MARKET DEVELOPMENTS

MEGHAN GALLOWAY
AND
RICHARD KANTOR
EDITORS

nova publishers
New York

For permission to use material from this book please contact us:
Telephone 631-231-7269; Fax 631-231-8175
Web Site: http://www.novapublishers.com

Library of Congress Cataloging-in-Publication Data

ISBN: 978-1-62257-965-5

Published by Nova Science Publishers, Inc. † New York

CONTENTS

PREFACE

A reverse mortgage is a special type of home loan for older homeowners that requires no monthly mortgage payments. Borrowers are still responsible for property taxes and homeowner's insurance. Reverse mortgages allow seniors to access the equity they have built up in their homes now, and defer payments of the loan until they die, sell, or move out of the home. The original purpose envisioned for reverse mortgages was to convert home equity into cash that borrowers could use to help meet expenses in retirement. Borrowers could choose between an income stream for everyday expenses, a line of credit for major expenses (such as home repairs and medical expenses), or a combination of the two. This book examines the changes that have taken place in the marketplace and in the consumers who use reverse mortgages, with a focus on consumer protection concerns.

Chapter 1 – A reverse mortgage is a special type of home loan for older homeowners that requires no monthly mortgage payments. Borrowers are still responsible for property taxes and homeowner’s insurance. Reverse mortgages allow seniors to access the equity they have built up in their homes *now*, and defer payment of the loan until they die, sell, or move out of the home. Because there are no required mortgage payments on a reverse mortgage, the interest is added to the loan balance each month. The rising loan balance can eventually grow to exceed the value of the home, particularly in times of declining home values or if the borrower continues to live in the home for many years. However, the borrower (or the borrower’s estate) is generally not required to repay any additional loan balance in excess of the value of the home. For most Americans, their home is the single largest asset they own. In 2009, half of homeowners age 62 and older had at least 55 percent of their net worth tied up in home equity. Home equity is accumulated over a lifetime of mortgage payments and house-price appreciation, but generally cannot be accessed without selling the home or taking out a loan. Reverse mortgages enable older homeowners to use that home equity to enjoy a more comfortable retirement *without* selling their home. Reverse mortgages are not the only option for accessing home equity without selling the home, however. Traditional home equity loans and home equity lines of credit (HELOCs) are possibilities. Reverse mortgages offer a different set of benefits, costs, and risks to the borrower than home equity loans or HELOCs. Reverse mortgages generally are easier to qualify for than home equity loans or HELOCs, which require adequate income and credit scores. Reverse mortgages do not require monthly mortgage payments and offer several important financial protections, but they have higher costs. Home equity loans and HELOCs have required monthly payments and offer fewer financial protections for the borrower, but they have lower costs.

Chapter 2 – Since the 1970s, parties have sought to create mortgage instruments that would enable elderly homeowners to obtain loans to convert their equity into income, while providing that no repayments would be due for a specified period or, ideally, for the lifetime of the borrower. These instruments have been referred to as reverse mortgages, reverse annuity mortgages, and home equity conversion loans. Reverse mortgages are the opposite of traditional mortgages in the sense that the borrower receives payments from the lender instead of making such payments to the lender. Reverse mortgages are designed to enable elderly homeowners to remain in their homes while using the equity in their homes as a form of income. In general, reverse mortgages may take one of two forms: term or tenure. Under a term reverse mortgage, the borrower is provided with income for a specified period. Under a tenure reverse mortgage, the borrower is provided with income for as long as he or she continues to occupy the property. For borrowers, the most risky reverse mortgage is the term reverse mortgage. Borrowers have been reluctant to enter such mortgages because at the end of the loan term the borrower would likely have to sell the home and move. For lenders, the most risky reverse mortgage is the tenure reverse mortgage. Lenders have been reluctant to originate such mortgages because the borrower is guaranteed lifetime income and lifetime occupancy of the home. This is risky because the mortgage debt grows over time, and the debt could exceed the value of the home if the borrower lives longer than his or her life expectancy. The use of tenure reverse mortgages has grown in recent years due to the availability of an Federal Housing Administration (FHA)-insured reverse mortgage. Under the FHA program, the risk of the borrower living too long is shifted to the federal government. Under prior law, FHA-insured reverse mortgages were subject to the FHA mortgage limit for the area in which a property is located. The Housing and Economic Recovery Act of 2008, P.L. 110-289, established a mortgage limit equal to the conforming loan limit for the Federal Home Loan Mortgage Corporation (Freddie Mac). Present law limits the aggregate number of FHA-insured reverse mortgages to 275,000 loans, and that limit has been exceeded. Notwithstanding the limit in present law, the Consolidated Appropriations Act, 2010, P.L. 111-117, provided that FHA may continue to insure HECMs through September 30, 2010.

In: Reverse Mortgages
Editors: Meghan Galloway and Richard Kantor
ISBN: 978-1-62257-965-5

Chapter 1

REVERSE MORTGAGES: REPORT TO CONGRESS*

Consumer Financial Protection Bureau

EXECUTIVE SUMMARY

A reverse mortgage is a special type of home loan for older homeowners that requires no monthly mortgage payments. Borrowers are still responsible for property taxes and homeowner's insurance. Reverse mortgages allow seniors to access the equity they have built up in their homes *now*, and defer payment of the loan until they die, sell, or move out of the home. Because there are no required mortgage payments on a reverse mortgage, the interest is added to the loan balance each month. The rising loan balance can eventually grow to exceed the value of the home, particularly in times of declining home values or if the borrower continues to live in the home for many years. However, the borrower (or the borrower's estate) is generally not required to repay any additional loan balance in excess of the value of the home.

For most Americans, their home is the single largest asset they own. In 2009, half of homeowners age 62 and older had at least 55 percent of their net worth tied up in home equity.[1] Home equity is accumulated over a lifetime of mortgage payments and house-price appreciation, but generally cannot be accessed without selling the home or taking out a loan. Reverse mortgages enable older homeowners to use that home equity to enjoy a more comfortable retirement *without* selling their home.

Reverse mortgages are not the only option for accessing home equity without selling the home, however. Traditional home equity loans and home equity lines of credit (HELOCs) are possibilities. Reverse mortgages offer a different set of benefits, costs, and risks to the borrower than home equity loans or HELOCs. Reverse mortgages generally are easier to qualify for than home equity loans or HELOCs, which require adequate income and credit scores. Reverse mortgages do not require monthly mortgage payments and offer several important financial protections, but they have higher costs. Home equity loans and HELOCs

---

* This is an edited, reformatted and augmented version of the Consumer Financial Protection Bureau, dated June 28, 2012.

have required monthly payments and offer fewer financial protections for the borrower, but they have lower costs.

Today, the market for reverse mortgages is very small. Only about 2 percent to 3 percent of eligible homeowners currently have a reverse mortgage, and only about 70,000 new reverse mortgages are originated each year.[2] But reverse mortgages have the potential to become a much more prominent part of the financial landscape in the coming decades. In 2008, the first baby boomers became eligible for reverse mortgages. The baby boom generation (48- to 66-year-olds in 2012) includes more than 43 million households, of which about 32 million are homeowners.[3] As of 2009, the median home equity for baby boomer households was $108,000.[4]

Nearly all reverse mortgages today are insured by the Federal Housing Administration (FHA)[a] through its Home Equity Conversion Mortgage (HECM) program. The insurance guarantees that borrowers will be able to access their authorized loan funds in the future, subject to the terms of the loan, even if the loan balance exceeds the value of the home or if the lender experiences financial difficulty. Lenders are guaranteed that they will be repaid in full when the home is sold, regardless of the loan balance or home value at repayment. Borrowers or their estates are not liable for loan balances that exceed the value of the home at repayment – FHA insurance covers this risk.

The original purpose envisioned for reverse mortgages was to convert home equity into cash that borrowers could use to help meet expenses in retirement. Borrowers could choose between an income stream for everyday expenses, a line of credit for major expenses (such as home repairs and medical expenses), or a combination of the two. It was anticipated that most, though not all, borrowers would use their loans to age in place, living in their current homes for the rest of their lives or at least until they needed skilled care. Upon the borrower's death, or upon leaving the home, the borrower or the estate would sell the home to repay the loan and would receive any remaining home equity.

Yet most of today's reverse mortgage borrowers do not use their loans to convert home equity into an income stream or a line of credit. Borrowers also do not typically live in their current homes until the end of their lives. Borrowers today are increasingly taking the full amount for which they qualify upfront as a lump sum. In many cases, borrowers are using that money to refinance an existing mortgage or other debt early in their retirement or even before reaching retirement. By refinancing with a reverse mortgage, these borrowers eliminate their monthly mortgage or debt payments, but the interest on the loan will chip away at their remaining home equity over time. In other cases, borrowers may be saving or investing the lump-sum proceeds, and may be earning less than they are paying in interest.

The range of products offered, the structure of the reverse mortgage market, and the consumers who use reverse mortgages have all changed dramatically in recent years. In the past, government investigations and consumer advocacy groups raised significant consumer protection concerns about the business practices of reverse mortgage lenders and other companies in the reverse mortgage industry. The new products in the market and the new ways that consumers are using reverse mortgages today add to the risks facing consumers.

It is within this context that Congress directed the Consumer Financial Protection Bureau (CFPB) to conduct a study on reverse mortgages as part of the Dodd-Frank Wall Street Reform and Consumer Protection Act.[5] In designing the study, the CFPB's objectives were to

---

[a] The FHA is a part of the U.S. Department of Housing and Urban Development (HUD).

(1) provide an authoritative resource on reverse mortgage products, consumers, and markets; (2) identify and assess consumer protection concerns; and (3) explore critical unanswered questions and update the public body of knowledge to reflect new market realities. This report presents the findings from that study.

This report examines the changes that have taken place in the marketplace and in the consumers who use reverse mortgages. The report places these changes within the broader context of the factors affecting consumer decision-making in a market poised to grow in reach and impact.

This report also examines consumer protection concerns that have been raised in the past and identifies emerging concerns.

E.1. Key Findings

1. **Reverse mortgages are complex products and difficult for consumers to understand.**
   - Lessons learned from the traditional mortgage market do not always serve consumers well in the reverse mortgage market. The rising balance, falling equity nature of reverse mortgages is particularly difficult for consumers to grasp.
   - Recent innovation and policy changes have created more choices for consumers, including options with lower upfront costs. However, these changes have also increased the complexity of the choices and tradeoffs consumers have to make.
   - The tools – including federally required disclosures – available to consumers to help them understand prices and risks are insufficient to ensure that consumers are making good tradeoffs and decisions.
2. **Reverse mortgage borrowers are using the loans in different ways than in the past, which increase risks to consumers.**
   - Reverse mortgage borrowers are taking out loans at younger ages than in the past. In FY2011, nearly half of borrowers were under age 70. Taking out a reverse mortgage early in retirement, or even before reaching retirement, increases risks to consumers. By tapping their home equity early, these borrowers may find themselves without the financial resources to finance a future move – whether due to health or other reasons.
   - Reverse mortgage borrowers are withdrawing more of their money upfront than in the past. In FY2011, 73 percent of borrowers took all or almost all of their available funds upfront at closing. This proportion has increased by 30 percentage points since 2008. Borrowers who withdraw all of their available home equity upfront will have fewer resources to draw upon to pay for everyday and major expenses later in life. Borrowers who take all of their money upfront are also at greater risk of becoming delinquent on taxes and/or insurance and ultimately losing their homes to foreclosure.
   - Fixed-rate, lump-sum loans now account for about 70 percent of the market. The availability of this product may encourage some borrowers to take out all of their funds upfront even though they do not have an immediate need for the funds. In

addition to having fewer resources to draw upon later in life, these borrowers face other increased risks. Borrowers who save or invest the proceeds may be earning less on the savings than they are paying in interest on the loan, or they may be exposing their savings to risky investment choices. These borrowers also face increased risks of being targeted for fraud or other scams.

- Reverse mortgage borrowers appear to be increasingly using their loans as a method of refinancing traditional mortgages rather than as a way to pay for everyday or major expenses. Some borrowers may simply be prolonging an unsustainable financial situation.

3. **Product features, market dynamics, and industry practices also create risks for consumers.**
   - A surprisingly large proportion of reverse mortgage borrowers (9.4 percent as of February 2012) are at risk of foreclosure due to nonpayment of taxes and insurance. This proportion is continuing to increase.
   - Misleading advertising remains a problem in the industry and increases risks to consumers. This advertising contributes to consumer misperceptions about reverse mortgages, increasing the likelihood of poor consumer decision-making.
   - Spouses of reverse mortgage borrowers who are not themselves named as co-borrowers are often unaware that they are at risk of losing their homes. If the borrowing spouse dies or needs to move, the non-borrowing spouse must sell the home or otherwise pay off the reverse mortgage at that time. Other family members (children, grandchildren, etc.) who live with reverse mortgage borrowers are also at risk of needing to find other living arrangements when the borrower dies or needs to move.
   - The reverse mortgage market is increasingly dominated by small originators, most of which are not depository institutions. The changing economic and regulatory landscape faced by these small originators creates new risks for consumers.
4. **Counseling, while designed to help consumers understand the risks associated with reverse mortgages, needs improvement in order to be able to meet these challenges.**
   - Reverse mortgages are inherently complicated, and the new array of product choices makes the counselor's job much more difficult. Counselors need improved methods to help consumers better understand the complex tradeoffs they face in deciding whether to get a reverse mortgage.
   - Funding for housing counseling is under pressure, making access to high-quality counseling more difficult. Some counselors may frequently omit some of the required information or speed through the material.
   - Some counseling agencies only receive payment if and when the reverse mortgage is closed (the counseling fee is paid with loan proceeds), which could undermine counselors' impartiality.
   - Some borrowers may not take the counseling sessions seriously. Additional consumer awareness and education may be necessary.
   - Counseling may be insufficient to counter the effects of misleading advertising, aggressive sales tactics, or questionable business practices. Stronger regulation,

supervision of reverse mortgage companies, and enforcement of existing laws may also be necessary.

5. **Some risks to consumers appear to have been adequately addressed by regulation, but remain a matter for supervision and enforcement, while other risks still require regulatory attention.**
   - Cross-selling,[b] previously a top consumer protection concern, appears to have been considerably dampened as a result of federal legislation, though some risks remain. Strong supervision and enforcement is necessary to ensure that industry participants abide by existing laws.
   - The risk of fraud and other scams is heightened for this population. Vigorous enforcement is necessary to ensure that older homeowners are not defrauded of a lifetime of home equity.
   - Special disclosures are required for reverse mortgages, but existing disclosures are quite difficult for consumers to understand.
   - There are general prohibitions against deceptive advertising, but there are no specific federal rules governing deceptive advertising with respect to reverse mortgages.

E.2. The CFPB'S Role

Under the Dodd-Frank Act, rulemaking and interpretive authority for consumer protection laws and regulations that apply to mortgages transferred to the CFPB on July 21, 2011.[6] The Dodd-Frank Act authorizes the CFPB to issue regulations it determines, as a result of this reverse mortgage study, are necessary or appropriate to accomplish the purposes of the Act. These regulations may include providing integrated disclosures and identifying practices as unfair, deceptive, or abusive.[7] The CFPB also has authority to supervise nonbank reverse mortgage companies and larger depository institutions and credit unions for compliance with federal consumer financial protection laws.

The findings of the study reveal several areas where the CFPB can play a role to protect consumers from risks posed by reverse mortgages and to help consumers make better decisions about reverse mortgages.

1. The CFPB can **issue regulations** under the federal consumer protection laws addressed specifically to protecting consumers considering a reverse mortgage.
   - The CFPB expects to undertake a project to improve and integrate TILA and RESPA disclosure requirements for reverse mortgages so that consumers can know before they owe when considering a reverse mortgage.
   - As part of this project, the CFPB will consider the 2010 proposal by the Board of Governors of the Federal Reserve System regarding reverse mortgages. The proposal would have placed limits on misleading advertising, improved

[b] Cross-selling occurs when a lender or mortgage broker requires or convinces a reverse mortgage borrower to purchase another financial product (e.g., an annuity, insurance policy, or investment product) with the proceeds of the reverse mortgage loan.

disclosures, and closed regulatory gaps related to cross-selling, among other things.[8]
- The CFPB will also consider whether other regulations are necessary and appropriate to protect consumers in the reverse mortgage market.

2. The CFPB can **develop improved approaches** to **engage** consumers considering a reverse mortgage and **empower** them to make better informed decisions.
   - The CFPB will continue to learn from stakeholders and counselors to better understand the primary obstacles to good consumer decision-making about reverse mortgages.
   - The CFPB will explore improved methods and approaches for helping consumers compare products, understand costs and risks, and evaluate tradeoffs.
3. The CFPB can **monitor the market** for unfair, deceptive, or abusive practices and compliance with existing laws.
   - The CFPB will take enforcement and supervisory actions if necessary.
4. The CFPB can **accept complaints** from consumers and work to **resolve** those complaints.
   - The CFPB is currently accepting reverse mortgage complaints through the web at www.consumerfinance.gov, phone at 1-855-411-CFPB, and mail.
   - The CFPB's Consumer Response team works with lenders, servicers, and other related companies to resolve consumer complaints and answer consumer inquiries.
5. The CFPB can **work with the Department of Housing and Urban Development (HUD)**, the parent agency of the FHA, to develop solutions to issues identified in this report over which HUD has influence.
   - The CFPB welcomes the opportunity to strengthen its partnership with HUD and improve outcomes for consumers.

E.3. About This Report

This report is organized into an introductory chapter, five main chapters – Product, Consumers, Market, Regulatory Structure, and Consumer Protection Concerns – and a final summary chapter.

Product. Contains HECM program requirements, key product options, costs and fees, and alternatives to reverse mortgages.

Consumers. Includes consumer motivations for using the product, borrower demographics, and an in-depth exploration of the ways borrower behavior has changed over the past two decades and how borrower behavior differs between different types of borrower.

Market. Discusses market volume, market dynamics, and the relationship between the secondary market and the primary market.

Regulatory Structure. Highlights the major federal and state consumer protection regulations and oversight mechanisms.

Consumer Protection Concerns. Assesses a range of concerns related to consumer protection in the reverse mortgage market.

1. INTRODUCTION

A reverse mortgage is a special type of home equity loan for older homeowners that requires no monthly mortgage payments. Borrowers are still responsible for property taxes and homeowner's insurance. Reverse mortgages allow seniors to access the equity they have built up in their homes *now*, and defer payment of the loan until they die, sell, or move out of the home.[c] These loans are called "reverse" mortgages because in many ways they function "in reverse" as compared to the traditional "forward" mortgages most homeowners use to purchase their homes. With a traditional mortgage, borrowers' home equity increases and the loan balance decreases over time as the borrower makes payments to the lender. With a reverse mortgage, borrowers' home equity *decreases* and the loan balance *increases* over time as borrowers receive cash payments from the lender and interest accrues on the loan.

Because there are no required monthly payments on a reverse mortgage, the interest is added to the loan balance each month. The rising loan balance can eventually grow to exceed the value of the home, particularly in times of declining home values or if the borrower continues to live in the home for many years. However, the borrower (or the borrower's estate) is generally not required to repay any additional loan balance in excess of the value of the home.[9]

For most Americans, their home is the single largest asset they own. In 2009, half of homeowners age 62 and older had more than 55 percent of their net worth tied up in home equity.[10] Home equity is accumulated over a lifetime of mortgage payments and house-price appreciation, but generally cannot be accessed without selling the home or taking out a loan. Reverse mortgages enable older homeowners to use that home equity to enjoy a more comfortable retirement *without* selling their home.

Reverse mortgages are not the only option for accessing home equity without selling the home, however. Traditional home equity loans or home equity lines of credit (HELOCs) are also possibilities. Reverse mortgages offer a different set of benefits, costs, and risks to the borrower than home equity loans or HELOCs. Reverse mortgages are generally easier to qualify for than home equity loans or HELOCs, which require adequate income and credit scores in order to qualify. Reverse mortgages do not require monthly mortgage payments and offer several important financial protections, but they have higher costs. Home equity loans and HELOCs have required monthly payments and offer fewer financial protections for the borrower, but they have lower costs.[11]

---

[c] Reverse mortgage borrowers must also meet certain obligations, such as remaining current on property taxes and insurance, maintaining the home in good repair, and living in the home as their primary residence. Borrowers who fail to meet these obligations can face foreclosure. This risk is discussed in more detail in Section 6.6.

The vast majority of reverse mortgages are insured by the Federal Housing Administration (FHA)[d] as part of its Home Equity Conversion Mortgage (HECM) program.[12] The FHA insurance guarantees that borrowers will be able to access their authorized loan funds in the future (subject to the terms of the loan), even if the loan balance exceeds the value of the home or if the lender experiences financial difficulty. Lenders are guaranteed that they will be repaid in full when the home is sold, regardless of the loan balance or home value at repayment. Borrowers or their estates are not liable for loan balances that exceed the value of the home at repayment – FHA insurance covers this risk.

Today, the market for reverse mortgages is very small. Only about 2 to 3 percent of eligible homeowners choose to take out a reverse mortgage.[13] Only about 582,000 HECM loans are outstanding as of November 2011, as compared to more than 50 million traditional mortgages and more than 17 million home equity loans and lines of credit.[14] But reverse mortgages have the potential to become a much more prominent part of the financial landscape in the coming decades. In 2008, the first baby boomers became eligible for reverse mortgages. The baby boom generation (48- to 66-year-olds in 2012) includes more than 43 million households, of which about 32 million are homeowners.[15] As of 2009, the median home equity for baby boomer households was $108,000.[16] Many boomers may find that they will need to use their home equity in order to maintain the lifestyle they expect to have in retirement.

The range of products offered, the structure of the reverse mortgage market, and the consumers who use reverse mortgages have all changed dramatically in recent years. In the past, government investigations and consumer advocacy groups have raised significant consumer protection concerns about the business practices of reverse mortgage lenders and other companies in the reverse mortgage industry. New products in the market and new ways that consumers are using reverse mortgages today add to the risks facing consumers.

It is within this context that Congress directed the Consumer Financial Protection Bureau (CFPB) to conduct a study on reverse mortgages as part of the Dodd-Frank Wall Street Reform and Consumer Protection Act.[17] In designing the study, the CFPB's objectives were to (1) provide an authoritative resource on reverse mortgage products, consumers, and markets; (2) identify and assess consumer protection concerns; and (3) explore critical unanswered questions and update the public body of knowledge to reflect new market realities. This report presents the findings from that study.

This report examines the changes that have taken place in the marketplace and in the consumers who use reverse mortgages. The report places these changes within the broader context of the factors affecting consumer decision-making in a market poised to grow in reach and impact.

This report also examines consumer protection concerns that have been raised in the past and identifies emerging concerns.

---

[d] The FHA is a part of the U.S. Department of Housing and Urban Development (HUD).

2. PRODUCT

Today, all but a handful of reverse mortgages are insured by the Federal Housing Administration (FHA)[e] as part of its Home Equity Conversion Mortgage (HECM) program. The HECM program started in 1989 as a small pilot program, was made permanent in 1998, and currently insures about 70,000 reverse mortgage loans per year.

Many of the original product design concepts for the HECM program were developed during the 1980s by private companies offering proprietary (non-government insured) reverse mortgages of various types. Throughout the 1990s, when the HECM program was still a small pilot, and again in the mid-2000s, in the midst of the housing boom, a range of proprietary products were available in the marketplace. For most consumers, however, the HECM offered a better value. Today, only one lender offers a proprietary product, which accounts for only a handful of loans per year.

The HECM program determines how much can be borrowed based on the value of the home, prevailing interest rates, and the age of the borrower (or youngest co-borrower). The loans require no monthly mortgage payments. Interest and fees are added to the principal balance each month, resulting in a rising loan balance over time. Borrowers may remain in the home indefinitely, even if the loan balance becomes greater than the value of the home – so long as the borrower meets certain conditions. In return for this protection, and protection against the possibility that their lender fails to make loan disbursements as agreed, borrowers pay a mortgage insurance premium (MIP) to FHA.

HECM borrowers have several options as to the structure of the MIP, the interest rate type (fixed or adjustable), and the way that they receive their loan proceeds. The range of options has increased in recent years, adding to the difficulty of the choices that prospective borrowers have to make around what is already a complex product. Prospective borrowers are required to attend mandatory pre-loan counseling, but the counseling may not be sufficient to fully equip prospective borrowers to make good decisions.

2.1. Reverse Mortgage Product Development

The first reverse mortgage in the U.S. was made in 1961 by a savings and loan company in Portland, Maine.[18] Throughout the next several decades, policymakers and mortgage companies explored ways for older homeowners to access their home equity.[19] In comparison to traditional mortgages that are limited by a number of years, reverse mortgages posed an "uncommon combination of risks" that could be difficult for lenders to assess.[20]

American Homestead took on these risks in 1984 with the first tenure-based reverse mortgage product.[21] Rather than setting a fixed term for the mortgage, American Homestead allowed the loan to stay in place until the borrower stopped occupying the home.[22] This tenure-based product provided the baseline for government-insured reverse mortgages. Senator John Heinz issued a proposal for FHA reverse mortgage insurance in 1983, and Congress ultimately passed a pilot program for HECMs in 1987.[23]

[e] The FHA is a part of the U.S. Department of Housing and Urban Development (HUD).

In 1988, President Ronald Reagan signed the act authorizing the FHA to insure reverse mortgages through the newly created HECM pilot program.[24] During the program's first decade, less than 40,000 HECM loans were made.[25] At the same time, lenders were experimenting with various proprietary, or non-government insured reverse mortgage product offerings. In 1998, the HECM program was authorized permanently and the FHA-insured product quickly came to dominate the market.[26] Throughout the early- to mid-2000s, rising home values and rapid increases in annual HECM production led lenders to again experiment with proprietary products, but volume remained small relative to the FHA's HECM program. At the peak of the real estate boom, perhaps 5 percent to 10 percent of reverse mortgages were proprietary products.[27] Today, only a handful of reverse mortgages are originated outside the HECM program.

Historically, proprietary lenders have struggled to compete with the amount of authorized loan proceeds offered in the HECM program. Proprietary products have typically only appealed to borrowers with high home values and/or borrowers who did not want to pay the high upfront MIP.[28] The proprietary market has all but disappeared today for two reasons: The overall housing market collapse that halted private mortgage securitizations; and recent changes to the HECM program that have made the HECM program more appealing to both consumer segments previously targeted by proprietary products.

Only one lender, Generation Mortgage, currently offers proprietary reverse mortgages. This product, called the Generation Plus loan, is aimed at the jumbo market with a minimum borrower age of 62 and a loan limit of $6 million.[29] The product is only available as a fixed-rate, lump-sum loan and carries an 8.875 percent interest rate and an origination fee of 1.5 percent of the initial principal balance.[30] Only 51 loans totaling about $48 million have been originated since this product was created in July 2010.[31]

Appendix I contains more detailed information about the proprietary products offered before the market collapse and the market dynamics present at that time.

2.2. The HECM Program

FHA insurance provides protections to both the lender and the borrower. Lenders are guaranteed that they will be repaid in full when the home is sold, regardless of the loan balance or home value at repayment. Borrowers are guaranteed that they will be able to access their authorized loan funds in the future (subject to the terms of the loan), even if the loan balance exceeds the value of the home or if the lender experiences financial difficulty. Borrowers or their estates are not liable for loan balances that exceed the value of the home at repayment – FHA insurance covers this risk. Figure 1 details the major features of HECM loans.

2.2.1. Recent Changes to the HECM Program

In 2008, FHA issued guidance clarifying that fixed-rate HECMs could be structured as closed-end loans, which enabled the development of a fixed-rate, lump-sum product.[32] In 2009, Congress increased the loan limit on HECM loans to $625,500.[33] This limit is still in effect today. In 2009 and 2010, FHA made changes to the amount of loan proceeds borrowers could receive and the pricing of the ongoing MIP. In 2010, FHA introduced a new product, the HECM Saver, which offers a lower upfront MIP in exchange for lower loan proceeds.

	Features & Requirements
Eligibility age	Borrower (or youngest co-borrower) must be at least 62 years old.
Home value	All homes are eligible, but FHA loan limits cap the amount of authorized loan proceeds on homes valued more than $625,500.
Authorized loan proceeds	At today's interest rates, borrowers receive between 51% and 77% of the appraised home value (or FHA loan limit, whichever is less) depending on age and product choice.
Mortgage Insurance Premium (MIP)	*Upfront:* 2% or 0.01% of home value (or FHA loan limit, whichever is less), depending on product choice. *Ongoing:* 1.25% per year on outstanding loan balance, assessed monthly.
Guarantee to borrowers	FHA guarantees borrowers that if the lender fails to make payments to the borrower as agreed, the FHA will make those payments on behalf of the lender.
Consumer protections	Mandatory pre-loan counseling; limits on costs and fees; right to remain in the home (subject to certain conditions); nonrecourse loan.
Protection for lenders/investors	FHA insurance guarantees that lenders/investors will be repaid in full, subject to certain conditions.

Figure 1. Key HECM features and requirements.

2.2.1a. Fixed-rate, closed-end HECMs

Historically, all HECMs were structured as open-end loans,[f] which meant that in practice nearly all HECMs carried an adjustable interest rate.[34] On March 28, 2008, FHA issued new guidance stating that fixed-rate HECMs could be structured as closed-end loans.[g,35] This regulatory clarification enabled the development of a fixed-rate, closed-end HECM in which borrowers are required to take all of their available proceeds as a lump sum at closing. This product now comprises about 70 percent of new HECM originations. The product is discussed in greater detail in Section 2.4.2. The factors that led to its development and market dominance are discussed in detail in the *Market* chapter.

2.2.1b. Change in loan limits

Historically, individuals with high home values received lower proceeds from HECM loans than they do today. FHA used a set of loan limits that varied by county and ranged from $200,160 to $362,790 as of 2007.[36] Despite its name, the loan limit capped the *value* of the home used to calculate proceeds, which in turn limited the amount of loan proceeds the borrower could obtain. Prospective borrowers with homes valued higher than the applicable limit could still obtain a HECM loan, but the amount they could borrow would be determined based on the loan limit rather than on the appraised value of the home.

In the Housing and Economic Recovery Act of 2008 (HERA), Congress replaced county-based loan size limits with a single national limit of $417,000.[37] In the American Recovery and Reinvestment Act (ARRA) passed in February 2009, Congress temporarily raised the nationwide loan limit to $625,500.[38] This temporary increase has been extended several times and is currently set to expire on December 31, 2012.[39] If extensions of the $625,500 limit are not implemented in the future, the program would revert to the $417,000 national loan limit.

[f] In an open-end loan (e.g., a line of credit), additional amounts can be borrowed after closing subject to the conditions of the loan. Any lender wanting to offer a fixed-rate HECM had to be willing to lend new money in the future at an interest rate fixed at origination. Few lenders were willing to take this risk.

[g] In a closed-end loan, the loan is for a fixed amount and additional principal amounts cannot be borrowed after closing.

As of 2009, the median home value for homeowners age 62 and older was $160,000.[40] Less than 10 percent of homeowners age 62 and older have home values greater than the current FHA limit of $625,500.[41]

2.2.1c. Change in loan proceeds & mortgage insurance premiums

The FHA has twice lowered the amount that borrowers can receive in loan proceeds, first in October 2009 and again in October 2010.[42] These changes were made in response to falling home values in an effort to improve the financial situation of the FHA insurance fund.[43] Additionally, in October 2010, FHA increased the ongoing MIP assessed monthly on the outstanding loan balance from 0.5 percent to 1.25 percent per year.[44]

2.2.1d. HECM Saver

Historically, FHA charged an upfront MIP of 2 percent of the appraised value of the home (or the applicable FHA loan limit, whichever is less), regardless of the balance of the loan at closing. On October 4, 2010, FHA introduced a new product option, the HECM Saver. It offers borrowers the option to virtually eliminate the upfront MIP – paying only 1/100th of 1 percent of the appraised value or applicable FHA loan limit – in exchange for lower proceeds.[45] This new option is discussed in greater detail below in Section 2.4.1.

2.3. HECM Program Requirements & Consumer Protections

HECM borrowers must meet certain program eligibility requirements as well as meet certain ongoing obligations as a condition of the loan.

2.3.1. Program Eligibility Requirements

Prospective borrowers must meet several requirements in order to be eligible for a HECM reverse mortgage.

1. **Age**: The borrower (or youngest co-borrower) must be at least 62 years old.[46]
2. **Ownership:** The borrower must hold title to the property.[47]
3. **Principal residence**: The borrower must occupy the property as a principal residence.[48]
4. **Sole mortgage**: Any existing mortgages (including home equity loans and HELOCs) on the property must be paid off at or before closing. HECM borrowers may use HECM proceeds to pay off an existing mortgage at closing.[49]
5. **Property standards**: The property must meet minimum housing quality standards as prescribed by FHA. If the property does not meet these standards, it must be repaired either prior to closing or shortly thereafter.[50]

2.3.2. Ongoing Obligations

As a condition of the loan, borrowers are required to continue to live in the home as their principal residence, pay property taxes and insurance, and maintain the property in good repair.

1. **Principal residence:** The borrower must continue to occupy the property as a principal residence. For co-borrowers, at least one borrower must continue to occupy the property as a principal residence. If the borrower (or last remaining co-borrower) lives someplace else for more than 12 months, the reverse mortgage may become due and payable. If the borrower does not repay the loan as requested, the lender can foreclose on the home.[51]
2. **Taxes & insurance:** The borrower must remain current on all property taxes and homeowner's insurance.[52] If the borrower fails to pay property taxes or maintain current homeowner's insurance, and fails to bring these accounts current when notified, the lender can foreclose and the borrower could lose their home.[53]
3. **Maintenance:** The borrower must keep the home in good repair. If the home falls into bad repair and the borrower does not make repairs when requested, the loan may become due and payable, and the lender may ultimately foreclose upon the home.[54]

2.3.3. Consumer Protections

HECM loans include several consumer protections:

1. **Right to remain in the home:** The borrower may live in the home indefinitely, regardless of how large the loan balance becomes, so long as the borrower complies with the three obligations listed in Section 2.3.2. For co-borrowers, if one borrower were to die, the surviving co-borrower would have the same right to live in the home indefinitely, provided the co-borrower continues to comply with the obligations in Section 2.3.2.
2. **FHA-approved lender:** Only FHA-approved lenders may make HECM loans.
3. **Non-recourse:** If the loan balance is greater than the value of the home at the time of the borrower's death, move-out, or foreclosure due to noncompliance with loan obligations, the lender cannot seek to recover the additional loan balance from the borrower's (or the estate's) other assets.[55] FHA insurance is designed to cover this excess loan balance.
4. **No prepayment penalty:** Borrowers may repay some or all of their loan at any time without being charged a prepayment penalty.[56]
5. **Counseling:** The borrower must receive counseling from a FHA-approved, independent third-party counseling agency prior to origination.[57]
6. **Disclosures:** FHA requires an extensive array of disclosures.[58]

2.3.4. Repayment Triggers

HECM loans can be declared due and payable when any of the following events occur:[59]

1. **Death:** The borrower (or last co-borrower) dies.
2. **Move-out:** The borrower (or last co-borrower) moves out of the home permanently.
3. **Extended absence:** The borrower (or last co-borrower) does not physically reside in the property for more than 12 months due to illness or other reasons.
4. **Sale or gift of the property:** The borrower (or last co-borrower) sells the property or otherwise transfers the title to a third party.

5. **Failure to fulfill obligations:** The borrower fails to pay taxes and insurance or to keep the home in good repair. The lender will give the borrower the opportunity to correct the problem prior to declaring a loan due and payable.

Once a loan has been declared due and payable, the borrower or the borrower's estate has six months to repay the loan, typically by selling the home.[60] If the balance of the loan is greater than the sales proceeds (subject to FHA procedures to ensure that the sales proceeds reflect the value of the home), the borrower or the estate does not have to pay the difference.[h, 61] If the borrower or the estate fails to sell the property or otherwise repay the loan within six months, the lender is required to start foreclosure proceedings.[62]

2.4. Key Product Decisions for the Prospective Borrower

The first decision consumers have to make is whether a reverse mortgage is right for their situation, or whether another product or course of action might be more suitable. Having decided upon a reverse mortgage, prospective HECM borrowers have an array of choices to make about what kind of loan they would like.

1. **Loan type:** The original HECM Standard product or the new HECM Saver product, which offers lower proceeds and lower upfront fees.
2. **Payment of loan proceeds:** Lump-sum, line-of-credit, monthly disbursement plan, or a combination.
3. **Interest rate:** Adjustable-rate or fixed-rate.

2.4.1. Loan Type Options

The first key choice is between the original HECM Standard loan and the new HECM Saver loan. The HECM Standard offers higher loan proceeds with higher upfront costs, while the HECM Saver offers lower upfront costs and lower loan proceeds. Figure 2 illustrates these differences.

During the Saver's first year, 6.0 percent of consumers applying for HECM loans chose that loan option.[63] Adjustable-rate borrowers and older borrowers were much more likely to choose the Saver products. These differences are discussed in more detail in Section 3.3.2.

2.4.1a. Calculating loan proceeds

The amount of loan proceeds a HECM borrower is authorized to receive depends on the borrower's age, the interest rate on the loan,[i] and the value of the home (or FHA loan limit, whichever is less). The complex formula is determined by FHA and standardized across

[h] If the borrower or the borrower's estate wants to *retain* the home and pay off the loan using other assets, the borrower's estate may settle the loan by paying the lesser of the loan balance or 95 percent of the appraised value of the home. *See* Section 6.7.2.

[i] Interest rate refers to the rate used to underwrite the loan for proceeds. For fixed-rate loans, this is the interest rate on the loan. The interest rate used to determine proceeds for adjustable-rate HECMs is known as the "expected rate" and is calculated using a 10-year index (plus the lender's margin) in lieu of the 1-month or 1-year interest rate actually used in calculating the interest rate on the loan. Nearly all adjustable-rate loans today use the 1-month LIBOR index, plus the lender's margin, to calculate the interest on the loan. These loans use the 10-year LIBOR Swap rate, plus the same margin, to determine the expected rate.

lenders. All other things being equal, younger borrowers receive lower proceeds than older borrowers. Borrowers choosing the Saver product receive lower proceeds than borrowers choosing the Standard product. Borrowers with higher interest rates will also receive lower proceeds in most cases.[64] Proceeds are calculated as a percentage of home value (or FHA loan limit, whichever is less), so higher home values will yield higher proceeds measured in dollars.

FHA publishes a series of "principal limit factors" for every combination of interest rates from 5 to 10 percent (in 0.125 percent increments) and borrower age from 62 to 90, separately for the Standard and Saver programs.[65] The principal limit factors are analogous to loan-to-value ratios in that, in most cases, they represent the percentage of the value of the home that the borrower is authorized to borrow (as calculated at the time of application).[j] For joint borrowers, the age of the youngest co-borrower is used. For fixed-rate products, the interest rate used to calculate proceeds is the same as the rate of the loan. For adjustable-rate products, a 10-year index rate is used instead of the actual rate of the loan (see footnote i).

The FHA calculations that determine the principal limit factor are the result of a complex mathematical model combining the interest rate assumption, life expectancy data, and other modeling assumptions (e.g., house price appreciation).

Figure 3 illustrates how the different inputs affect the calculated principal limit factor. The green lines show the principal limit factors for loans at 5 percent interest, which is typical of the market in 2012, while the red lines show the principal limit factors at a higher 8 percent interest rate. The dark lines show the principal limit factors for HECM Standard loans, while the light-shaded lines show the principal limit factors for HECM Saver. All four lines increase gradually with borrower age.

	Loan type	
Features	**HECM Standard**	**HECM Saver**
Upfront Mortgage Insurance Premium (MIP)	• 2.0% of appraised value* • *Example: $4000*	• 0.01 of appraised value* • *Example: $200*
Loan proceeds	• Larger. • Maximum loan proceeds range from 62% to 77% of appraised value*, depending on age, at today's interest rates.** • *Example: $130,400*	• Smaller. • Maximum loan proceeds range from 51% to 61% of appraised value*, depending on age, at today's interest rates.** • Proceeds are 12.6 percentage points lower on average across all ages and interest rates • *Example: $108,600*

* Or applicable FHA loan limit, whichever is less. **Using a 5% interest rate (see footnote i).
Example uses a $200,000-year-old borrower, and a 5% interest rate.

Figure 2. Key differences between Standard and Saver HECMs.

[j] The principal limit factor is applied to the lesser of the appraised value of the home or the applicable FHA loan limit. Thus, for borrowers whose home values exceed the applicable FHA loan limit, the actual loan-to-value ratio would be lower than the principal limit factor. The principal limit factor determines the initial authorized loan proceeds – the actual loan-to-value ratio will change over time with the rising loan balance and house price appreciation (or depreciation).

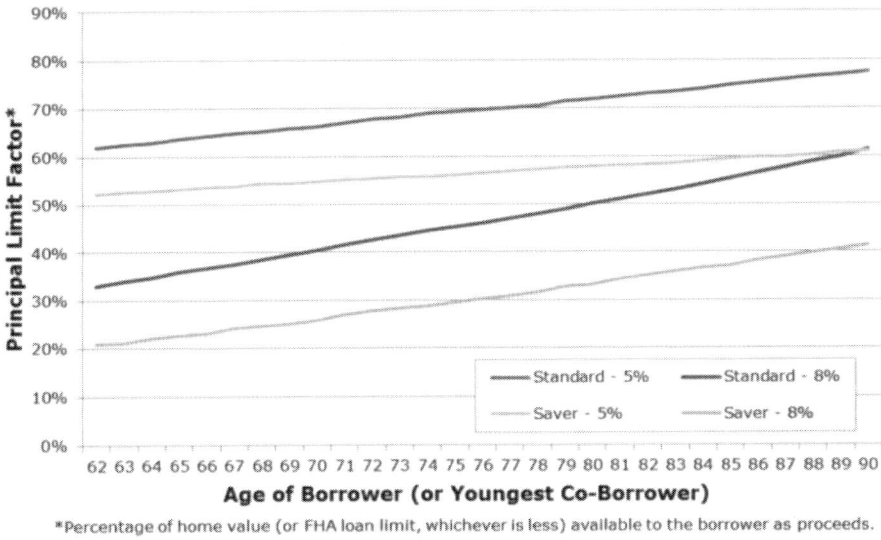

Source: Published FHA Principal Limit Factors.
Note: Interest rate refers to the rate used to underwrite the loan for proceeds. See footnote i on page 24).

Figure 3. Principal limit factors* for Standard and Saver loans at 5% and 8% interest.

The principal limit factor is multiplied by the appraised value of the home (or the applicable FHA loan limit, whichever is less) to calculate the "initial principal limit," or the maximum dollar amount the borrower is authorized to borrow. In practice, few borrowers are authorized to receive the entire initial principal limit. Most borrowers' *net* principal limit is reduced by upfront mortgage insurance and closing costs, which are financed into the loan in lieu of being paid in cash at closing. Borrowers with an existing traditional mortgage, home equity loan, or home equity line of credit (HELOC) must use their reverse mortgage proceeds to pay off the other loan(s) at closing,[66] further reducing the amount of actual cash that borrowers receive. Borrowers have several choices regarding how they receive their funds, which are discussed in Section 2.4.3.

2.4.1b. Complex trade-offs

The HECM Saver was designed as a lower-cost product for seniors who do not need access to as much money as the HECM Standard would provide. The tradeoffs between the two products are more complex than just differences in upfront costs, however. The HECM Saver reduces the upfront MIP from 2 percent to 0.01 percent of the home value (or FHA loan limit, whichever is less). In today's market, HECM Savers generally carry interest rates one-quarter to one-half of a percentage point higher than HECM Standards, and both HECM Savers and HECM Standards carry the same 1.25 percent ongoing MIP.[67] Thus, at today's interest rates, the HECM Saver could cost more in interest over the life of the loan than a HECM Standard would. Depending on how long the borrower keeps the loan, the increased interest on a HECM Saver could in some cases outweigh the reduced upfront cost.

In cases where the borrower anticipates that the loan balance at repayment could be greater than the home value (whether due to longer-than-expected borrower life, rising interest rates, or slow or negative home price appreciation), the tradeoff between the HECM Standard and the HECM Saver is even more complex. The HECM Saver product provides lower proceeds to the borrower at the outset of the loan, which means that the loan is less likely to exceed the value of the home at repayment than with a HECM Standard. But in cases where the loan balance *does* exceed the value of the home at repayment, the borrower receives less funds and devotes a greater portion of home equity to interest with a HECM Saver than with a HECM Standard.

2.4.2. Interest Rates

Today, most HECM borrowers have a choice between a fixed-rate product and a monthly-adjustable product based on the 1-month LIBOR index.[68] In the early years of the program, most HECM loans used an annually adjustable rate based on the 1-year constant maturity treasury rate. The annually adjustable rate option has all but disappeared today.

Prior to 2007, only a handful of lenders offered fixed-rate HECMs.[69] Starting in 2007, a larger array of lenders began offering fixed-rate HECMs, but volume remained low until mid-2009, when the fixed-rate option suddenly became the dominant product. Around 70 percent of HECMs originated today are fixed-rate loans.[70] The *Market* chapter discusses the rise of the fixed-rate product option in greater detail.

Importantly for consumers, today the fixed-rate HECM is *only* available with a lump-sum disbursement option, and is structured as a closed-end loan in which borrowers are not permitted to borrow additional funds at a future date. These restrictions are not dictated by HECM regulations, but are a result of market forces.[71] Fixed-rate HECMs also carry a higher interest rate at origination than adjustable-rate HECMs.

Borrowers who choose adjustable-rate HECMs, in contrast, can choose from any of six different options for receiving their loan proceeds. Adjustable-rate loans – including those where the borrower takes all or almost all of their funds at closing – are structured as open-end loans in which borrowers can, if they wish, pay off part of their loan and free up that part of their credit line for later use.[72] Adjustable-rate borrowers also benefit from a unique credit line growth feature. If a borrower does not take all the proceeds at the start of the loan, then the total amount that can be borrowed later will be higher. The disbursement options and the credit line growth feature are discussed in Section 2.4.3.

2.4.3. Disbursement of Loan Proceeds

Borrowers who choose adjustable-rate HECMs – whether Standard or Saver – can choose from several options for receiving the loan proceeds.

HECM regulations authorize five different disbursement options:[73]

1. **Line of credit** – a line of credit accessible at the borrower's discretion
2. **Term** – a fixed monthly disbursement for a fixed number of years
3. **Tenure** – a fixed monthly disbursement for as long as the borrower lives in the home
4. **Modified term** – a smaller fixed monthly disbursement for a fixed number of years, in combination with a line of credit accessible at the borrower's discretion
5. **Modified tenure** – a smaller fixed monthly disbursement for as long as the borrower lives in the home, in combination with a line of credit accessible at the borrower's discretion

In practice, a sixth disbursement option also exists – a **lump sum** at closing. While the lump sum does not formally exist as a separate disbursement option in the HECM regulations, all HECM borrowers are permitted to withdraw a lump sum at closing.[74] Importantly, in today's market, the fixed interest rate option (discussed in Section 2.4.2) is *only* available with a lump-sum disbursement. These fixed-rate, lump-sum loans are structured as closed-end loans in which borrowers are not permitted to borrow additional funds at a future date.[75]

Adjustable-rate borrowers whose principal balance outstanding is less than the allowable principal limit benefit from two additional features. First, they may change their disbursement plan at any time for a nominal fee. Borrowers with a line of credit may decide to convert some or all of their remaining line of credit into a monthly disbursement plan. Likewise, borrowers with a monthly disbursement plan may decide to reduce or eliminate their monthly disbursement in order to create a line of credit in addition to or in lieu of the monthly disbursements.

Second, line-of-credit plans (or partial line-of-credit plans in conjunction with a monthly disbursement plan) benefit from an unusual credit line growth feature. If the loan is not fully drawn, the unused portion of the credit line is compounded at the same rate as the loan balance, and the borrower can take advantage of that expanding credit line at a later date. FHA calculates a new maximum allowable loan balance each month as if the loan had been fully drawn at closing, and the difference between the maximum allowable loan balance and the actual loan balance is available to the borrower, as shown in Figure 5. Monthly disbursement plans benefit from the same feature, but the expanding loan balance limit is factored into the monthly disbursement amount calculation at the outset, so borrowers receive higher monthly disbursements than they would without the credit line growth feature.

Figure 5 illustrates how the unused credit line grows over time using a hypothetical borrower who was authorized for $200,000 in net proceeds but took only $100,000 in cash at closing and did not take any further draws during the next seven years. By the end of year seven, the unused $100,000 grows to an available credit line of $134,578 (assuming a 3 percent interest rate plus 1.25 percent mortgage insurance premium). This increased credit line is available to borrowers as long as they remain in their homes and fulfill their other loan obligations as described in Section 2.3.2, regardless of the level of appreciation (or depreciation) of their homes.

Historically, most borrowers chose a line-of-credit plan. Among loans originated in the 1990s, 71 percent of borrowers chose a line of credit while 29 percent of borrowers chose one of the monthly disbursement plans (term, tenure, modified term, or modified tenure). In 2007, 87 percent of borrowers chose a line of credit, and 13 percent chose a monthly disbursement plan.[76] However, by the late 2000s, most line-of-credit borrowers were taking a substantial portion of their available funds upfront. The median borrower in 2007 took out 82 percent of their available funds within the first year, and three-quarters of borrowers took at least half of their available funds within the first year.[77]

Starting in early 2009, the fixed-rate product, which requires a lump-sum disbursement, began to dominate the market. During FY 2011, 69 percent of loans originated were fixed-rate, lump-sum.[78] Of the remaining 31 percent, the vast majority are line-of-credit plans. Among current originations, likely no more than 20 to 30 percent of adjustable-rate loans, or no more than about 6 to 10 percent of loans overall, have a monthly disbursement plan.[79]

Figure 6 shows a hypothetical example comparing the fixed-rate, lump-sum option to several different adjustable-rate, line-of-credit scenarios. The example uses a 68-year-old borrower with a $250,000 home. At today's interest rates, this borrower qualifies for $163,000 in initial proceeds with the HECM Standard product (the example does not deduct for upfront MIP and closing costs, but these costs are the same across scenarios). The scenarios show the additional amount that the borrower is eligible to receive if she spreads her disbursements out over six years (the typical length of a HECM loan) instead of taking all of her funds upfront. A borrower who takes only one-third of available proceeds upfront, and takes additional disbursements each year for the following five years, receives $15,190 more in proceeds and owes $16,607 less in interest after six years than the borrower who takes a lump sum upfront.

Features	Interest rate type: Adjustable	Interest rate type: Fixed
Available payment options	All: Line of credit, Term, Tenure, Modified Term, Modified Tenure, Lump-sum	Lump-sum only
Interest rate	• Averaged 2.5% in FY 2011 • Lower at origination than fixed rate, but can change over the life of the loan.	• Averaged 5.1% in FY 2011 • Higher at origination, but will not change.
Loan structure/ prepayment	Open-end loan.* Can prepay all or some of the loan at any time and re-use credit line.	Closed-end loan.** Can prepay all or some of the loan at any time, but re-use of the credit line is not permitted.
Credit line growth	Unused credit line grows over time at the same rate as the interest plus mortgage insurance premium assessed on the loan balance.	No credit line growth.

Note: *HECM regulations do not specifically permit nor prohibit closed-end, adjustable-rate loans, though in practice the CFPB is not aware of any lenders making these loans. **According to FHA Mortgagee Letter 2008-08, fixed-rate reverse mortgages can be open-end or closed-end, though in practice the CFPB is not aware of any lenders making open-end, fixed-rate HECMs.

Figure 4. HECM loan features by rate type.

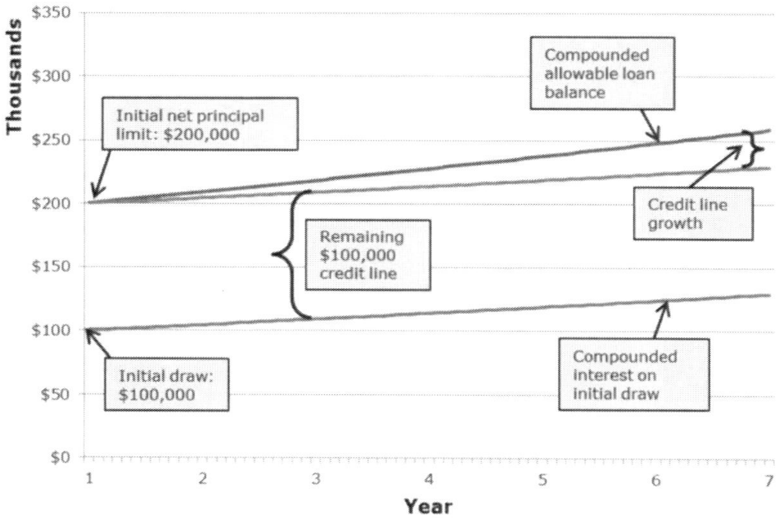

Note: This example assumes a 3 percent interest rate and a 1.25 percent monthly mortgage insurance premium. The amount of credit line growth is dependent on the interest rate. A higher interest rate would result in greater credit line growth over time.

Figure 5. Illustration of credit line growth.

	Total amount received over 6 years	Total amount paid in interest + MIP over 6 years	Loan balance after 6 years
Fixed-rate lump sum	$163,000	$73,933	$236,933
	Adjustable-rate plans		
Line of credit - 3 equal disbursements over 3 years	$170,583	$64,932	$235,515
Line of credit – two-thirds of available proceeds upfront, 5 additional disbursements over next 5 years	$170,595	$64,920	$235,515
Line of credit – one-third of available proceeds upfront, 5 additional disbursements over next 5 years	$178,190	$57,326	$235,515

Note: This example uses a 5.0 percent interest rate for the fixed-rate, lump-sum option. For the adjustable-rate scenarios, it uses a 2.9 percent starting interest rate with an increase of 1 percent in each of the following three years. If interest rates increased more quickly, the amount of interest owed, but also the additional credit line available, would be larger after 6 years. All scenarios include the 1.25 percent ongoing MIP.

Figure 6. Example loan scenarios.

2.5. Special-Purpose HECM Loans

The vast majority of borrowers (94 percent in FY 2011) used the regular HECM products to tap their existing home equity to pay for expenses and/or to pay off an existing traditional mortgage. However, the HECM program offers two additional special-purpose product types: HECM for Purchase and HECM Refinance. Both special-purpose loans are available with either fixed or adjustable interest rates and with the Standard or Saver insurance premium/loan proceeds structure.

2.5.1. HECM for Purchase: Buying a Home with a Reverse Mortgage

A HECM reverse mortgage can be used to buy a home. The HECM for Purchase program was introduced in 2008 to allow a borrower to use a HECM to purchase a new home, rather than borrowing against a home they already own.[80] Older homeowners interested in downsizing, moving closer to family, or moving for other reasons may find this special-purpose HECM loan more useful than the ordinary HECM products.

The borrower can use the HECM for Purchase in lieu of a traditional mortgage to finance part of the home's cost. As with most traditional mortgage transactions, the borrower must supply a down payment to supplement the HECM for Purchase financing, which can be paid out of proceeds from the sale of their current home or from other savings or assets. However, the down payment requirements under HECM for Purchase are substantially higher than in a traditional mortgage transaction.

The same loan-to-value calculations ("principal limit factors") for ordinary (non-Purchase) Standard or Saver HECM loans are applied to the HECM for Purchase program. For example, at today's interest rates (using a 5 percent interest rate), a 72-year-old borrower would qualify for HECM Standard loan proceeds of approximately 67 percent of the value of the new home (assuming the home is worth less than the $625,500 FHA loan limit). This borrower would be able to finance 67 percent of the value of the new home (or $134,000 for a

$200,000 home) using the HECM for Purchase and would have to supply a 33 percent down payment (or $66,000), plus closing costs. Borrowers must make their new homes their principal residence within 60 days of closing the loan.

The HECM for Purchase option comprised 1.8 percent of all HECMs originated in FY 2010, rising to 2.3 percent during FY 2011.

2.5.2. HECM Refinance: Refinancing an Existing HECM Loan

The HECM Refinance program allows borrowers in limited circumstances to refinance their existing HECM loans to obtain better terms. Because the balance on a reverse mortgage rises over time, refinances are much rarer in the reverse mortgage market than in the traditional mortgage market. In many cases, within a few years of taking out the loan, the growing loan balance (including interest and fees) on the existing HECM will exceed the proceeds a borrower would be eligible to obtain under a new HECM, making a refinance impossible. HECM-to-HECM refinances are usually only possible in cases where a borrower's home has appreciated significantly, interest rates have fallen substantially, and/or the borrower has drawn only a small portion of the authorized loan proceeds on the existing HECM.

Prior to 2004, there were no special procedures for refinancing a HECM. Any borrower wishing to refinance would have submitted a new loan application, paid a new round of upfront fees, including the upfront MIP, and paid off the old HECM at closing of the new HECM. In March 2004, FHA published a new rule implementing Section 201 of the American Homeownership and Economic Opportunity Act of 2000. The new rule provided for a special refinance option in which the borrower was only required to pay the upfront MIP on the *difference* between the original appraised value and the new appraised value (or FHA loan limit, whichever is less) used to underwrite the refinance.

The first refinances under the new program were done in 2005. Between FY2005 and FY2008, the market share for HECM Refinance loans hovered between 3.6 percent and 6.8 percent of all HECMs originated. HECM Refinances peaked in FY 2009 with 9,754 loans, or 8.5 percent of HECM production. In FY 2011, HECM refinances fell to only 2.3 percent of all HECMs.

2.6. Costs and Fees

Reverse mortgages have both upfront and ongoing costs and fees associated with them. FHA mortgage insurance premiums (MIP), interest, and upfront origination fees and closing costs are the largest costs.

2.6.1. Upfront Costs & Fees

Upfront costs and fees consist of the upfront MIP, the origination fee, closing costs, and a counseling fee.

Upfront MIP: FHA assesses a one-time, nonrefundable initial MIP equal to 2 percent (HECM Standard) or 0.01 percent (HECM Saver) of the appraised value of the home (or the applicable FHA loan limit, whichever is less).[81]

Home value	Maximum origination fee	Maximum origination fee as % of loan proceeds Principal limit factor (Loan proceeds-to-home value ratio)		
		30%	50%	70%
$100,000	$2,500	8.3%	5.0%	3.6%
$150,000	$3,000	6.7%	4.0%	2.9%
$200,000	$4,000	6.7%	4.0%	2.9%
$300,000	$5,000	5.6%	3.3%	2.4%
$400,000	$6,000	5.0%	3.0%	2.1%

Figure 7. Maximum HECM origination fees as % of loan proceeds at various home values and principal limit factors.

Origination Fee: Lenders may charge an origination fee up to $2,500 for homes valued at $125,000 or less. For homes valued at $125,000 or more, the maximum allowable origination fee is calculated at 2 percent of the appraised value of the home up to $200,000, plus 1 percent of the amount greater than $200,000. The total origination fee is capped by regulation at a maximum of $6,000.[82] However, because the payout to the borrower is typically only 30 to 70 percent of the borrower's home value (depending on age and interest rate), the origination fee can still represent a large percentage of the loan amount, as shown in Figure 7. Borrowers typically pay for the origination fee using loan proceeds, reducing the amount that the borrower actually receives.

Today, origination fees are typically waived on fixed-rate HECMs and may be partially discounted on adjustable-rate HECMs. This is due to market conditions explained more thoroughly in the *Market* chapter. Should market conditions change, lenders may return to charging the maximum origination fee.

Closing Costs: Third-party fees for the appraisal, title search, insurance, surveys, inspections, recording fees, mortgage taxes, credit checks and other fees are typically paid for with loan proceeds, reducing the amount that the borrower actually receives.

Counseling Fee: Historically, HUD-funded counseling agencies provided counseling to prospective reverse mortgage borrowers free of charge. In the 2011 budget cycle, funding for this program was cut. As a consequence, many counseling agencies have begun charging prospective borrowers a fee. HUD requires that the fee be "reasonable and customary," and agencies must waive the fee for clients with incomes less than twice the poverty level.[83] Some counseling agencies assess this fee at time of counseling, while others will allow it to be paid at closing using loan proceeds.

2.6.2. Ongoing Costs & Fees

Ongoing costs and fees consist of the monthly MIP, monthly servicing fee, and monthly interest.

Monthly MIP: FHA assesses an ongoing MIP equal to 1.25 percent of the loan balance (principal drawn plus accumulated interest, MIP, and fees) per year on all loans, whether HECM Standard or HECM Saver.[84] The 1.25 percent rate is an annual rate, but it is calculated and added to the loan balance on a monthly basis.[85] Because of the negative-amortization feature of the loan, the MIP compounds in the same way that the interest does. Each month, borrowers are being charged MIP on a growing loan balance that includes prior interest and prior MIP.

Servicing Fee: As with traditional mortgages, the servicing fee is embedded in the interest rate. Each month, servicers receive between 30 and 144 basis points (0.30 to 1.44 percent) before the accrued interest is credited to the secondary market investors.[86] This fee is intended to cover the cost of sending the borrower account statements, disbursing loan proceeds, and ensuring that borrowers keep up with loan requirements such as real estate taxes and homeowner's insurance premiums.[k] It also compensates Ginnie Mae issuer-servicers for the financial risks they undertake, as explained in Section 4.4.3a.

Interest: Each month, interest accrues on the loan and is credited to the investors who own the loan. The interest compounds over time, and is paid to the investors all at once when the loan is repaid.

2.7. Alternatives to Reverse Mortgages

Reverse mortgages are best suited to seniors who need or want to supplement their retirement resources; who do not have sufficient cash flow from other sources to qualify for a traditional home equity line of credit; who want to remain in their home; and who can reasonably expect to remain in the home long enough to justify the upfront costs of the loan. Financially sophisticated borrowers may also find that a reverse mortgage makes sense as a financing tool within a comprehensive retirement planning strategy under certain circumstances.

Before choosing a reverse mortgage, consumers should carefully evaluate whether another product or course of action would allow them to achieve their financial goals at lower cost. Alternative products include a home equity line of credit (HELOC) and specialized products and programs offered at the state and local level. Alternative courses of action include refinancing a traditional mortgage to lower the monthly payments, selling the home and downsizing, and/or applying for federal, state, or local programs that may provide financial assistance to seniors.

2.7.1. Home Equity Line of Credit (HELOC)

Like reverse mortgages, HELOCs offer the borrower the opportunity to convert home equity into cash, but they do so with a very different set of eligibility criteria, costs, risks, and benefits than a reverse mortgage. For some borrowers who can qualify, a HELOC may provide a cheaper method of achieving their financial goals with acceptable risks and downsides. For other borrowers, the increased costs of a reverse mortgage may be outweighed by the added protections and fewer obligations of a reverse mortgage, even if they can qualify for a HELOC. Many prospective reverse mortgage borrowers also may be

---

[k] The servicing fee has not always been embedded in the interest rate. Historically, lenders deducted a "servicing fee set-aside" from the borrower's initial principal limit before determining the net principal limit (the amount of cash the borrower can actually access). Lenders then charged a $30 to $35 servicing fee each month, paid out of the reserved loan proceeds. As discussed in Section 4.5.1, this practice was discontinued in mid-2009 by all major lenders in favor of the embedded structure.

unable to qualify for a HELOC. Figure 8 compares the costs, risks, and benefits of a HECM as compared to a HELOC.

2.7.2. Specialized Products & Programs

In additional to HECM and proprietary reverse mortgages, alternative financial products and other forms of financial assistance are available at the state and local level for seniors who need help staying in their homes. These products were historically considered lower-cost alternatives to HECM or proprietary reverse mortgages. Other forms of assistance also may be available at no cost to the consumer. Alternative products generally fall into four categories: tax credits or loan advances for paying property taxes, property tax deferrals, deferred payment loans for home improvements, and specialized reverse mortgage loans offered in conjunction with state housing finance agencies.

Feature	HECM	HELOC
Eligibility		
Age	Must be 62 or older.	None.
Income	None currently, though a basic financial assessment may be a requirement in the future.*	Must have sufficient income to make monthly payments.
Credit	None currently, though a basic credit check may be a requirement in the future.*	Must pass lender's underwriting criteria.
Costs/Benefits		
Upfront costs	*Historically:* High (origination fee, upfront MIP, closing costs). *Currently:* Lower than in the past with HECM Saver option and waiving/ discounting of origination fees, though generally still higher than HELOCs.	Generally no origination fee, although some lenders may charge an early cancellation fee if the line is closed within a certain number of years.[87] No MIP.
Mortgage Insurance Premium (MIP)	*HECM Standard:* 2% of home value** upfront. *HECM Saver:* 0.01% of home value** upfront. *Ongoing:* 1.25% per year on outstanding loan balance, assessed monthly.	No MIP.
Interest rate	*Fixed rate:* 4.5% to 5% *Adjust. rate:* LIBOR + 2.25% to 3% (Fully indexed: 2.5% to 3.25% as of April 2012).	Typically Prime + 1% to 2%, though can be higher depending on credit. (Fully indexed: 4.25% to 5.25% as of April 2012).
Maximum Loan to Value Ratio (LTV)	*At origination:* 51% to 77% at today's rates, depends on age and product choice. *Through life of loan:* No limit.	*At origination:* Generally 80%, some allow up to 90%. *Through life of loan:* Not designed to be a negative-amortization product. Credit line may be cut if LTV exceeds lender criteria.
Risks/ Protections		
Future credit line availability	*Fixed rate:* no future credit line *Adjustable rate:* future credit line guaranteed, increases at same rate as interest + MIP	Future credit line may be cut or suspended if home prices decline, overall credit conditions tighten, or the borrower's credit picture declines.
Foreclosure risk due to nonpayment	Limited to tax & insurance defaults	Defaults on monthly payments as well as tax & insurance.
Obligations		
Monthly mortgage payments	None.	Required, can face foreclosure if unable to make monthly payments.
Taxes & insurance	Required, can face foreclosure if fail to make payments.	Can be escrowed by lender.
Primary residence	Required.	Required.

Note: *FHA has indicated that it is considering proposing an upfront financial assessment in response to rising tax and insurance defaults, as discussed in Section 6.6. FHA has indicated that it expects to publish new regulations in the 4th quarter of 2012.[88] ** Home value or FHA loan limit, whichever is less.

Figure 8. Comparison of costs, risks, and benefits of HECMs vs. HELOCs.

2.7.2a. Circuit breaker tax credits or tax grants

The most common form of assistance in paying property taxes available for senior citizens and other eligible consumers is the Circuit Breaker tax credit or tax grant. Offered by over half of the states, Circuit Breaker programs provide a mechanism for tax relief for qualifying seniors.[89] While requirements vary among the states, in order to qualify consumers generally must have paid an amount in real estate taxes that exceeds a certain percentage of their income and cannot earn more than the income limits set by the state or locality for the tax year. Consumers receive the assistance either in the form of a tax credit when filing income taxes or a grant in the form of a check. Recent budget cuts have affected certain states' ability to offer Circuit Breaker programs and the ability of states to continue to provide this assistance is not certain.[90]

2.7.2b. Property tax deferrals

Property tax deferral programs allow taxpayers, usually 65 or older and meeting annual income limits, to delay payment of property taxes until the property is sold or until the death of the taxpayer. There are generally no origination fees or insurance premiums, and interest rates, if any, can vary among states and programs. Many programs limit the amount consumers can borrow, and some programs do not allow consumers to obtain a property tax deferral loan if the consumer already has a reverse mortgage on the property.[91] Approximately half the states have some permutation of a property tax deferral program.[92]

2.7.2c. Deferred payment loans

Deferred payment loans provide eligible homeowners with one-time, lump-sum advances that may be used for repairing or improving the consumer's home. As with other alternative products, eligibility requirements vary among the state and local programs. Many contain income limits or minimum age requirements. These loans may only be used for specific purposes, such as bringing a house up to code or making a home handicapped-accessible by adding a ramp. Generally, deferred payment loans are offered at a low or zero interest rate and repayment of principal and interest is required when the home is sold or the borrower dies.[93] Select programs may offer grants or forgivable loans for emergency repairs.[94]

2.7.2d. Specialized reverse mortgage loans from state housing finance agencies & nonprofit partnerships

Some states have implemented programs to provide financial assistance to the elderly through specialized reverse mortgage loans, as discussed further below.[95]

Connecticut

Starting in 1993, Connecticut's Housing Finance Authority partnered with Department of Social Services to provide the Reverse Annuity Mortgage Program.[96] Borrowers must be 70 years or older and at least one borrower must have costs associated with long-term care.[97] Borrowers' income cannot exceed $81,000, and the maximum loan available amount is 70 percent of the appraised home value, not to exceed $417,000. Loan payments are made monthly for five or ten years, with the borrower having the option to take out a $5,000 one-time, lump-sum payment at the time of closing. The program currently offers a 7.0 percent fixed interest rate.

Montana

The Montana Board of Housing implemented its Reverse Annuity Mortgage Loan Program in October of 1990.[98] Borrowers must be 68 years of age or older and meet income requirements. Loan payments are made for 10 years, with a lump sum advance of up to $10,000 available at the closing for payment of prior mortgages or liens, repairs to the home, and advances for certain closing costs. The program currently offers a 5.0 percent interest rate.

Massachusetts

Since 1984, the Homeowner Options for Massachusetts Elders (H.O.M.E.) nonprofit agency has partnered with community lenders to offer reverse mortgages and lines of credit to elder homeowners.[99] H.O.M.E. assists Massachusetts residents ages 60 and above (or 50 and above if facing foreclosure) who meet annual income requirements. In addition to offering counseling, referral, and foreclosure prevention services, H.O.M.E. has a variety of loan products including the Term Reverse Mortgage, the Modifiable In-Home Care Reverse Mortgage, the Senior Equity Line of Credit, and combination options. H.O.M.E. considers loans to be a "last resort" and endeavors to find other alternatives.[100]

2.7.3. Alternatives to a Reverse Mortgage

Some consumers may be better off not taking a reverse mortgage and instead pursuing an alternative course of action. Many consumers considering a reverse mortgage may not realize that they are eligible for government benefit programs.[101] One reverse mortgage counseling agency reports finding other solutions for 50 percent of the potential borrowers it counsels.[102] The National Council on Aging estimates that prospective reverse mortgage borrowers could be eligible for more than $378 million in benefits.[103] Available benefits include both federal programs such as Supplemental Security Income (SSI), as well as state and local programs such as energy assistance and the special-purpose loans discussed in Section 2.7.2.

Homeowners struggling with existing mortgage payments but whose income could support a smaller payment may find that a traditional mortgage refinance will suit their needs at a lower cost. Downsizing is another alternative to a reverse mortgage. Selling the current home and buying or renting a smaller home may free up enough equity to cover a consumer's needs. Furthermore, the smaller home could decrease maintenance and tax expenses. Consumers in poor health or who need assistance might consider retirement communities, assisted living facilities, or moving in with relatives.

3. CONSUMERS

As of 2010, there were roughly 24 million homeowner households in the U.S. headed by someone age 62 and older.[104] Home equity makes up a large portion of senior homeowners' net worth. In 2009, half of homeowners age 62 and older held more than 55 percent of their net worth in home equity.[105] By some estimates, older homeowners held more than $3 trillion in home equity as of the third quarter of 2011.[106]

Although the potential pool of borrowers is quite large, only about 2 to 3 percent of eligible households actually have a reverse mortgage.[107] For the most part, older homeowners are simply not interested in reverse mortgages. Older homeowners who *do* consider a reverse mortgage and complete counseling are much more likely than the general population of older homeowners to have an existing traditional mortgage, a home equity line of credit (HELOC), or other consumer debt. Among older homeowners who do have debt, prospective reverse mortgage borrowers owe more on average than households not seeking a reverse mortgage.[108]

Over the past two decades, the HECM program grew dramatically from a small pilot program to more than 100,000 loans per year in the late 2000s, before falling to about 70,000 loans per year in 2010 and 2011.[109] It is difficult to say whether shifts in borrower characteristics over time are the result of this expansion or a result of broader demographic changes and economic conditions. However, today's reverse mortgage borrowers look very different from borrowers in the early years of the program.

Today's borrowers are taking out reverse mortgages at substantially younger ages, and are more likely to have existing traditional mortgage debt than in the past. Today's borrowers also are much more likely to take all of their available proceeds upfront than in the past. Younger borrowers and those with lower home values are especially likely to take all of their proceeds upfront.

The market is poised to change again, as the large cohort of baby boomers make their way into retirement. As shown in Figure 9, Census figures project that the number of people over age 60 will reach 75 million by 2020, and 92 million by 2030.[110] Given homeownership rates among older homeowners, there are likely to be nearly 40 million eligible homeowner households headed by someone 62 or older by 2030.[111] It is too early to tell whether the aging boomers will choose to use reverse mortgages in greater or lesser proportions – or in similar or different ways – than the current generation of older homeowners.

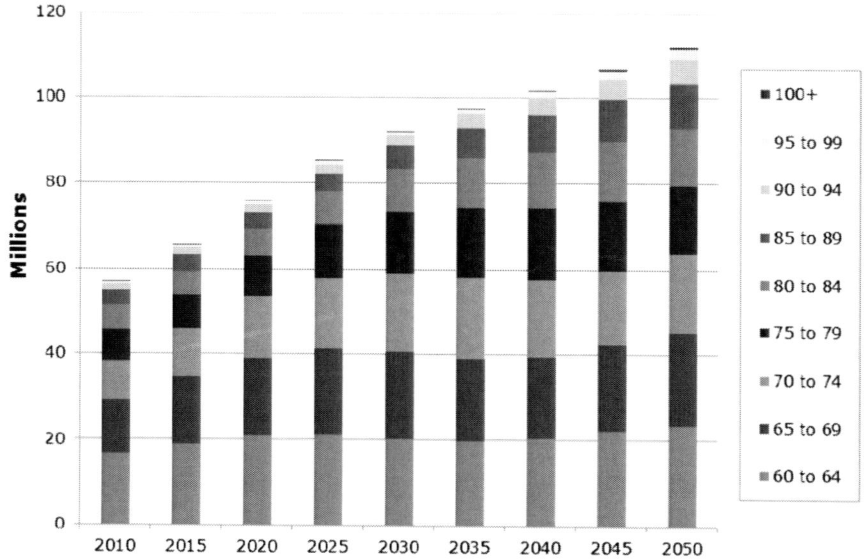

Source: U.S. Census Bureau

Figure 9. Projection of population age 60 and over, 2010 to 2050.

3.1. Consumer Awareness, Attitudes, and Motivations

While the population of older homeowners eligible for reverse mortgages is poised to grow significantly in the coming years, the number of eligible homeowners that will actually choose to take out a reverse mortgage is much more uncertain. Older homeowners today are largely uninterested in reverse mortgages, and market penetration is very low. Only about 2 to 3 percent of eligible homeowners today have a reverse mortgage.[112] It is difficult to predict whether the baby boomers will choose to take out reverse mortgages in higher proportions than today's eligible homeowners.

3.1.1. High Awareness

Evidence from two national AARP-sponsored surveys of consumers age 45 and older suggests that the low market penetration is not due to lack of awareness. In 2007, 70 percent of survey respondents indicated that they had heard of a reverse mortgage before, up from 51 percent in 1999.[113] Yet respondents who said they might consider a reverse mortgage in the future *decreased* from 19 percent to 14 percent over the same time period.[114]

A 2007 survey by Harris Interactive, a polling organization, similarly found that 72 percent of baby boomers (then aged 43-61) and 86 percent of respondents aged 62 and older indicated that they were aware of reverse mortgages. The awareness level of reverse mortgages was roughly the same as the awareness level of fixed-rate traditional mortgages (76 percent among baby boomers, 84 percent among respondents aged 62+).[115]

Although most older consumers are aware of the product, eligible homeowners are largely not interested in taking out reverse mortgages. One survey of homeowners 62 and older conducted in the late 2000s found that after the HECM program was described, 71 percent of respondents said they were not interested (21 percent said they wanted to learn more, and only 4.3 percent said they would participate).[116] Among those who are sufficiently interested in the product to attend counseling, only about 60 percent actually go through with the transaction.[117] Figure 10 illustrates the drop-off between awareness and interest.

3.1.2. Low Interest

Surveys of consumers suggest that consumers are reluctant to take out reverse mortgages for a number of reasons. These reasons include a general wariness about the product, a belief that the product should be used only as a last resort, a desire to own the home free and clear after many years of making mortgage payments, and a desire to leave the home to children or other heirs as an inheritance.

A 2007 poll of the general adult population found that 36 percent of consumers had an unfavorable or very unfavorable impression of reverse mortgages, while 39 percent were neutral and 25 percent had a favorable or very favorable impression.[118] As shown in Figure 11, consumers were much more wary of reverse mortgages than fixed-rate traditional mortgages.

Historically, senior homeowners have felt that a reverse mortgage should only be used as a last resort. A 2001 study of low-income reverse mortgage borrowers in Massachusetts found that borrowers typically did not seek out a reverse mortgage until they had exhausted their savings and were behind on their bills.[119] In a 2006 AARP survey, reverse mortgage borrowers were more likely to have looked into reverse mortgages as a means to pay for "basic necessities and essential expenses" (50 percent) than as a means to have "more money to spend on extras" (38 percent).[120] A survey conducted in the late 2000s of age-eligible homeowners indicates that this "last resort" orientation continues, as many respondents commented that they "thought it [HECM] was an attractive program for those who needed it," with some respondents adding that they "hoped they would not need the program."[121]

The 2001 Massachusetts study of low-income reverse mortgage borrowers suggests that at least among earlier generations of older homeowners, the desire to own the home free and clear and pass that home on to one's children was a strong reason for consumers to decide against a reverse mortgage. Borrowers reported struggling with the decision to use the equity in their homes. Some needed assurances from their children that their children were "financially set," while some homeowners interviewed for the study who received reverse mortgage counseling ultimately decided against the loan on the same grounds.[122] Lenders interviewed for the 2000 evaluation of the HECM program stated that they were having difficulty marketing the loans because of a "Depression-era mentality among the current elderly generation that views debt of any kind as risky and unwise."[123]

There is some evidence that current seniors and the aging baby boomers may be more amenable to taking on debt and less attached to the idea of leaving an inheritance, though there is still an interest in leaving bequests. Between 2004 and 2007, the median household debt increased by 38 percent among households headed by an adult aged 50 to 61.[124] A 2010 industry poll found that when asked to choose between leaving their children an inheritance and being able to pay all their bills so their children would not worry about them, 27 percent of eligible homeowners said they wanted to leave their children an inheritance and 68 percent said they wanted to be able to pay their bills.[125] However, survey participants may not view these options as mutually exclusive, so some caution is warranted in interpreting these results. It is not yet clear whether baby boomers will be any more likely to take out reverse mortgages than the current generation of older homeowners. In a 2011 survey of leading-edge baby boomers (65-year-olds in 2011), only 12 percent of respondents indicated that they would consider a reverse mortgage in the future.[126]

3.1.3. Low Take-Up

Data from the 2006 AARP survey of reverse mortgage counseling participants indicate that interested consumers who ultimately decided against taking out a reverse mortgage did so for many of the same reasons that drive the overall reluctance of consumers to take out reverse mortgages. The belief that reverse mortgages should only be used as a last resort is echoed in the primary reasons that counseling participants cited for not going through with the loan.

Nearly 60 percent of counseling participants who decided against the loan appear to have reconsidered whether they really needed the loan and whether it was worth the cost.[127] Fully 30 percent said that the primary reason they did not take out the loan was because the costs were too high. Another 28 percent said that the loan was not necessary at this time.[128] And 10 percent said that they wanted to continue to own their home free and clear or wanted to ensure that their heirs would be able to inherit the home.[129]

Other reasons given for not going through with the loan included lower proceeds than expected, a complicated process, concerns about debt, and expensive home repairs required as a condition of the loan.

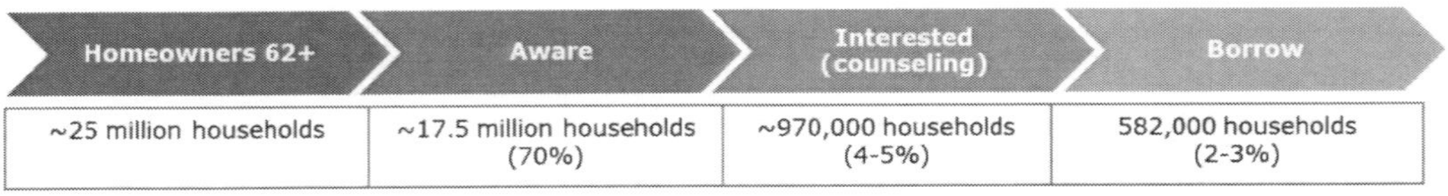

Figure 10. Estimated market penetration, 2011.

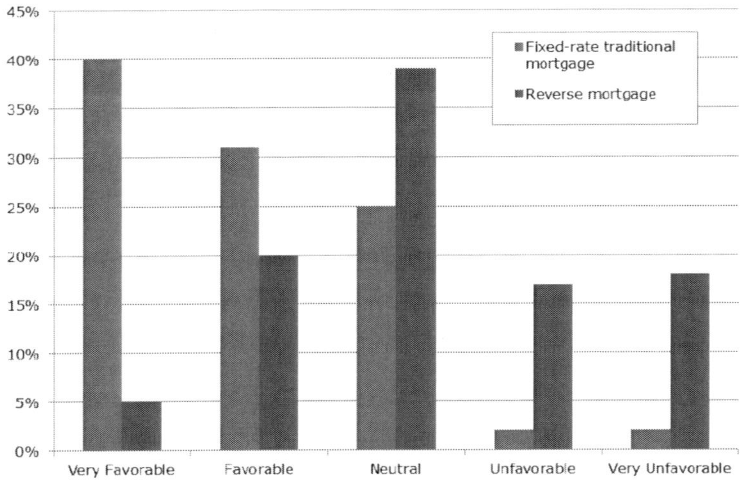

Source: Harris Interactive Poll.

Figure 11. Consumer impressions of mortgage products, 2007.

3.1.4. Motivations of Prospective Borrowers

Prospective reverse mortgage borrowers are generally motivated by a combination of two things: a need or desire for additional cash, and a desire to remain in their current home.

3.1.4a. Need or desire for more cash

A recent study conducted by MetLife and the National Council on Aging (NCOA) seems to indicate that the last few years have produced stark changes in the primary *purpose* for which prospective borrowers are seeking additional cash. According to the 2006 AARP survey, the most common reasons prospective reverse mortgage borrowers looked into the product were to improve their quality of life and/or plan for emergencies. According to the 2010 MetLife/NCOA study, the overwhelming reason that prospective borrowers looked into the product was as a means to manage debt, especially among counseling participants in their 60s.[130] Figure 12 displays the results of these two studies.

However, these data need to be interpreted with caution. The samples for the two studies were drawn differently. The AARP study was a phone survey of individuals who had obtained counseling through an AARP-endorsed housing counselor as much as three years prior to the survey. The MetLife study used data collected during counseling sessions over a three-month period. In addition, the questions asked in the two studies were not identical. Importantly, AARP provided counselees with separate answer choices for paying off mortgage debt and non-mortgage debt, while MetLife/NCOA grouped these responses into a single category. It seems likely that there is some overlap between the two categories in the 2006 AARP study (i.e., some respondents chose both mortgage and non-mortgage debt as a reason for looking into reverse mortgages) but we do not know how much. Moreover, in both studies, respondents were allowed to select multiple responses. With this type of question, it can be difficult to discern the primary motivations for consumer behavior. While there are other reasons to think that recent borrowers are more likely than previous borrowers to be most concerned about managing debt, more research on borrower motivations is needed.[1]

3.1.4b. Desire to remain in the current home

According to a 2010 industry poll, 81 percent of reverse mortgage borrowers say they plan to remain in their current home for the rest of their life.[131] Reverse mortgage borrowers are only slightly more likely to indicate a desire to remain in their current home than other eligible homeowners, 77 percent of whom said they wanted to stay in their current home for the rest of their lives.[132] These homes often have strong emotional ties – 43 percent of reverse mortgage borrowers and 36 percent of eligible homeowners still live in the home where they raised their children.[133]

However, comparatively few reverse mortgage borrowers actually do remain in their homes for the rest of their lives. Historically, the median reverse mortgage borrower repaid their loan after about 5 to 6 years,[134] despite having a life expectancy at origination of 11 years.[135] Recent developments in the housing market have resulted in fewer borrowers repaying their loans early, but this may be a temporary phenomenon. Repayment behavior is discussed in greater detail in Section 3.4.2.

3.1.5. High Satisfaction Reported among Recent Borrowers

Despite the general unease about reverse mortgages expressed by older consumers, reverse mortgage *borrowers* have reported high levels of initial satisfaction with the loans. More than four out of five borrowers in the 2006 AARP survey said that the loan had "completely" (58 percent) or "mostly" (25 percent) met their financial needs. Similarly, large majorities of borrowers agreed or strongly agreed that the reverse mortgage had helped them remain at home (79 percent), improved their quality of life (87 percent), and given them peace of mind (94 percent).[136] The 2010 poll conducted for the National Reverse Mortgage Lenders Association reported that 52 percent of borrowers would definitely recommend a reverse mortgage to a family member or a friend, and 28 percent would probably recommend it.[137]

However, to date no studies have been conducted on the long-term financial impact of reverse mortgages or borrowers' long-term satisfaction. The borrower satisfaction surveys conducted thus far have contacted borrowers whose loans are only a few years old. Reverse mortgages may well have different impacts, and borrowers may have different opinions of them, five to ten years into the loan. In addition to assessing long-term borrower satisfaction with the loans, more research is needed to understand what borrowers do after they repay the loans. As noted above, many borrowers do not actually remain in the home until they die. More research is needed with both *current* borrowers who have had their loans for many years, and with *former* borrowers who have repaid their loans, in order to learn more about the impacts on borrowers five to ten years after origination.

---

[1] As discussed in Section 3.2.4, today's counselees are significantly more likely to report having an existing mortgage than in years past.

3.2. Borrower Demographics

Reverse mortgage borrowers today are different from earlier borrowers in several important respects. Today's borrowers are taking out the loans at younger ages than earlier cohorts and are more likely to be married than in the past. They also are more likely to have traditional mortgage debt than in the past. These shifts coincide with the rapid expansion of the HECM program, from less than 10,000 loans per year in the late 1990s to over 100,000 loans per year in 2008 and 2009.[138] Recent borrowers constitute a much larger group than earlier borrowers. It is difficult to say whether shifts in borrower characteristics over time are a result of this transition from a very niche product to a wider set of borrowers, or whether the shift in borrower characteristics is a result of broader demographic changes and economic conditions.

Today's prospective reverse mortgage borrowers also differ from the underlying population of older homeowners, especially with respect to levels of debt. Prospective reverse mortgage borrowers are more likely to have a traditional mortgage and other types of debt than the general population of older homeowners. Among those that have traditional mortgages, reverse mortgage counseling participants have higher balances than the underlying population of older homeowners with a mortgage.

3.2.1. Age

Over the last two decades, reverse mortgage borrowers have started taking out the loans at younger and younger ages. Throughout the 1990s, more than half of borrowers were in their 70s, with borrowers in their 80s slightly more common than borrowers in their 60s. Beginning in the mid-2000s, a surge of younger borrowers in their 60s reshaped the age distribution. During this time period, the HECM program also dramatically expanded, from less than 10,000 loans per year to over 100,000 loans per year in 2008 and 2009. As shown in Figure 13, the proportion of borrowers in their 60s has more than doubled to 47 percent in FY2011, while borrowers in their 70s have slid to only 36 percent.

	2010		2006	
Reason for interest	Age 62-69	Age 70+	Borrowers	Non-borrowers
Pay off debt	73%	62%	-	-
Mortgage debt	-	-	40%	40%
Non mortgage debt	-	-	28%	27%
Increase income for every day expenses	31%	36%	50%	40%
Enhance quality of life	26%	28%	73%	68%
Plan ahead for emergencies	21%	24%	78%	66%

Sources: 2010 data - *Changing Attitudes, Changing Motives*, MetLife 2012. 2006 data – AARP, *Reverse Mortgages: Niche Product or Mainstream Solution?*, 2007.

Figure 12. Motivation among reverse mortgage counseling participants, 2006 & 2010.

Figure 14 tracks the evolving age distribution of HECM borrowers and compares it to the underlying senior population in 2010. The first two charts show the distribution of borrowers' ages at origination during the first and second decades of the program. The third chart shows the age distribution for the most recent fiscal year, FY2011, and the fourth chart provides a comparison to the overall senior population. This fourth chart includes 60-and 61-year olds in red bars for additional context.

Not only are recent borrowers younger at origination than earlier borrowers, but a dramatic spike in loan volume appears among the youngest eligible borrowers. While the median borrower in FY 2011 was 69.5, the most common age for borrowers was 62.[139] This surge of borrowers at the entry age of the program suggests a bottleneck of younger borrowers waiting to become eligible. The fourth chart in Figure 14, which shows the underlying senior population, does not have such a large concentration of 62-year-olds.[140] The distinctly taller bars for ages 62-64 in the third chart (FY 2011 borrowers) and ages 60-63 in the fourth chart (2010 population—one year earlier) represent the leading edge of the Baby Boomers.

With the exception of the spike at age 62, the age profile of HECM borrowers more closely mirrors the underlying population now than ever before. However, reverse mortgages do not provide equal value to borrowers of all ages. Borrowers in their 60s receive the lowest amount of proceeds, and stand to lose the most amount of home equity to compounded interest over a longer number of years. Section 3.4 discusses in greater detail the changing ways that borrowers are using the product. Section 3.5 discusses the increased risks to younger borrowers.

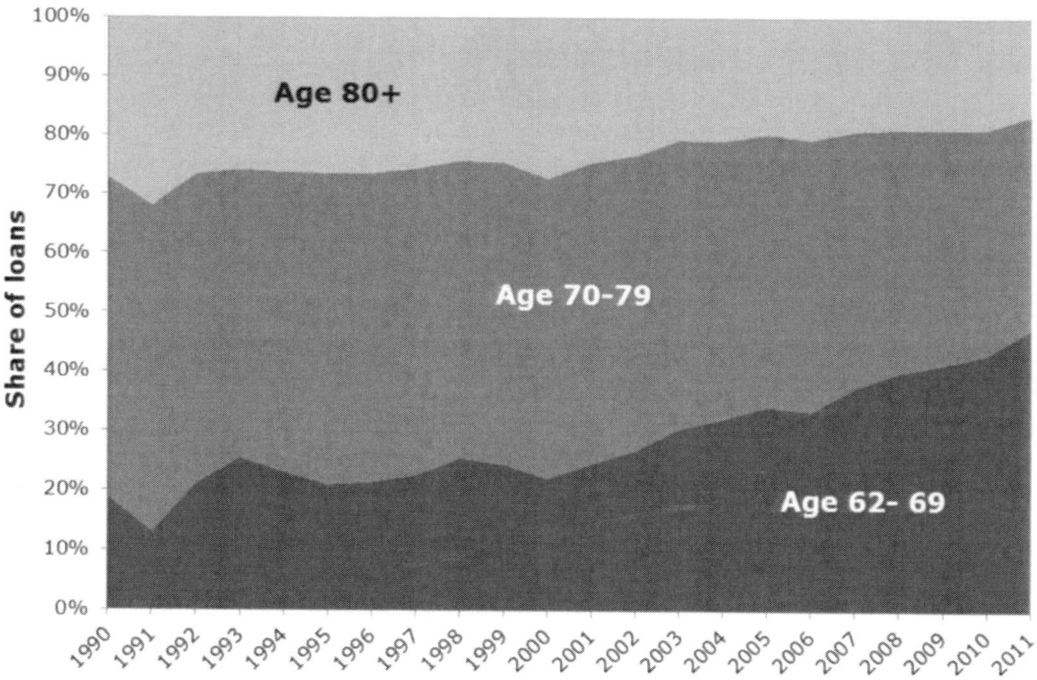

Source: CFPB analysis of FHA data.

Figure 13. Share of loans by age at origination, FY1990-2011.

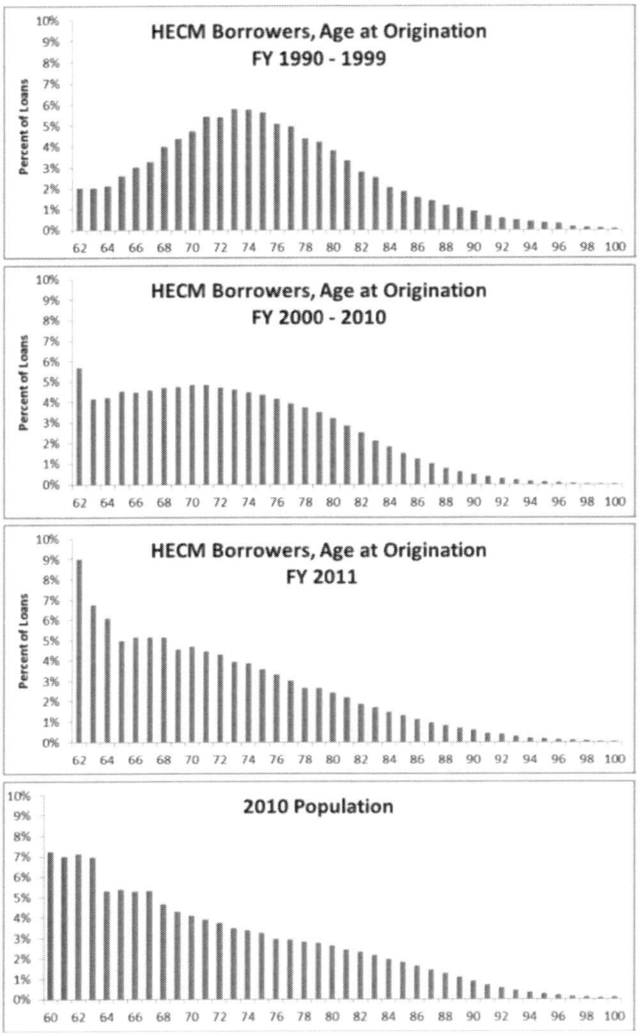

Source: CFPB analysis of FHA and U.S. Census Bureau data.

Figure 14. Evolving age distribution of HECM borrowers, with 2010 senior population.

3.2.2. Gender & Marital Status

Historically, the typical reverse mortgage borrower was a single female in her 70s.[m] With the increase of younger borrowers over the past decade, the proportion of couples has increased as well. Couples comprised 30 percent of borrowers in the 1990s, increasing to 37 percent in the late 2000s.[141] Single male borrowers, meanwhile, have also become more common.

Figure 15 shows this transition. While the share of single females has fallen from an average of 56 percent in the 1990s to an average of 43 percent in the late 2000s, single females are still the largest segment of reverse mortgage borrowers.

[m] FHA data does not actually record the marital status of borrowers, but rather whether there are one or two borrowers on the reverse mortgage. A small number of borrowers recorded as single may in fact be married or partnered, but chose not to include their spouse/partner on the reverse mortgage note. This can be risky for the non-borrowing spouse/partner, as discussed in Section 6.7.

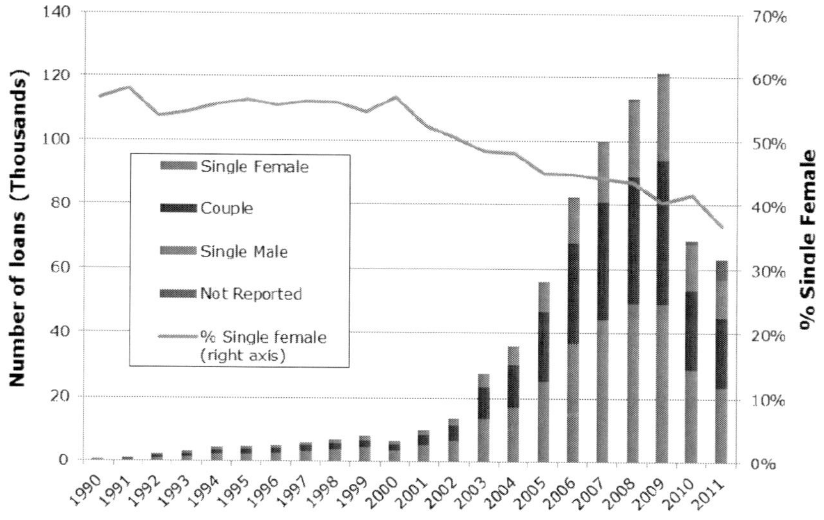

Source: CFPB analysis of FHA data.

Figure 15. Share of loans by gender & marital status, 1990-2011.

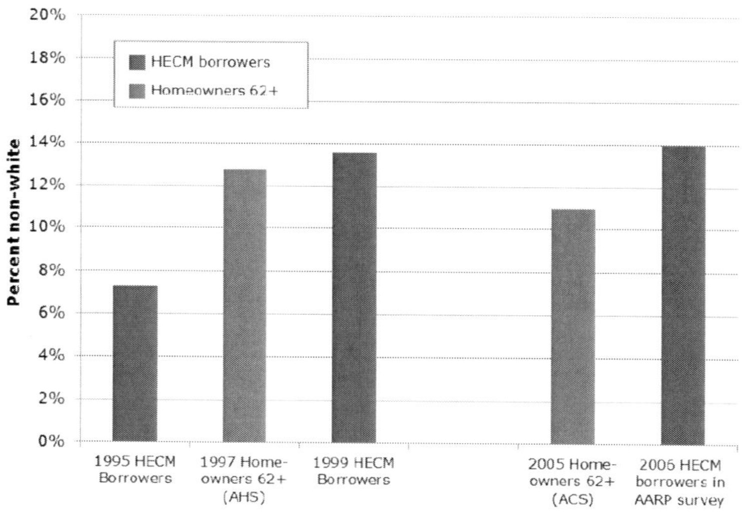

Source (Homeowners age 62+): 1997 American Housing Survey (AHS), 2005 American Community Survey (ACS).

Source (HECM borrowers): 1995 and 1999 HECM Evaluation Reports. Donald L. Redfoot et al., AARP, *Reverse Mortgages: Niche Product or nstream Solution? Mai* (Dec. 2007, 2006 data).

Figure 16. Race & ethnicity of HECM borrowers compared to homeowners age 62+.

3.2.3. Race/Ethnicity

There is no publicly available race and ethnicity data for HECM borrowers, so we have to rely on published program evaluations and survey data. Early in the HECM program, some observers raised concerns that nonwhite homeowners were under-represented among borrowers. In a 1995 analysis, only 7 percent of borrowers were nonwhite, while the underlying population of homeowners age 62 and over was 11 percent nonwhite in 1997.[142] By 1999, the proportion of nonwhite HECM borrowers had risen to nearly match the underlying population.[143] In 2006, nonwhite reverse mortgage borrowers in an AARP survey were actually over-represented compared to the underlying population.[144]

In 2010, the Federal Reserve Board held four public hearings and requested comments on possible amendments to Regulation C, the implementing regulation of the Home Mortgage Disclosure Act (HMDA).[145] Public comments spanned a range of issues including amending Regulation C to require the reporting of reverse mortgages, which are currently excluded from the regulation's requirements.[146] The Dodd-Frank Act transferred rulemaking authority for HMDA to the CFPB.[147]

3.2.4. Financial Position

Consumers who seek out reverse mortgages are more likely to have a traditional mortgage than the general population of older homeowners – and that difference is growing. In 2006, 47 percent of reverse mortgage counseling participants reported having a traditional mortgage or HELOC.[148] In contrast, only 42 percent of homeowners over age 62 had mortgage debt in 2007.[149] By 2010, 67 percent of counseling participants reported having mortgage debt,[150] while only 43 percent of homeowners over age 62 had mortgage debt in 2009.[151]

As shown in Figure 17, these differences between HECM counselees and the general population of older homeowners diverge dramatically when we look just at the late-2000s time frame (2009 homeowner data and 2010 counseling participant data). Homeowners in their 60s are more than twice as likely to have mortgage debt as homeowners age 70 and older (61 percent vs. 29 percent), because homeowners pay down their mortgages as they age. HECM counseling participants in their 60s are about 20 percent (12 percentage points) more likely than the general population of homeowners in their 60s to have mortgage debt. Meanwhile, HECM counseling participants in their 70s are more than *twice as likely* to have mortgage debt than all homeowners of the same age.

	Percent of homeowners with mortgage debt	
Year, by age group	**Homeowners, Age 62+**	**HECM Counseling Participants**
Mid-2000s	42%	47%
Late 2000s	43%	67%
Age 62-69	*61%*	*73%*
Age 70+	*29%*	*62%*

Source (Homeowners age 62+): CFPB analysis of Survey of Consumer Finance data, 2007 (mid-2000s) and 2009 (late 2000s).

Source (HECM counseling participants): Donald L. Redfoot et al., AARP, *Reverse Mortgages: Niche Product or Mainstream ion? Solut* , Dec. 2007 (2006 data: mid-2000s). MetLife, *Changing Attitudes, Changing Motives* , 2012. (2010 data: late 2000s).

Figure 17. Proportion older homeowners and HECM counseling participants and with mortgage debt.

Data obtained by the CFPB from one reverse mortgage lender confirms that reverse mortgage borrowers commonly have existing mortgage debt. In 2010, 64 percent of borrowers using this lender (69 percent of borrowers age 62-69 and 61 percent of borrowers age 70 and over) used at least some portion of their reverse mortgage proceeds to pay off an existing mortgage.[152]

Prospective reverse mortgage borrowers are not only more likely to have mortgage debt than their counterparts in the general population, but those who do have a mortgage also owe more on their homes than comparable older homeowners. Figure 18 compares the amount of mortgage debt (measured as a percent of home value) reported by HECM counselees who had a mortgage in 2010 with the amount of mortgage debt owed by general-population homeowners in 2009 (the closest year available). Overall, HECM counselees were about 10 percentage points more likely to owe at least 25 percent of their home's value than all older homeowners. The lender data obtained by the CFPB is broadly consistent with these findings.

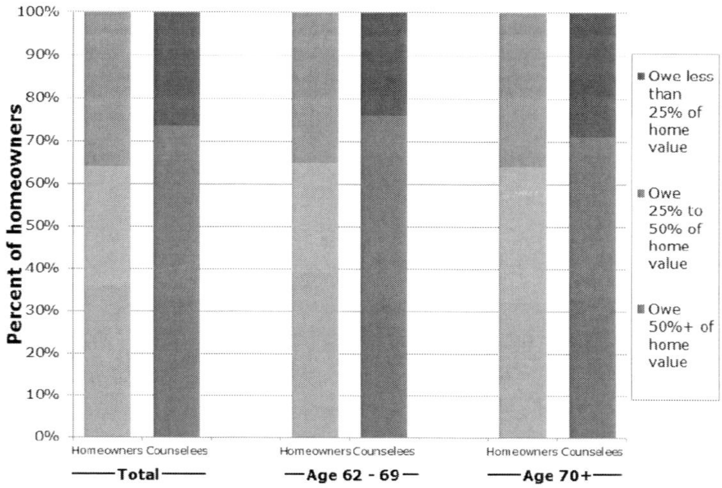

Source (Homeowners): CFPB analysis of Survey of Consumer Finances data, 2009.
Note: Homeowners are limited to homeowners ages 62+ who have a mortgage.
Source (Counselees): MetLife Mature Market Institute, *Changing Attitudes, Changing Motives*, 2012. (2010 data)

Figure 18. Amount of mortgage debt, homeowners and HECM counselees with mortgages.

Whereas the difference in *likelihood* of having a mortgage between reverse mortgage counseling participants and the general population of older homeowners is more pronounced for homeowners age 70 and over, the difference in the *proportion of home value owed* is larger for homeowners in their 60s.

Finally, prospective reverse mortgage borrowers also are more likely to have more debt overall than the general population of older homeowners. Figure 19 uses the same 2010 counseling data and 2009 population data to compare the debt characteristics of HECM counselees with the general population of older homeowners. Overall, HECM counselees are 18 percentage points more likely to have some type of mortgage or consumer debt than the general population of homeowners age 62 and older. For HECM counselees in their 60s, the difference is smaller (9 percentage points more likely) while for HECM counselees age 70 and over, the difference is even greater (27 percentage points, or more than twice as likely).

Historically, reverse mortgage borrowers have had somewhat lower incomes than older homeowners generally. Figure 20 shows the income distribution of reverse mortgage borrowers in 2009.

There is some evidence to suggest that the baby boom generation – whose members are just beginning to become eligible for reverse mortgages – will carry more debt into retirement than earlier generations. Between 2004 and 2007, the median household debt increased by 38 percent among households headed by an adult aged 50 to 61.[153]

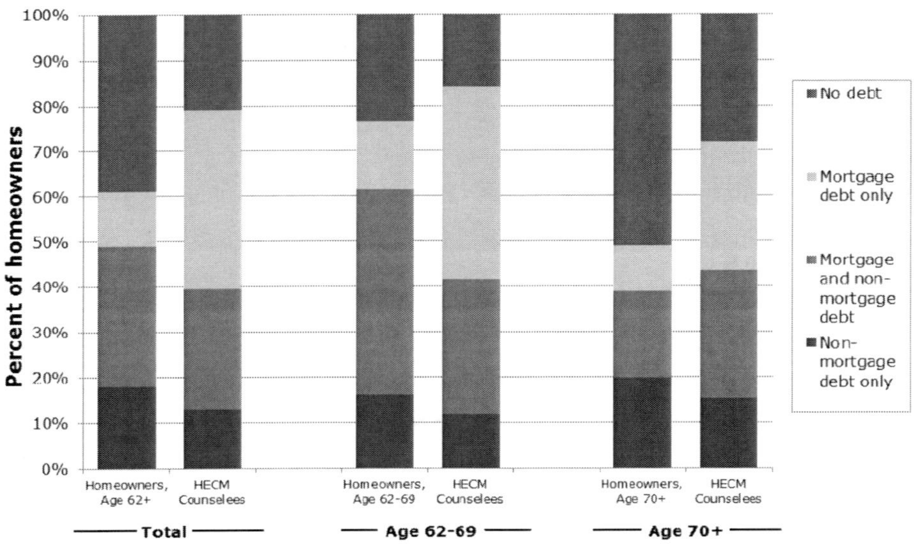

Source (HECM counselees): MetLife Mature Market Institute, *Changing Attitudes, Changing Motives*, 2012 (2010 data).
Source (Homeowners 62+): CFPB analysis of Survey of Consumer Finances data (2009 data).

Figure 19. Debt characteristics of older homeowners and HECM counselees, late 2000s .

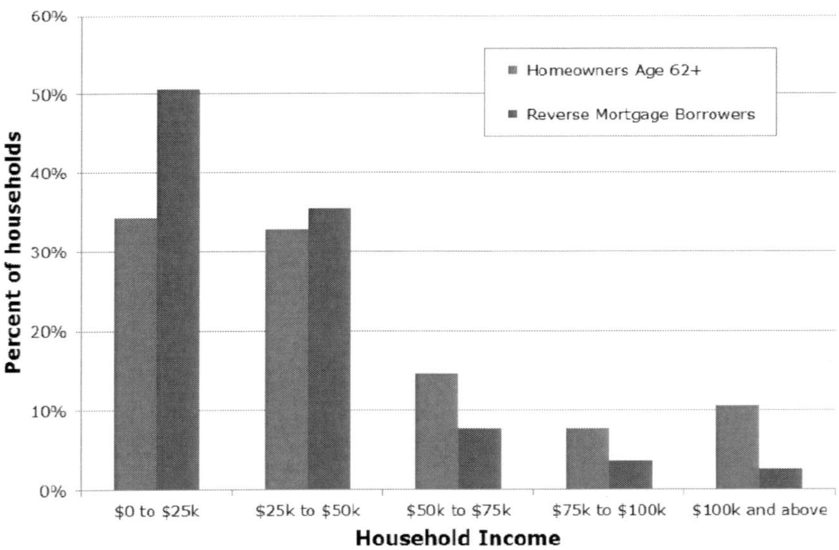

Source: CFPB analysis of American Housing Survey data, 2009.

Figure 20. Income distribution of reverse mortgage borrowers, 2009.

3.3. Borrower Behavior Differs by Segment

Not all reverse mortgage borrowers are alike. FHA data reveals several interesting differences between different consumer segments.

3.3.1. Fixed-Rate, Lump-Sum Product More Popular with Younger Borrowers and Lower-Home-Value Borrowers

Younger borrowers are more likely to take out fixed-rate, lump-sum loans than older borrowers. As shown in Figure 21, borrowers in their 60s are about 30 percentage points more likely to take out fixed-rate loans than borrowers over age 85. Data obtained by the CFPB from a reverse mortgage lender add additional context to this observation. Among this lender's customers, younger borrowers are much more likely to use their reverse mortgage to pay off an existing lien at closing. This suggests that one reason younger borrowers are choosing fixed-rate, lump-sum loans in higher proportions than older borrowers may be because they are using the loan to pay off an existing mortgage.

Borrowers with lower home values are also more likely to take out fixed-rate, lump-sum loans than borrowers with higher home values. As shown in Figure 22, borrowers with home values less than $100,000 are 25 percentage points more likely to take out fixed-rate, lump-sum loans than borrowers with home values greater than $500,000. Unlike in Figure 21, the lender data on the proportion of borrowers paying off a lien at closing exhibits a contrary trend to the data on borrowers choosing a fixed-rate loan. This could be because borrowers with lower home values receive lower proceeds, in dollar terms, than borrowers with higher home values. Borrowers with low home values who own their homes free and clear and choose a fixed-rate, lump-sum loan may view the overall dollar amount of proceeds to be insufficient to warrant saving a portion for later use.

Age	% of borrowers choosing a fixed-rate, lump-sum loan (market-wide FHA data)	% of borrowers paying off a lien at closing* (data restricted to one lender)
Less than 65	77%	70%
65 - 69	76%	69%
70 - 74	70%	68%
75 - 79	63%	64%
80 - 84	57%	59%
85+	47%	48%

Source: Fixed-rate market share: CFPB analysis of FHA data. Pay off lien at closing: CFPB analysis of data provided by a reverse mortgage lender. *In this data, "lien" generally refers to an existing mortgage, but could also include a federal lien or judgment. The lien payoff data is from one lender only, and so cannot be interpreted as representative of the entire market.

Figure 21. Fixed-rate, lump-sum usage and lien payoffs by age group, FY2010.

Appraised value	% of borrowers choosing a fixed-rate, lump-sum loan (market-wide FHA data)	% of borrowers paying off a lien at closing* (data restricted to one lender)
Less than $100,000	83%	48%
$100,000 - $200,000	73%	60%
$200,000 - $300,000	65%	66%
$300,000 - $400,000	61%	68%
$400,000 - $500,000	61%	72%
$500,000+	57%	76%

Source: Fixed-rate market share: CFPB analysis of FHA data. Pay off lien at closing: CFPB analysis of data provided by a reverse mortgage lender. *In this data, "lien" generally refers to an existing mortgage, but could also include a federal lien or judgment. The lien payoff data is from one lender only, and so cannot be interpreted as representative of the entire market.

Figure 22. Fixed-rate, lump-sum usage and lien payoffs by home value, FY2010.

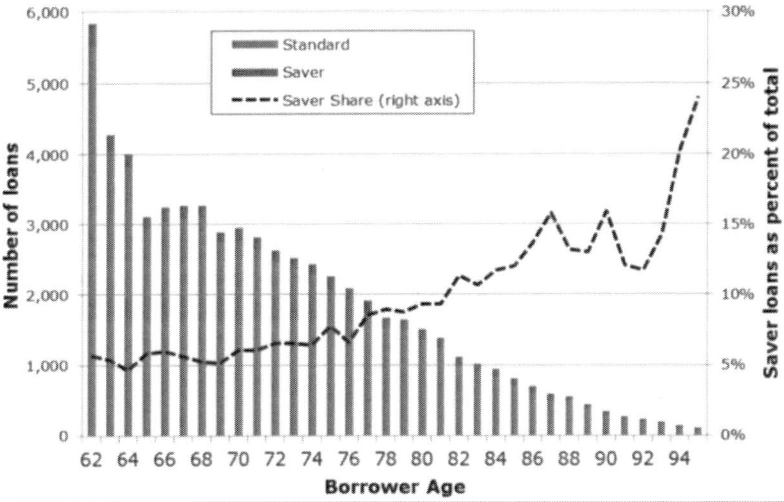

Source: CFPB analysis of FHA data

Figure 23. HECM Saver volume and share by borrower age, FY 2011.

3.3.2. Saver Product More Popular with Older Borrowers and Adjustable-Rate Borrowers

As discussed in Sections 2.2.1d and 2.4.1, a new product called the HECM Saver was introduced in October 2010 that virtually eliminated the upfront FHA mortgage insurance premium in exchange for offering loan lower proceeds to the borrower. Overall, the new Saver product has had very low uptake (7 percent in FY 2011), but as Figure 23 shows, the uptake increases significantly with age. The oldest homeowners are particularly well-suited to benefit from the Saver's lower upfront fees and may need to access less of their home equity.[n]

The Saver product also has proved much more popular among adjustable-rate borrowers than among fixed-rate borrowers. As shown in Figure 24, the Saver reached 28 percent market share among adjustable-rate borrowers in early 2011 before retreating to 18 percent in late 2011. In contrast, only 2 percent of fixed-rate borrowers chose the Saver product in 2011. This makes sense, as the Saver is designed to appeal to borrowers who do not need as much money, while the adjustable-rate loan appeals most to borrowers who do not need all of their proceeds upfront. It seems likely that borrowers who need less proceeds overall are also less likely to need all of their proceeds upfront. Thus, borrowers who do not need a lot of proceeds are both more likely to choose the Saver product (in order to take advantage of lower upfront mortgage insurance) and more likely to choose the adjustable-rate product (in order to save on interest costs and benefit from the credit line growth).

3.4. Shifts in Borrower Usage Patterns

Borrowers today are taking out more cash upfront than in the past. This trend has been building slowly over time, but was exacerbated in 2009 when the new fixed-rate product

[n] The older the borrower, the less benefit the borrower will derive from the Standard product because the borrower has fewer years of life expectancy over which to spread the higher upfront fees of the Standard product.

requiring borrowers to take the full amount up front was introduced. Meanwhile, the housing crash in 2008 appears to have triggered a significant slowdown in the rate at which borrowers repay their loans, but it is too soon to tell whether this trend will continue or revert to historical norms when the housing market recovers.[154]

3.4.1. More Borrowers Take More Cash Upfront

Over the last two decades, borrowers have been taking more and more of their reverse mortgage proceeds upfront.[155] In 1990, the median borrower took out 36 percent of authorized loan proceeds within the first year.[156] Throughout the 1990s and 2000s, the proportion of proceeds taken out upfront crept upwards. By 2008, the median borrower was taking out 88 percent of authorized loan proceeds within the first year – nearly a full draw.[157]

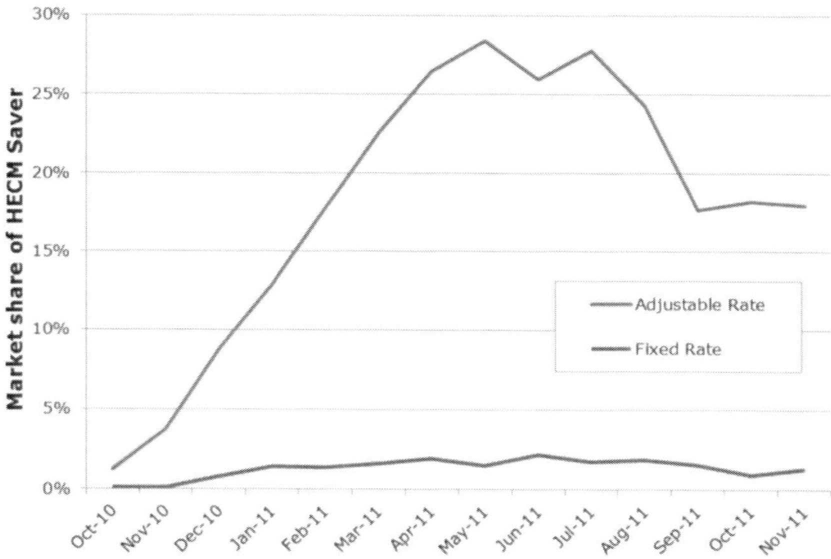

Source: CFPB analysis of FHA data.

Figure 24. HECM Saver market share, by rate type.

As the market shifted toward fixed-rate lump-sum products in early 2009, the proportion of borrowers who took all of their loan proceeds upfront increased markedly. The increase in median upfront cash draws through 2008 suggests that many of the borrowers who chose fixed-rate loans since mid-2009 would have taken out most of their available proceeds upfront regardless of which product they chose. Many of these borrowers appear to be using the reverse mortgage not as a method for generating income to supplement expenses in retirement, but as a method to refinance their existing mortgage without incurring monthly mortgage payments. Data from one lender indicate that borrowers who use most or all of their proceeds in order to refinance an existing mortgage are more likely to choose a fixed-rate, lump-sum loan than borrowers who own their homes free and clear or who have only a small existing mortgage.[158] Borrowers who refinance an existing mortgage with a reverse mortgage face increased risks, which are discussed in greater detail in Section 3.5.

However, as shown in Figure 25, the market adoption of the fixed-rate, lump-sum product in early 2009 coincides with a 32 percentage point increase in the proportion of borrowers taking 90 percent or more of their available funds at closing. These figures strongly suggest that the fixed-rate, lump-sum product is largely responsible for increasing the proportion of borrowers taking all of their funds upfront.

There appears to be a significant segment of borrowers who are taking fixed-rate, lump-sum loans and taking sizeable cash payouts. According to data from one lender covering the two-year period after the fixed-rate product had come to dominate the market, nearly one-third of borrowers who owned their homes free and clear or had only a small existing mortgage balance chose a fixed-rate loan.[159] As noted in Section 3.3.2, this phenomenon is particularly pronounced among borrowers with lower home values. During the same time period, 28 percent of this lender's fixed-rate, lump-sum borrowers took home more than $50,000 in cash at closing.[160]

Data on how borrowers use these funds are not available. Some may be paying off other, non-mortgage debt, investing in home improvements, or taking care of other major expenses. However, to the extent that borrowers' immediate expenses are less than their total proceeds, these fixed-rate borrowers may be saving or investing a portion of the proceeds. These borrowers may be earning less on the money than they are paying in interest on the loan, and might be better served by choosing an adjustable-rate loan that benefits from the line-of-credit growth feature discussed in Section 2.4.3. These borrowers also face increased risks of making poor investment choices or being targeted for fraud or other scams.

Loan type	**2008**	**2010**
Adjustable rate	98%	30%
Less than full draw (<90% at closing)	*57%*	*25%*
Full draw (90%+ at closing)	*41%*	*5%*
Fixed rate (lump sum)	2%	70%
Total	100%	100%
Borrowers taking 90%+ at closing	**43%**	**75%**

Source: CFPB analysis of FHA data.

Figure 25. Borrowers taking a full draw at closing, 2008 & 2010.

Around 70 percent of borrowers have chosen the fixed-rate product since mid-2009. Some of these borrowers have high upfront cash needs due to an existing mortgage, while other borrowers are taking large sums in cash for reasons that are less well understood. In contrast, borrowers who have chosen to stay with the adjustable-rate product are, for the most part, taking out much less in cash up front. After the introduction of the fixed-rate product, the upfront cash draw of the median *adjustable-rate* borrower plummeted. Figure 26 reveals this emerging segmentation between fixed-rate borrowers, who take a lump-sum at closing, and adjustable-rate borrowers, who are increasingly taking lower draws at closing. By mid-2011, the median *adjustable-rate* borrower was taking out only 45 percent of available proceeds in cash.[161]

3.4.2. Typical Loan Terms Have Lengthened

Historically, the median reverse mortgage borrower repaid the loan after about 5 to 6 years,[162] despite having a life expectancy at origination of about 10 to 11 years.[163] An analysis conducted in 2007 found that borrowers in their 60s at origination were less likely to live in the home for the rest of their lives than borrowers who were in their 70s or 80s at origination. Borrowers in their mid-60s at origination paid off their loans 6 to 8 times more quickly than would have been expected based on underlying age-specific mortality rates. Borrowers in their mid-70s paid their loans off about 2 to 3 times more quickly, and borrowers in their mid-80s paid their loans off about 1.5 times more quickly, than underlying mortality rates would suggest.[164]

Starting in 2007, borrower payoff behavior changed markedly. Borrowers started repaying their loans more slowly. Figure 27 shows the cumulative proportion of loans paid off over time for each origination year from 2001 through 2010. The loans originated between 1990 and 2000 behaved similarly to each other, and are aggregated together to provide historical context.

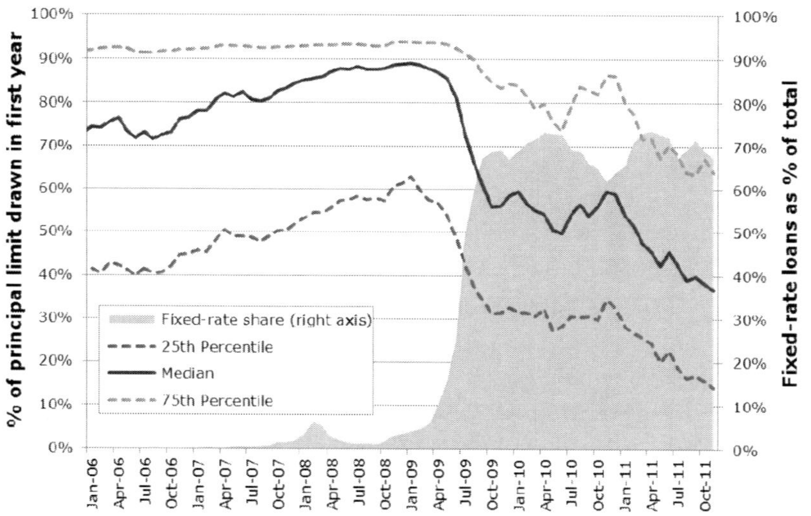

Source: CFPB analysis of FHA data.

Figure 26. Initial cash draws of adjustable-rate borrowers, 2006-2011.

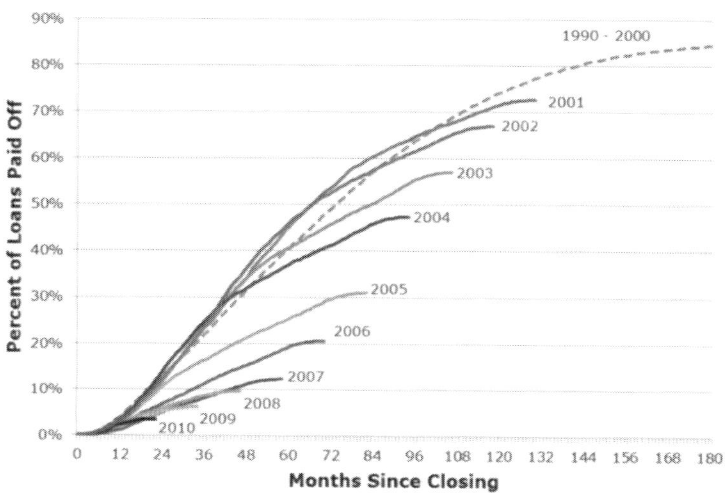

Source: CFPB analysis of FHA data.

Figure 27. Cumulative proportion of loans paid off, by origination year, 1990-2010.

The 2005 origination year offers a clear example of how much loan terms have lengthened. Loans originated in 2005 reached their sixth year during 2011. Historically, at least 50 percent of borrowers would have paid off their loans by the sixth year. As shown in Figure 27, however, only 30 percent of loans originated in 2005 had been paid off by the sixth year.

The 2001 through 2006 lines all have clear bends where they switch from a steeper to a flatter trajectory. The points at which the lines bend correspond approximately with the year 2007. This pattern is easiest to see for the 2005 origination year. The 2005 line separates from the rest of the pack at 24 months, which is in 2007. The same is true for the 2003 origination year (the curve bends at about 48 months, which is in 2007) and every other origination year from 2001 through 2006. The origination years 2007 and later are all on a lower trajectory from the very beginning.

The timing of this shift in borrower behavior suggests that the housing crash may be significant in explaining payoff behavior. The height of the housing bubble was in 2006 and early 2007.[165] By the end of 2008, many borrowers may have had little remaining equity in their homes due to the rising reverse mortgage balance coupled with home price declines. With little equity remaining, many borrowers who would otherwise have moved may not have had the financial resources to do so.

Borrowers in origination years 2007-2010, who took out their loans during and after the housing crash, are already exhibiting lower pay-off rates than any prior origination year. For these borrowers, the overall market environment may be contributing to less mobility than in previous years.

When the dataset is restricted to just states hardest hit by the foreclosure crisis, the pattern is similar to that observed in Figure 27, but more pronounced. Compared to historical norms, payoff speeds increased during the boom, and then flattened out even more markedly than in Figure 27. The pattern also holds throughout the age distribution of reverse mortgage borrowers. As shown in Figure 28, the curves are flatter for borrowers in their 60s and steeper for borrowers 70 and older (reflecting shorter life expectances and more payoffs due to deaths in the older cohort), but the overall pattern is strikingly similar.

3.5. New Risks to Consumers

This chapter has identified five key trends present among reverse mortgage borrowers:

- Today's prospective borrowers are more likely to have substantial existing mortgage debt and/or consumer debt than the general population of older homeowners, and they are more likely to have mortgage debt than borrowers in the past.
- Borrowers are taking more cash upfront than in the past.
- Borrowers are more likely to be in their 60s at origination than in the past.
- Borrowers in their 60s are more likely to have substantial existing mortgage debt than older borrowers.
- Borrowers in their 60s are more likely than older borrowers to choose a fixed-rate, lump-sum product.

Taken together, these facts suggest that borrowers today are increasingly using reverse mortgages as a way to refinance existing mortgage debt – while eliminating their monthly mortgage payments – early in their retirement or even before reaching retirement. Data obtained by the CFPB from one reverse mortgage lender supports this conclusion. This pattern of use is very different from what was originally intended when the product was first developed, and poses several significant risks to the consumer.

The original purpose envisioned for reverse mortgages was to enable older borrowers to convert home equity into cash they could use to help meet expenses in retirement.[166] Borrowers could choose between an income stream for everyday expenses, a line of credit for major expenses (such as home repairs and medical expenses), or a combination of the two. It was anticipated that most, though not all, borrowers would use their loans to age in place, living in their current homes for the rest of their lives or at least until they needed skilled care. Upon the borrower's death, or upon leaving the home, the borrower or the estate would sell the home to repay the loan and would receive any remaining home equity.

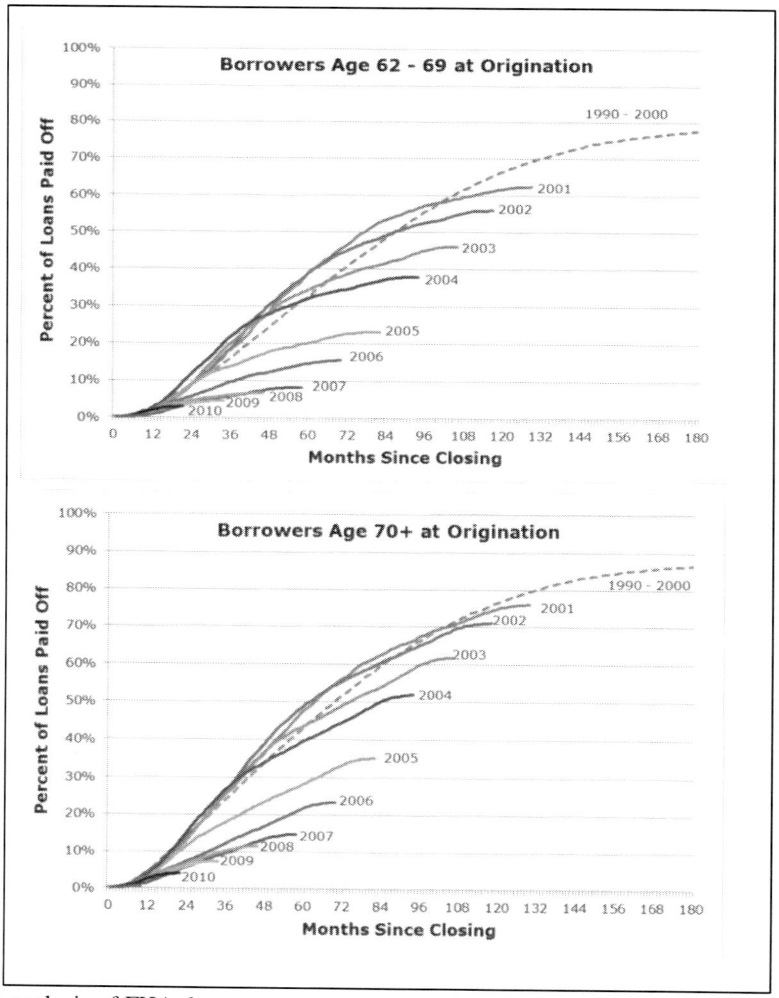

Source: CFPB analysis of FHA data.

Figure 28. Cumulative proportion of loans paid off, by age and origination year, 1990-2010.

When borrowers instead use reverse mortgages as a method of refinancing an existing mortgage (or other debt), they essentially devote their existing home equity to servicing the debt on the property. While they gain additional cash flow (that previously was going to mortgage payments) for a period of time, they lose the ability to use their home equity as a cushion against other major expenses in retirement, such as needed home repairs or medical expenses. This risk is greater for the new surge of borrowers in their 60s with sizeable traditional mortgage balances and long life expectancies.

Refinancing a traditional mortgage with a reverse mortgage may well be a good choice for borrowers in their 60s who have adequate retirement resources to cover everyday expenses and who are unable to continue working or whose employment income does not support the current mortgage. This type of borrower receives something of considerable value – the ability to remain in the current home indefinitely – in exchange for assuming a rising loan balance that will slowly consume the borrower's remaining equity.

Even for this relatively stable prospective borrower, however, choosing a reverse mortgage early in retirement is a riskier decision than it is for older borrowers with similar financial circumstances. Borrowers in their 60s have longer life expectancies than borrowers in their 70s. If borrowers in their 60s succeed in aging in place, they will most likely use up all of their home equity, but they will receive considerable benefit in exchange for that home equity. But if borrowers in their 60s *do not* succeed in aging in place indefinitely – if, due to health or other reasons they need to move at some point in their 70s or 80s – they are at high risk of having used up all of their home equity and having no financial resources with which to finance their move.

Meanwhile, if prospective borrowers *do not* have adequate savings and other retirement resources and are instead struggling to make ends meet, using a reverse mortgage to refinance an existing traditional mortgage can result in even greater long-term financial risk to the borrower. Some prospective borrowers' financial situations may be fundamentally unsustainable. Using a reverse mortgage to hold on to the home for the near term may simply postpone hard decisions, provide little long-term benefit to the borrower, and consume most or all of the borrower's home equity in the process. This type of borrower is at high risk of getting behind on taxes and insurance, and facing foreclosure on the reverse mortgage.

According to an industry poll, the vast majority of older homeowners say that they want to live in their homes for the rest of their lives.[167] Nonetheless, some do downsize.[168] Some portion of younger borrowers might be using reverse mortgages as a medium-term financing tool to increase cash flow prior to downsizing or otherwise selling their homes. In this case, there is less reason to be concerned that younger borrowers may be jeopardizing their long-term financial stability by tapping their home equity too early. However, traditional mortgage products may be more suitable for these borrowers than a reverse mortgage. Reverse mortgages carry a sizeable insurance premium to cover the risk that at the time the loan is repaid the loan balance will exceed the value of the home, either because the borrower outlived the actuarial tables or because home prices declined. If younger borrowers do not intend to live in the home long enough to need this coverage, traditional mortgage or HELOC financing may be a better option for those who can qualify.

In sum, reverse mortgage borrowers in their 60s, especially those seeking to refinance a sizeable traditional mortgage balance, are at higher risk than other borrowers of finding themselves with few financial resources with which to cover unexpected expenses or finance a move later in life. Prospective borrowers in their 60s with few other retirement resources may simply be prolonging an unsustainable financial situation by using a reverse mortgage to refinance a traditional mortgage. And prospective borrowers in their 60s seeking to use a reverse mortgage as a way to increase cash flow for a few years before moving may find that traditional mortgage products are better suited to their situation.

Some borrowers also appear to be taking a lump sum upfront *without* refinancing a traditional mortgage. They too face increased risks of having fewer resources to draw upon later in life. Borrowers who save or invest the proceeds may be earning less on the savings than they are paying in interest on the loan, or they may be exposing their savings to risky investment choices. These borrowers also face increased risks of being targeted for fraud or other scams.

4. Market

The reverse mortgage market has changed dramatically in the past few years. Proprietary products, which had proliferated during the mortgage boom in 2006 and 2007, completely evaporated in the subsequent recession. In late 2007, Ginnie Mae[o] introduced a new securitization model that led to the development of a new fixed-rate product in which borrowers are required to take all of their authorized loan proceeds upfront in a lump sum. In early 2008, FHA issued guidance stating that this fixed-rate product could be structured as a closed-end loan. In April 2009, Fannie Mae,[p] which had been the dominant secondary-market purchaser of HECM loans since the program's inception, began scaling back its presence in the market. In its place, Ginnie Mae-backed HECM Mortgage-Backed Securities (HMBS) have become the nearly exclusive secondary-market instrument.

In mid-2009, changes in the interest rate environment coupled with the exit of Fannie Mae and the shift to the Ginnie Mae securities altered the cost and benefit calculus – for both consumers and lenders – of adjustable rate HECMs as compared to the new fixed-rate, lump-sum HECMs. In less than six months, the market share of fixed-rate HECMs swung from less than 10 percent to more than 60 percent of originated HECMs. Since August 2009, the market share of the fixed-rate, lump-sum product has ranged between 60 percent and 75 percent.

In October 2010, FHA introduced a variety of policy changes including a new product, the HECM Saver, which virtually eliminates the upfront mortgage insurance premium in exchange for lower proceeds available to the borrower. FHA also lowered the loan proceeds available to Standard HECM borrowers.

In early 2011, the two largest reverse mortgage lenders, Wells Fargo and Bank of America, announced their exit from the market. In April 2012, the largest remaining lender, MetLife, also announced its exit. These three lenders had large retail lending operations. With their departure, the market has become much more heavily dependent on mortgage brokers and small correspondent lenders.

---

[o] Ginnie Mae is a special-purpose government-sponsored secondary market facilitator dedicated to facilitating the securitization of FHA-insured mortgages.

[p] Fannie Mae and Freddie Mac are government-sponsored enterprises, also known as GSEs, dedicated to facilitating the securitization of traditional, non-FHA insured residential mortgages.

4.1. Size of the Market

During the first decade of the HECM program's existence, less than 10,000 loans were made each year. The program initially was authorized only as a demonstration program with specific caps on the number of loans that could be insured. In 1998, Congress made the HECM program permanent and expanded FHA's authority to insure reverse mortgages.[169] In the early 2000s, volume began to grow steadily, reaching 50,000 loans per year by 2005.

Figure 29 provides three different measures of HECM origination volume over time:

- **Number of loans.** The number of loan originations peaked in FY 2009 at 115,000 and fell to 72,000 by FY 2011.[170] In total, 740,000 loans have been originated under the HECM program; about 582,000 are still outstanding.
- **Home value.** The dollar volume of originations can be measured by the home value at origination (or applicable FHA loan limit, whichever is less). Known as the maximum claim amount, this represents the maximum future value of the loan to investors at repayment, including compounded interest.[171] By this measure, about $166 billion (not adjusted for inflation) has been originated over the history of the program. As of November 2011, $136 billion is outstanding.[172]
- **Initial Principal Limit.** The initial principal limit is generally the actual cash amount borrowers are authorized to receive.[173] For fixed-rate borrowers, this would represent the actual initial balance on the loan. For adjustable-rate borrowers, the initial balance is often less. By this measure, nearly $114 billion in loans (not adjusted for inflation) has been originated since the program's inception. As of November 2011, about $92 billion is outstanding.[174]

Figure 30 chronicles the increase in average home values and initial principal limits for HECM loans over time.

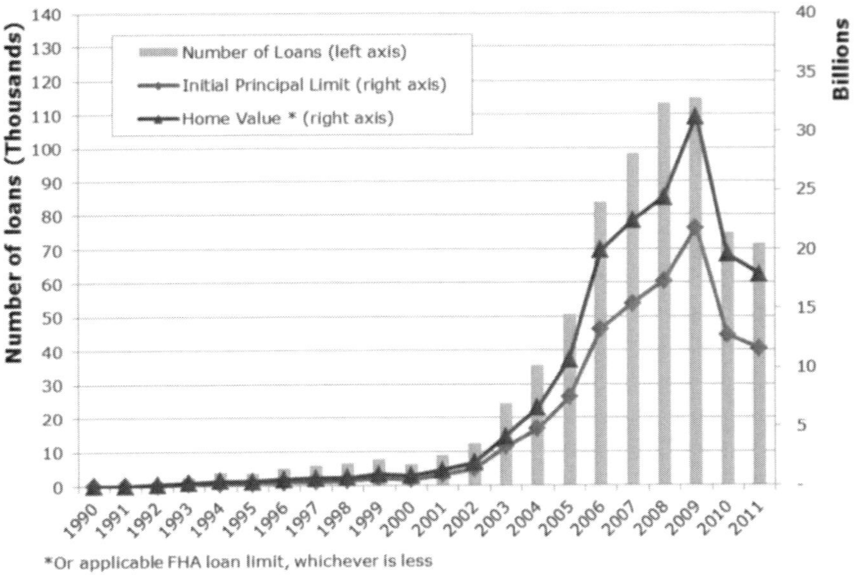

Source: CFPB analysis of FHA data.

Figure 29. HECM loan volumes, FY 1990-2011.

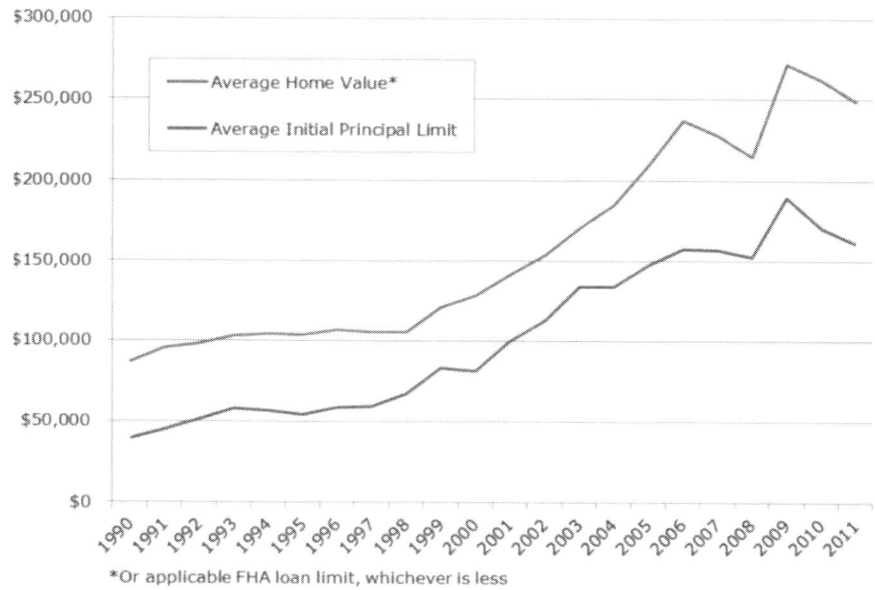

Source: CFPB analysis of FHA data.

Figure 30. Average home values* and initial principal limits for HECM loans, 1990-2011.

The proprietary market is almost nonexistent today. Only one lender, Generation Mortgage, offers a product. Appendix I details the development of the proprietary market prior to the housing crash.

4.2. A Complex Market

Much like the traditional mortgage market, the reverse mortgage market includes several types of companies that fill different and sometimes overlapping roles. Loan originators are companies that take borrowers' applications and arrange loans. Lenders underwrite and fund the loans. The originator and the lender can be the same, or separate, companies.

Reverse mortgage lenders, like traditional mortgage lenders, do not typically want to hold reverse mortgage loans on their books until maturity. Instead, they sell the loans to a secondary market investor, or ultimate owner of the loan. By selling the loans into the secondary market, lenders free up capital to make new loans. The terms prevailing in the secondary market drive the pricing and product availability decisions made by lenders and brokers, ultimately having a profound impact on the options available to consumers.

Like traditional mortgage loans, reverse mortgage loans are originated through three channels: retail, wholesale, and correspondent.

- **Retail.** Large lenders employ a retail sales force to make loans directly. In the retail channel, the originator and the lender are the same company.
- **Wholesale.** Large lenders have business relationships with a network of independent brokers who facilitate and prepare loans for the large lender. The large lender then

makes the loans using its funds. In the wholesale channel, the originator and the lender are different companies (the broker is the originator).

- **Correspondent.** Correspondent lenders are not able to or do not wish to sell loans directly into the secondary market. These lenders have business relationships with other companies that do deal directly with the secondary market. The correspondent lender makes loans on its own behalf, using its own funds, and then sells the loans to the other company. Correspondent lenders generate loans through their own retail loan officers, brokers, and sometimes through other correspondent lenders.

In the traditional mortgage market, the government-sponsored enterprises (GSEs) Fannie Mae and Freddie Mac play an important role in purchasing mortgages from lenders. They package loans into securities and sell those securities to investors. In the reverse mortgage market, neither GSE is involved in purchasing HECMs. Today, the primary method of selling HECMs into the secondary market is through Ginnie Mae, a special-purpose government-sponsored secondary market entity that facilitates the securitization FHA-insured mortgages.[175] Unlike the GSEs, Ginnie Mae does not purchase and securitize loans itself. Instead, it provides a government guarantee for securities packaged by individual securities issuers through its HECM Mortgage Backed Securities (HMBS) program.

Securities issuers can be one of two types of companies. Some issuers are also retail lenders. These retail lender-issuers package securities containing loans that they originated themselves, bought from correspondent lenders, or sourced through brokers. Other issuers are niche secondary-market intermediaries (referred to here as aggregator-issuers) that package securities primarily composed of loans bought from correspondent lenders or sourced through brokers.

After packaging a security, issuers sell the security to Wall Street broker-dealers who place the securities with investors in the secondary market. The investors interested in purchasing HMBS are typically institutional investors such as pension funds, domestic banks, hedge funds, and money managers.[176]

Ginnie Mae issuers are required to be the servicer of record for all the loans in their securities, which means that the issuer is responsible for servicing the loans in the future. While issuers may subcontract some of the day to day tasks of servicing the loan,[177] they retain several financial and procedural obligations (discussed in greater detail in Section 4.4.3a). Thus, issuers are referred to throughout this report as issuerservicers.

Figure 31 illustrates the reverse mortgage market relationships as they exist today.

4.2.1. Unique Market Challenges for Reverse Mortgages

Reverse mortgages are more complicated to sell and service than traditional mortgages. In a traditional mortgage, the exchange of money is straightforward. For a fixed-rate, lump-sum reverse mortgage, the cash flows are less predictable – the money is repaid in a lump sum at an uncertain date instead of being paid periodically over time. Historically, however, nearly all reverse mortgages were structured as adjustable-rate, line-of-credit or monthly disbursement plans. For these products, the exchange of money is not only less predictable, but also more complicated than in the traditional mortgage market. The reverse-mortgage market has to contend with the extra question of which entity will provide the cash to make future payments to the borrower. Figure 32 illustrates this difference in cash flows between traditional mortgages and adjustable-rate reverse mortgages. The challenges this dynamic creates are discussed in greater detail in Section 4.4 and 4.5.3.

4.3. The HECM Market Today

The HECM market today is fragile, although there is substantial appetite for reverse mortgage securities among investors. High-profile exits of the largest lenders in 2011 and 2012 have left the origination side of the market fragmented and unstable with more than 2,000 loan originators in a market that does just 70,000 loans a year.[178] Meanwhile, the issuer-servicer conduit to the secondary market is heavily concentrated with only five companies actively securitizing new originations. The fixed-rate, lump-sum product continues to dominate the market with about 70 percent market share. Current market conditions make this product especially profitable to lenders, which has led to competition and innovation in consumer pricing.

4.3.1. Lender Exits Create New Dynamics in the Primary Market

The two largest originators, Wells Fargo and Bank of America, exited the market in 2011. Together, they comprised 36 percent of the market. Wells Fargo cited concerns over the reputational risks of foreclosing on seniors due to tax and insurance defaults. Bank of America cited a need to refocus on its core business lines in the aftermath of the crisis.[179] Financial Freedom, which had been a driving force in the industry in the early to mid-2000s but had been slowly losing market share in recent years, also announced its exit in 2011.[180]

MetLife, the third-largest originator prior to the exit of Wells Fargo and Bank of America, expanded rapidly in 2011 to absorb much of the market share left behind. By the fourth quarter of 2011, MetLife had captured 25 percent of the market between its retail and wholesale channels. But on April 26, 2012, MetLife announced its exit from the reverse mortgage business as part of the wind-down of its banking charter.[181]

Figure 33 shows how the key players in the market have changed between the fourth quarters of 2010 and 2011. The companies shaded in orange are no longer accepting new business.

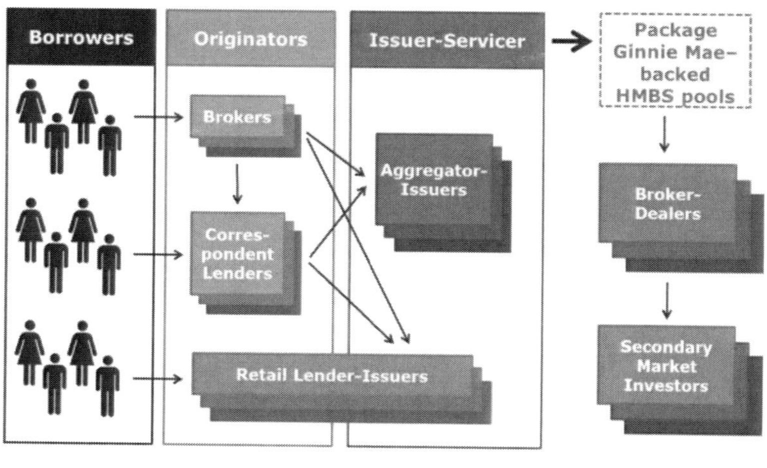

Figure 31. Today's reverse mortgage market.

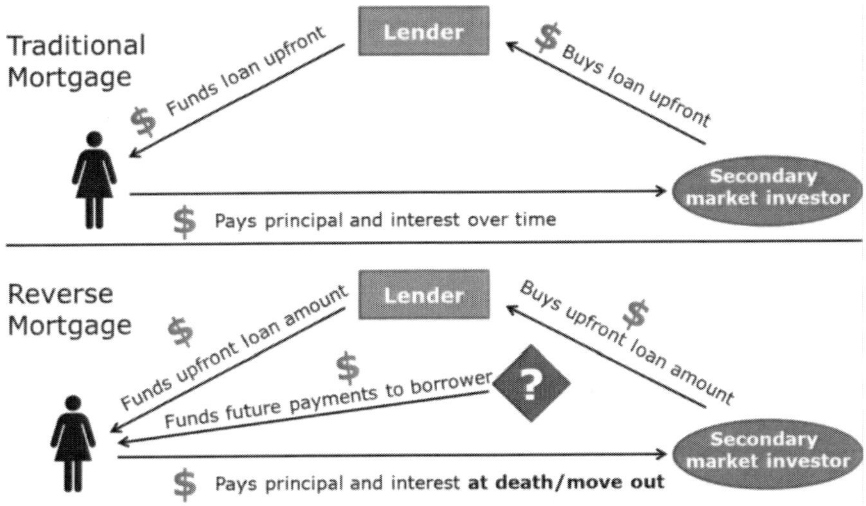

Figure 32. Difference in cash flows between traditional and reverse mortgages.

Top 10 Originators	Q4 2011 Retail # loans	Retail % of total market	Wholesale # loans	Wholesale % of total market	Total # loans	Total % of total market
METLIFE BANK, N.A.	2,539	18%	966	7%	3,505	25%
ONE REVERSE MORTGAGE LLC	1,263	9%	0	0%	1,263	9%
URBAN FINANCIAL GROUP	313	2%	627	5%	940	7%
GENWORTH FINANCIAL HM EQ ACC	381	3%	554	4%	935	7%
WELLS FARGO BANK NA	817	6%	0	0%	817	6%
GENERATION MORTGAGE COMPANY	322	2%	428	3%	750	5%
AMERICAN ADVISORS GROUP	626	5%	0	0%	626	5%
SECURITY ONE LENDING	256	2%	205	1%	461	3%
THE FIRST NATIONAL BANK LAYTON	298	2%	0	0%	298	2%
REVERSE MORTGAGE USA, INC	279	2%	0	0%	279	2%
Total Top 10	**7,094**	**51%**	**2,780**	**20%**	**9,874**	**71%**
Total	**10,818**	**78%**	**3,046**	**22%**	**13,864**	**100%**

Top 10 Originators	Q4 2010 Total # loans	Total % of total market
WELLS FARGO BANK NA	4,678	25%
BANK OF AMERICA NA CHARLOTTE	2,048	11%
METLIFE BANK, N.A.	1,519	8%
ONE REVERSE MORTGAGE LLC	1,005	5%
GENERATION MORTGAGE COMPANY	360	2%
1ST AA REVERSE MORTGAGE INC	336	2%
URBAN FINANCIAL GROUP	266	1%
FINANCIAL FREEDOM ACQUISITION	218	1%
SECURITY ONE LENDING	201	1%
AMERICAN ADVISORS GROUP	178	1%
Total Top 10	**10,809**	**59%**
Total	**18,384**	**100%**

Source: CFPB analysis of FHA data.

Figure 33. Top 10 originators, Q4 2010 & Q4 2011.

A number of nonbank originators with very different business models have emerged as the remaining major players in the industry. Urban Financial Group is a largely wholesale-driven lender relying on a network of brokers and is owned by Wall Street finance firm Knight Group. One Reverse Mortgage, a subsidiary of Quicken Loans, a privately held nonbank mortgage company, is an entirely retail, call-center-driven originator. Generation Mortgage is a nonbank, mostly wholesale-driven lender with some retail presence, backed by Guggenheim Partners, a privately held financial services firm. Genworth Financial Home Equity Access is an affiliate of a large insurance company, also relying largely on wholesale. Of these top four remaining originators, two (Urban Financial Group and Generation) are also active Ginnie Mae issuers. The other two (One Reverse and Genworth) are approved Ginnie Mae issuers but are not yet actively issuing securities.[182]

4.3.2. Fragmented Originations

As shown in Figure 33, prior to the exit of MetLife, only 51 percent of loans were originated by the top 10 retail lenders. Smaller retail or correspondent lenders originated 27 percent, and brokers in the wholesale channel originated 22 percent. The loss of MetLife's 18 percent retail share and the final wind-down of Wells Fargo and Bank of America will make the originations market more heavily dependent on small brokers and independent mortgage companies than it has been. With the exception of One Reverse Mortgage, the remaining top lenders in the business are more wholesale-oriented than those that have exited. A recent industry report found that originations growth in the wholesale channel had surged in recent months, while retail originations had actually declined.[183]

The reverse mortgage industry today is a crowded marketplace with low overall loan volume of only about 70,000 loans per year. Issuers need loans to fill their securitization pipelines, but there are few borrowers. In today's market, at least half of all loans are originated through wholesale and small correspondent lenders, and borrowers are scattered across many originators. In 2011, the industry had over 2,000 small originators, most of them brokers, doing a handful of loans a month.[184] Competition among large lender-issuers for brokers' and correspondents' business is intense. According to industry rate sheets obtained by the CFPB, a large proportion of the secondary market premiums earned by issuers – that is, the amount paid by an investor to the issuer that exceeds the loan balance advanced to the borrower – is passed through to brokers and correspondents.

Some brokers, community banks, and small mortgage companies are primarily traditional mortgage businesses that may only do a reverse mortgage once every few months. Other brokers and small originators are dedicated reverse mortgage companies or divisions that are actively looking for customers. For these small companies, the difference between producing three loans a month and four loans a month is very important to the bottom line. Without the advertising budgets or brand-name recognition of the larger lenders, small originators struggle to find interested clients. Given the size of the premiums that wholesale lenders and issuers are offering, aggressive sales tactics among originators could be a cause for concern.

Many brokers also turn to lead-generation services, which sell lists of names of people who have supposedly expressed interest in a reverse mortgage.[185] As discussed in Section 6.9.2, these lead-generation companies do not always follow good business practices, which can lead to frustration and wasted money for originators, and a poor experience for the consumer.

4.3.3. Heavily Concentrated Conduit to the Secondary Market

Today, almost all HECM loans are packaged into Ginnie Mae securities.[186] The Ginnie Mae-based market is barely three years old and still faces challenges.[187] As shown in 34, only five issuer-servicers are actively packaging HECM securities from new originations.[188] A larger number of entities are authorized issuer-servicers, but some have yet to actually issue any securities, preferring instead to sell their loans to existing issuer-servicers. The capacity of the issuer-servicer sector to buy loans and bundle securities shrank considerably with the departure of Wells Fargo, Bank of America, and Financial Freedom in 2011 and MetLife in 2012. In January 2011, Ginnie Mae also tightened its issuer requirements by increasing the net worth requirement from $1 million to $5 million, which further limited the number of lenders eligible to become issuers.[189]

The newest issuer is Live Well Financial, which obtained Ginnie Mae approval in January 2012 and issued its first security in April 2012.[190] Nationstar Mortgage, a nonbank mortgage company, has recently acquired the reverse mortgage servicing portfolios of Bank of America and MetLife (pending regulatory approval).[191] While Nationstar is not currently securitizing new originations, it could do so in the future.

Industry participants have indicated that an accounting question about how to treat securitized loans is limiting the number of issuers actively issuing securities. Ginnie Mae requires the issuer to repurchase the loan when it reaches 98 percent of the maximum claim amount, as discussed in Section 4.4.3a.[192] This requirement may mean that, under generally accepted accounting principles, issuers cannot claim "true sale" status for securitized loans and would have to continue to report securitized loans as liabilities on their balance sheets. Several large lenders approved by Ginnie Mae to issue HECM securities say they are refraining from securitizing reverse mortgages because of this uncertainty.

4.3.4. Fixed-Rate, Lump-Sum Product Dominates the Market

Prior to 2009, nearly all HECMs carried adjustable interest rates. In the very early years of the program, the rates adjusted annually based on the one-year constant maturity treasury (CMT) rate. In the late 1990s, monthly adjustable loans replaced annually adjustable loans as the dominant rate option, though the monthly adjustments were calculated using the same one-year CMT rate used in calculating annually adjustable HECMs. In October 2007, FHA published a rule allowing monthly adjustable rates to be calculated using the one-month LIBOR.[193] By mid-2009, the monthly adjustable LIBOR had become the dominant adjustable-rate option.[194]

In late 2007, a fixed-rate product previously offered by only one or two banks became more widespread, though volume remained low through 2008 and early 2009. The development of this product was enabled through the introduction of the Ginnie Mae securitization mechanism in late 2007, and a regulatory clarification issued by FHA in early 2008 that permitted the fixed-rate product to be structured as a lump-sum, closed-end loan.[195] In mid-2009, Fannie Mae, the longtime buyer of HECM loans, began to exit the market. The new fixed-rate, lump-sum product rocketed from less than 10 percent of the market to more than 60 percent in less than six months. Since then, fixed-rate loans have ranged between 65 percent and 75 percent of the market. Figure 35 illustrates this transition from a mostly adjustable-rate to a mostly fixed-rate market. The events that led to this transition are discussed in more detail in Sections 4.4 and 4.5.

4.3.5. High Secondary Market Premiums Prompt Lower Fees and Interest Rates

Due to complex market forces discussed in greater detail in Section 4.5, issuers have been receiving exceptionally high premiums in the secondary market for some time. In mortgage finance, *premium* refers to the amount a secondary market investor pays the lender at the time of the loan's sale that is above and beyond the loan balance advanced to the borrower. In the reverse mortgage market, the premium is paid to the Ginnie Mae issuer, which typically pays a portion of the premium to the broker, retail loan officer, or correspondent lender that originated the loan. Premiums do not translate directly into profit. In today's market, some portion of the high premiums get returned to consumers as waived origination fees and/or lender-paid closing costs. Issuers and originators also must cover their expenses.

Issuer	Channels	Rate types	Volume Jan 2012	Volume 2011
Urban Financial Group	Small retail, larger wholesale, correspondent	Fixed & adjustable	$132m	$1,556m
Generation Mortgage	Small retail, larger wholesale, correspondent	Fixed & adjustable	$80m	$1,046m
Reverse Mortgage Solutions	Mostly correspondent	Fixed only	$121m	$871m
Sunwest Mortgage	Mostly wholesale	Fixed & adjustable	$41m	$354m
Live Well Financial	Mostly wholesale and correspondent	Fixed & adjustable	first issuance April 2012	

Source: Ginnie Mae, interviews with industry participants.

Figure 34. Active Ginnie Mae issuers securitizing new originations, May 2012.

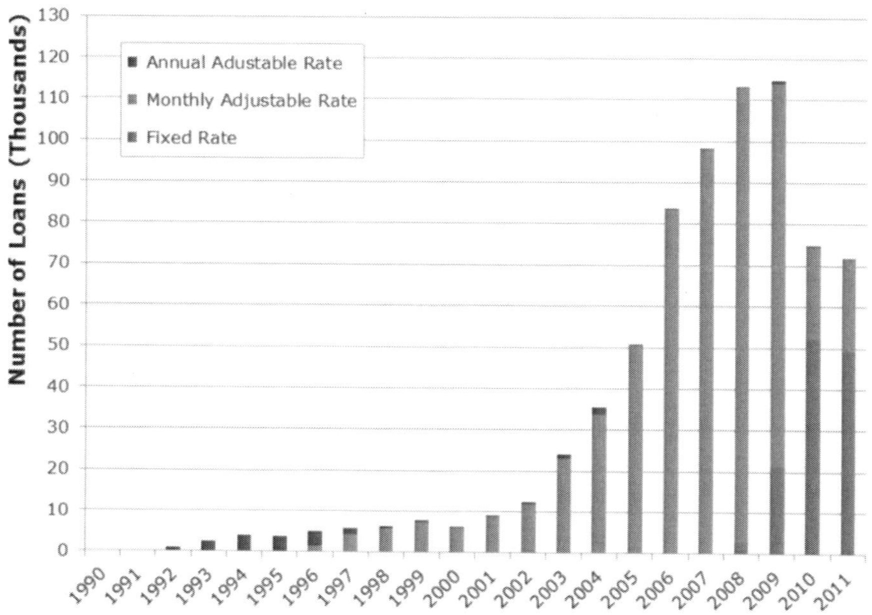

Source: CFPB analysis of FHA data.

Figure 35. HECM loan volumes by rate type, FY 1990-2011.

In early 2012, investors in Ginnie Mae HECM securities were willing to pay between 10 and 12 percent of the loan balance as a premium on fixed-rate HECMs.[196] Adjustable-rate HECMs were commanding premiums of 6 to 9 percent of the loan balance.[197] HECM Saver pools were on the lower end of those ranges.[198] In contrast, typical premiums in the traditional mortgage market for market-rate loans are in the 1 to 4 percent range.

Enabled by the high secondary market premiums, competition has led issuers and lenders to reduce or eliminate origination fees, to begin paying closing costs on behalf of the borrower, and more recently to reduce interest rates. For reasons discussed in detail in Section 4.5.4b, most of these pricing changes have occurred on fixed-rate, lump-sum loans only. For most of 2011, the typical interest rate on a fixed-rate HECM was 5.06 percent. In March 2012, several major lender-issuers reported that their primary fixed-rate product was priced at 4.75 percent with zero origination fee.[199] In early April, just before exiting the market, MetLife introduced a 4.5 percent fixed-rate product with zero origination fee.[200] The latest available data on the market as a whole put the average fixed-rate product at 5.0 percent in March 2012. However, this data is based on FHA insurance endorsements of closed loans, which lag several months behind consumer prices in the market.[201]

4.4. The Evolution of the HECM Secondary Market

Ginnie Mae securities have been the dominant secondary market vehicle for only the past three years. In the 23 years since the HECM program's inception, the secondary market has evolved considerably. Previously, both Fannie Mae and Wall Street securitization houses participated in the HECM secondary market. Throughout the HECM program's history, the various secondary market structures have had to contend with the unique challenge of future cash flows to the borrower described in Section 4.2.1.

4.4.1. Fannie Mae Enables Early HECM Lending

From the inception of the HECM program until the mid-2000s, Fannie Mae was the only secondary market investor. During the 1990s, HECM production was less than 10,000 loans a year. Fannie Mae held these loans on its balance sheet and did not package the loans into securities. In its loan purchase agreement with lenders, Fannie Mae agreed to provide the funds for future payments to borrowers.[202] At the time, nearly all HECMs were adjustable-rate, line-of-credit or monthly disbursement loans.[203] There was little or no variation in the interest rate margin, which was effectively set by Fannie Mae. As the only investor, Fannie Mae set the terms under which it was willing to purchase loans. Fannie Mae reimbursed the lender for the upfront funds provided to the borrower but paid little, if any, premium.[204] Lenders covered their expenses and made their profits primarily on the basis of upfront origination fees charged to the borrower.[205] If the lender also serviced the loan on behalf of Fannie Mae, it would also earn monthly servicing fees.

4.4.2. Wall Street Gains Interest as the HECM Program Grows

In 1998, Congress authorized the HECM program permanently, ending its status as a pilot program.[206] Between 2002 and 2005, HECM production increased significantly, reaching 50,000 loans in FY2005 and nearly 84,000 loans in FY2006.[207] In late 2006, Wall

Street emerged as an alternative source of secondary market investors. Using a securitization structure similar to that developed by Lehman Brothers in 1999 to securitize proprietary reverse mortgages, Bank of America Securities and later Deutsche Bank and RBS Greenwich Capital issued a series of private-label HECM securities between August 2006 and September 2007.[208] In this case, the securities' investors were responsible for funding future payments to borrowers. The securitization trust included a small pool of liquid assets for this purpose, which was replenished as individual borrowers died, moved out, or otherwise repaid their loans.

The AAA-rated securities were attractive to investors because they offered a different risk profile as compared to other available investments. The underlying loans also carried FHA insurance guaranteeing repayment of principal and interest regardless of the value of the home at the end of the loan.[209] The Wall Street securitization houses were able to sell the securities into the market at higher prices than Fannie Mae was paying for the underlying loans. This enabled Wall Street to offer lenders higher premiums than Fannie Mae was offering for the same type of loans.[210] As a result, secondary market share slowly shifted from Fannie Mae to the Wall Street securitization model. In FY2007, roughly 25 percent of HECMs (by dollar volume) were sold to Wall Street.[211]

4.4.3. Ginnie Mae Enters the Market

By late 2007, Ginnie Mae had developed yet another alternative using a new securitization structure.[212] As shown in Figure 36, the new structure altered the division of risk and responsibility within the market. In the private-label structure pioneered by Lehman Brothers and Bank of America, Wall Street securities houses purchased whole loans from lenders and made the securitization trust responsible for funding future payments to borrowers. In the Ginnie Mae model, secondary market securities investors purchase only the portion of the loan paid to the borrower in cash at the time of closing, and the reverse mortgage issuer-servicer is responsible for funding future payment to borrowers. Those future payments are then packaged into separate securities and sold into the market at a later date. A single reverse mortgage could be broken up into dozens of different Ginnie Mae securities.

The issuer-servicer role was a new role for reverse mortgage market participants to play. In the old model, lenders simply sold their loans to Fannie Mae or a Wall Street investment bank and might or might not continue to service the loans on behalf of the investor in exchange for a monthly servicing fee.[q] In the new model, lenders had a choice: they could either become issuer-servicers and begin bundling securities themselves, or they could sell their loans to another market participant (usually a large lender or specialty servicer) that was an approved Ginnie Mae issuer-servicer.

4.4.3a. New risks for Ginnie Mae issuers

Becoming a Ginnie Mae issuer-servicer entailed accepting several risks and responsibilities that were previously borne by Fannie Mae or investors in Wall Street securities. First, issuer-servicers needed capital to fund the future repurchase of the loan. Because the FHA insurance program accepts loans for assignment (sale) to FHA once the

---

[q] Specialty reverse mortgage servicers were available to accept the servicing contract if the lender preferred not to develop a servicing business line. The major subcontracted servicers in the market today are Reverse Mortgage Solutions, an aggregator-issuer and servicer, and Celink, which specializes in subcontracted servicing only.

loan value reaches 98 percent of its maximum claim amount (the appraised value at origination or applicable FHA loan limit, whichever is less), the Ginnie Mae securitization agreements require the issuer-servicer to repurchase the loan from the pools when that threshold is reached.[213] If the loan is in good standing, the issuer-servicer can then assign (sell) the repurchased loan to FHA and receive reimbursement. However, the reimbursement can take up to 60 days to process, during which time the issuer-servicer must cover the cost of holding the loan.[214] More importantly, if the loan is not in good standing (e.g., if the borrower has failed to pay taxes or insurance on the property), FHA will not accept the loan for assignment.[215] In this case, the issuerservicer must continue to hold and service the loan until the borrower becomes current, until maturity, or until foreclosure.[216]

Second, issuer-servicers needed ready, flexible access to capital in order to fund future payments to borrowers, which could be in unpredictable amounts at unpredictable times. Under the Fannie Mae and Wall Street models, the loan's investor had funded these future draws. Under the Ginnie Mae model, the issuer-servicer was responsible.

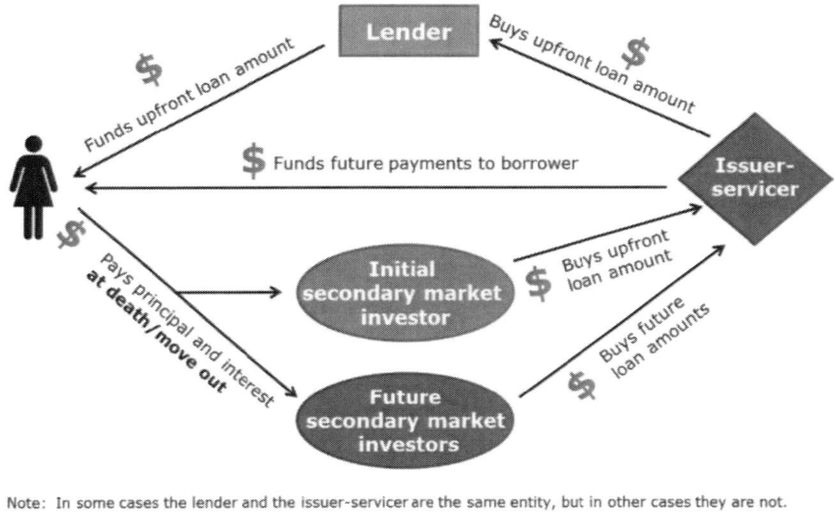

Figure 36. Ginnie Mae securitization model.

Third, there was the risk that future market conditions might make it difficult to securitize and sell the future cash draws. If an issuer packaged an adjustable-rate, line-of-credit HECM into a security at LIBOR + 2.5 percent today, and two years from now the borrower requested a large cash draw but the secondary market was demanding LIBOR + 3 percent, the issuer would have to take lower revenue or even a loss on that particular draw in order to securitize it.

4.4.3b. Development of the fixed-rate, lump-sum product

Of the three new risks to Ginnie Mae issuer-servicers described above, the first risk applies equally to all HECMs. The second two risks, in contrast, are largely eliminated if the reverse mortgage is a fixed-rate, lump-sum loan as opposed to an adjustable-rate, line-of-credit or monthly disbursement loan. With a fixed-rate, lump-sum loan, there are no future draws to fund or securitize.

Prior to the introduction of the Ginnie Mae securitization structure, fixed interest rates were technically an available option under HECM regulations, but only a small handful of fixed-rate loans were done each year. Historically, all HECMs had been structured as open-end loans, meaning that lenders wanting to offer a fixed-rate HECM had to be willing to take the interest rate risk of lending new money in the future at an interest rate fixed at origination.[217] Very few lenders were willing to take that risk, and neither was Fannie Mae. Prior to November 2008, Fannie Mae did not purchase fixed-rate HECMs.[218]

However, because adjustable-rate, open-end loans carried the additional risks and capital requirements under the new Ginnie Mae securitization model described above, issuer-servicers and Ginnie Mae gave new consideration to the idea of a closed-end, fixed-rate, lump-sum HECM. Industry participants approached FHA to inquire whether fixed-rate, lump-sum HECMs could be considered closed-end loans. On March 28, 2008, FHA issued new guidance stating that fixed-rate HECMs could be structured as closed-end loans, opening the door for widespread origination of the fixed-rate, lump-sum product.[219]

Ginnie Mae further bolstered the development of the new fixed-rate, lump-sum product through its issuer program. Initially, Ginnie Mae was more willing to approve applications to issue fixed-rate HECM securities than applications to issue adjustable-rate HECM securities, because of the additional financial risks adjustable-rate issuance posed to issuer-servicers. As late as early 2011, several nonbank issuers had approval for fixed-rate issuance only.[220]

4.4.4. Market Crash Leads to New Market Realities

The housing market crash in 2008 triggered a series of changes in the secondary market for HECMs that fundamentally reshaped the market and the offerings to consumers.

The last private-label HECM securitization had been done in September 2007. During the turbulent markets of 2008, Fannie Mae and the new Ginnie Mae securities were the only options for originators looking to sell their loans. The first Ginnie Mae security was issued in November 2007, but it failed to attract interest from investors.[221] Investors were wary from the unfolding mortgage and economic crisis and were unfamiliar with the new securitization structure. The anticipated cash flows from these securities were quite different than Ginnie Mae traditional mortgage-backed securities, and re-securitization mechanisms (which provide a wider array of cash-flow structures appealing to different types of investors) were not yet available.[r] As 2008 came to a close, only a handful of successful Ginnie Mae securities – some fixed-rate and some adjustable-rate – had been issued.[222] The vast majority of HECM loans in 2008 were still adjustable-rate loans sold to Fannie Mae.

While the new Ginnie Mae securitization model worked better with fixed-rate, lump-sum loans (as discussed in Section 4.4.3a) and the FHA had issued critical guidance in March 2008 stating that fixed-rate, lump-sum HECMs could be structured as closed-end loans, the new product did not immediately gain much market share. The most likely explanation for this is that, at the time, borrowers received more loan proceeds with adjustable-rate loans.

---

[r] As in the traditional mortgage market, investors in reverse mortgage-backed securities have different preferences for the type of cash flows and the risk profile of the securities they purchase. Ginnie Mae program rules require that all Ginnie Mae HECM Mortgage Backed Securities (HMBS) have a simple structure in which each investor receives a pro rata portion of loan repayments when they occur. This structure only appeals to a limited number of investors. In order to appeal to a wider array of investors, Ginnie Mae needed a structure to allow market participants to create a wider array of cash flow structure and risk profiles by creating new securities out of a set of underlying HMBS pools (i.e., re-securitizing the HMBS pools).

As discussed in Section 2.4.1a, FHA determines the proceeds that a borrower can receive based on the borrower's age and the interest rate on the loan. For adjustable-rate loans, the "expected rate," or the sum of the lender's margin plus a 10-year index, is used instead of the actual interest rate on the loan.[223] Throughout 2008, fixed-rate HECMs carried higher interest rates than the expected rate on adjustable-rate HECMs due to underlying interest rate conditions. This meant that borrowers would receive substantially lower proceeds with the fixed-rate HECM than with the adjustable-rate product.[s]

Beginning in April 2009, however, the fixed-rate, lump-sum product began to rapidly gain market share. Within six months, this product dominated the market. A number of factors contributed to this market shift, most notably changes in the interest-rate environment and disruptions in the secondary market. These changes altered lender incentives and increased the proceeds available to consumers with fixed-rate loans compared to adjustable-rate loans.

In late 2008 and early 2009, lenders raised margins on adjustable-rate HECM loans from an average of 1.5 percent in July 2008 to an average of 2.6 percent by March 2009. Several factors may have contributed to these margin increases, including changes to Fannie Mae pricing policies and sharp drops in underlying interest rates due to the Federal Reserve's quantitative easing program to stabilize the economy.[224] In April 2009, Fannie Mae – which was under pressure from its regulator to reduce the size of its portfolio – began to withdraw from the market by reducing the prices it paid lenders for their loans. These Fannie Mae pricing changes pushed margins on adjustable-rate HECMs higher still.[225] By June 2009, average margins were 2.94 percent.[226]

In April 2009, a spike in the LIBOR swap rate combined with the margin increases on adjustable-rate HECMs to alter the choices faced by reverse-mortgage borrowers. The "expected rate" used to determine proceeds on adjustable-rate loans is the sum of the lender's margin and the 10-year LIBOR swap rate.[t] The combined increase in these two components (shown in Figure 37) was enough to push the adjustable "expected" rate higher than the interest rate on fixed-rate loans for the first time in the history of the HECM program (shown in Figure 38). This meant that for the first time, fixed-rate loans offered higher loan proceeds than adjustable-rate loans, making fixed-rate loans substantially more attractive to borrowers than they had ever been.

At the same time that this shift in relative proceeds was occurring, Fannie Mae was withdrawing from the market and pushing market share into Ginnie Mae securities. For over a year, issuers and their broker-dealer partners had been slowly educating the investor community about the value of Ginnie Mae-backed HECM securities compared to alternative investments.[227] At the same time, Ginnie Mae had developed a structure for re-securitizing the HMBS pools that made them more attractive to a larger array of investors.[228] The Ginnie Mae-based market was ready to absorb more loans just as Fannie Mae was retreating. Ginnie Mae market share picked up dramatically in the space of only a few months in mid-2009.[229]

---

[s] Loan proceeds are inversely related to the interest rate.

[t] As discussed in Section 2.4.1a, according to FHA policy, adjustable-rate HECMs are underwritten for the purpose of determining the "initial principal limit" (i.e. the maximum amount of proceeds) using the 10-year LIBOR swap rate instead of the one-month LIBOR index used to actually price the loans. The loans are underwritten using the 10-year swap rate plus the lender's margin; this composite rate for underwriting purposes is known as the "expected rate."

By September 2009, Fannie Mae estimated that its market share of new loans was only about 10 percent.[230] Most or all of the other 90 percent was going into Ginnie Mae securities.

As discussed in Section 4.4.3b, Ginnie Mae had been reluctant to provide approval for adjustable-rate issuers because of the risks retained by these issuers. As a result, several issuers were *only* purchasing and securitizing fixed-rate loans in early 2009.[231]

In sum, secondary market forces in mid-2009 had both made the market better equipped to provide fixed-rate loans, and altered pricing conditions such that borrowers preferred fixed-rate loans. In the space of less than six months, fixed-rate loans went from less than 10 percent to more than 60 percent market share. Figure 37 and Figure 38 illustrate this transition.

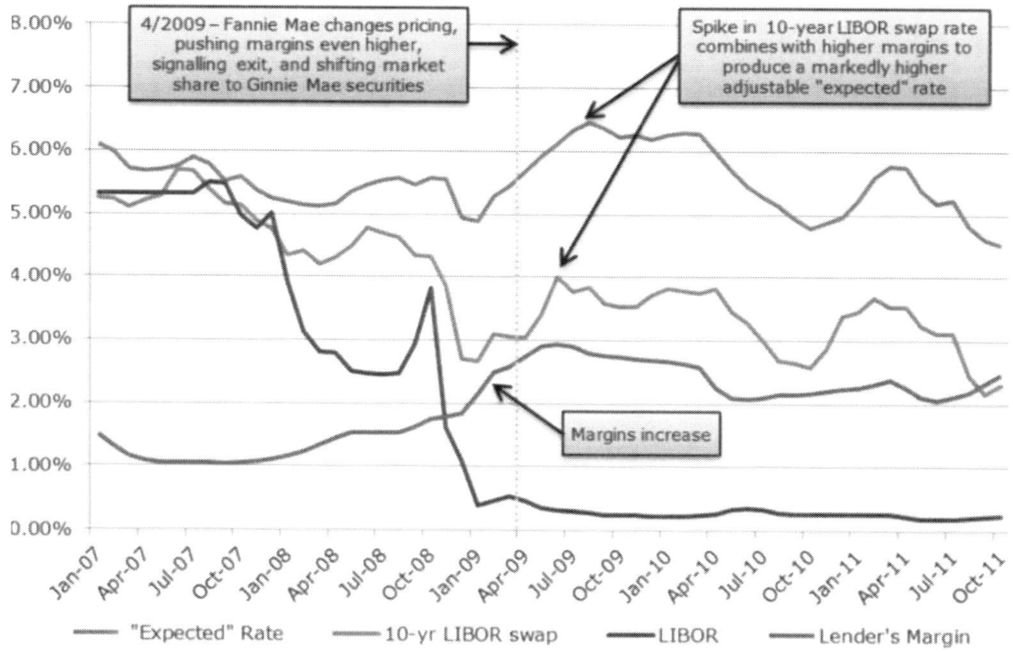

Source: CFPB analysis of FHA data, Wall Street Journal (LIBOR), Federal Reserve (10-year LIBOR Swap).

Figure 37. Increased margins and spike in LIBOR swap rate produce higher "expected" rate.

4.5. Continued Dominance of the Fixed-Rate, Lump-Sum Product and New Approaches to Pricing

Since the market swung toward fixed-rate, lump-sum loans in mid-2009, these loans have continued to dominate the market. As discussed in Section 4.4, part of the reason that fixed-rate, lump-sum HECMs were able to capture more than two-thirds of the market in less than six months in 2009 was that the fixed-rate, lump-sum product provided more proceeds to consumers. By late 2011, initial loan proceeds had largely equalized between the fixed-rate and the adjustable-rate products. Yet fixed-rate, lump-sum HECMs still claimed about 70 percent market share in early 2012.

There are several factors that contribute to this outcome. First, in the absence of a difference in proceeds, consumers clearly have a preference for fixed interest rates. Second, the Ginnie Mae-based secondary market is still immature, and challenges in the market may be limiting the capacity of some market actors to offer adjustable-rate loans. Third, pricing in the secondary market favors fixed-rate loans. That pricing difference may (a) encourage some loan originators to recommend the fixed-rate product versus the adjustable-rate product to prospective borrowers, and (b) result in higher fees for the adjustable-rate product that could deter consumers from selecting this product. These factors are explored more fully in the following sections.

4.5.1. Initial Loan Proceeds Have Equalized between Fixed- and Adjustable-Rate Loans

In this era of very low interest rates, a previously little-known provision of FHA underwriting policy has emerged as a key force affecting market dynamics and, ultimately, the choices offered to consumers. Since the HECM program's inception, FHA has used an interest rate “floor” for underwriting purposes.[232] The floor rate has the effect of setting an upper limit on maximum allowable proceeds.[233] If prevailing interest rates fell below the floor, originators were free to charge borrowers the lower rate, but borrowers would not receive any additional loan proceeds as a result. Historically, the floor rate was set at 5.5 percent, which for much of the program's history was well below prevailing interest rates and thus had little practical impact.

Starting in early 2009, prevailing interest rates had fallen such that the floor rate began to affect market dynamics. Figure 39 shows the same chart as Figure 38, this time with the FHA floor rate. In early 2009, the interest rate for fixed-rate loans begins to track the floor rate very closely. In October 2010, FHA lowered the floor for the first time in the history of the HECM program, from 5.5 percent to 5.0 percent.[234] Interest rates on fixed-rate loans promptly fell to meet the new floor and stayed at 5.0 percent through the end of 2011.

Lenders, counselors, consumer advocates, and other industry participants interviewed for this study unanimously report that as a general rule, the single most important thing to prospective reverse mortgage borrowers is how much money they can receive from the loan proceeds.[235] Without the ability to offer more proceeds to borrowers, lenders and originators did not have a strong incentive to reduce the interest rates on fixed-rate loans below the floor. Some lenders reported experimenting with offering below-floor rates in 2010 and 2011, but they found that without higher proceeds, lower rates were ineffective in attracting more borrowers.[236]

As noted in Section 4.3.5, more recently the continued high premiums in the secondary market coupled with intense competition among issuers for loans has prompted lenders to reduce rates below the floor. As of April 2012, many lenders were offering a .75 percent fixed-rate loan with no origination fee, but several industry participants report that prevailing rates are still higher than they would be without the FHA floor.[237]

In 2010, however, in lieu of lowering interest rates below the FHA floor, lenders began experimenting with ways to increase proceeds. The first innovation was the abolishment of the servicing fee set aside. Since the inception of the program, lenders had reduced borrowers' net loan proceeds by an amount intended to cover the cost of future servicing fees. Starting in March 2010, several large lenders incorporated the servicing fees into the interest rate (as is standard practice in the traditional market) and eliminated the servicing fee set aside. This increased borrower proceeds by several thousand dollars.[238]

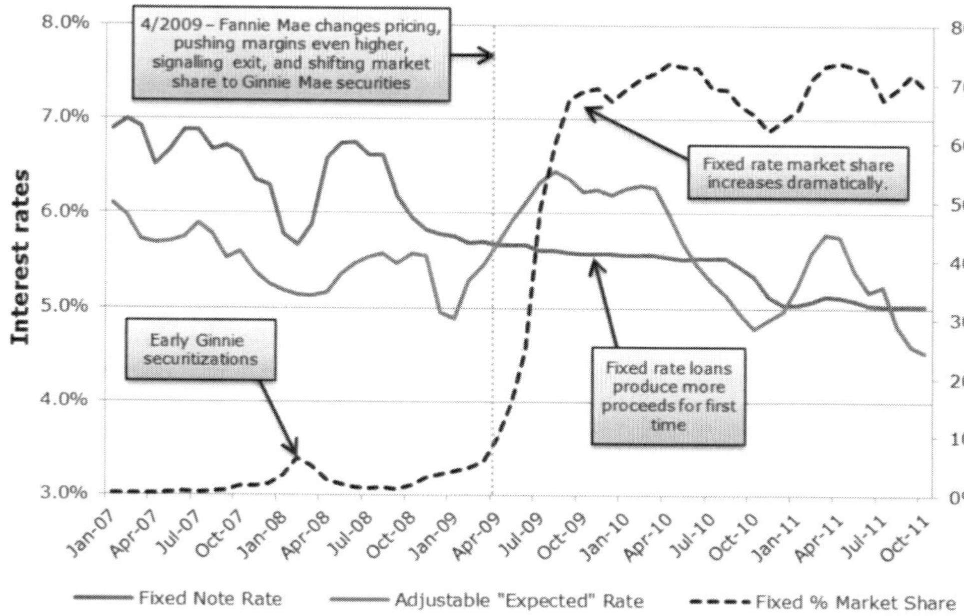

Source: CFPB analysis of FHA data.

Figure 38. Interest rates and fixed-rate market share.

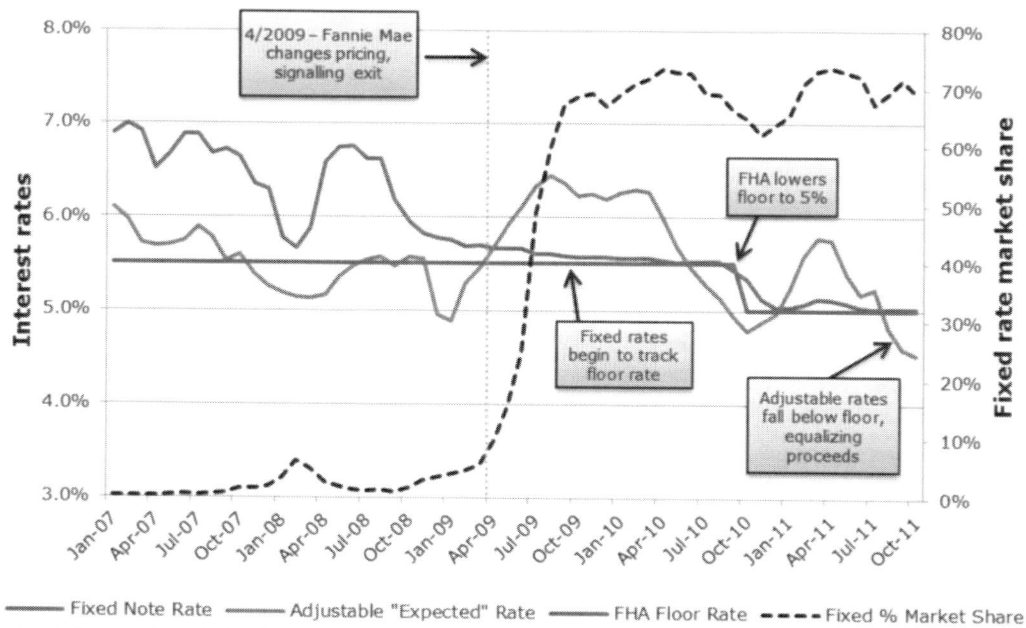

Source: CFPB analysis of FHA data.

Figure 39. Interest rates, FHA floor rate, and fixed-rate market share.

At first, most lenders eliminated the servicing fee set aside on fixed-rate loans only. Within a few weeks, the no-servicing fee set aside fixed-rate loan had become the industry standard.[239] Wells Fargo, however, eliminated the servicing fee set aside on fixed and adjustable rate loans simultaneously.[240] Adoption was slower for adjustable-rate loans, but within 12 months servicing fee set-asides were virtually non-existent on both fixed-and adjustable-rate loans.[241]

Starting in April 2010, lenders began experimenting with reducing or eliminating origination fees as well.[242] Some lenders even began paying the upfront mortgage insurance premium or other closing costs on behalf of borrowers.[243] These pricing changes generally differed between fixed-rate and adjustable-rate products and are discussed in more detail in Section 4.5.4b.

By mid-2010, average margins on adjustable-rate HECMs had fallen to 2.1 percent (down from nearly 3 percent in mid-2009 when the market first transitioned from Fannie Mae to Ginnie Mae securities), a sign that the market was becoming more competitive. After fluctuating in late 2010 and early 2011, the 10-year LIBOR swap rate fell to its lowest level yet, pushing the "expected rate"[244] used to determine the proceeds on adjustable-rate HECMs below the floor in late 2011, as shown in Figure. Immediately, margins started to tick up again as lenders were able to capture higher premiums in the secondary market while holding the expected rate steady as underlying interest rates continued to slide. With the FHA floor in place, the increased margins did not affect the amount of proceeds borrowers received. The higher margins did increase the interest rate on the loans, however, which means that borrowers' equity will get depleted more quickly.

With both adjustable and fixed rates at or below the floor, consumers in late 2011 were presented with roughly equal proceeds regardless of whether they chose a fixed-rate, lump-sum loan or an adjustable-rate, line-of-credit or monthly payment loan. Yet fixed-rate market share continues to range between 65 percent and 75percent, due to a combination of consumer preferences for fixed interest rates generally, challenges in the market to offering adjustable-rate loans, and pricing in the secondary market.

4.5.2. Consumers Prefer Fixed Interest Rates

Lenders and counselors interviewed for this study universally agreed that with initial proceeds roughly equal, many borrowers are simply uninterested in considering an adjustable-rate loan. After several years of housing-crisis headlines about the dangers of adjustable interest rates, borrowers appear to be transplanting the lessons from the traditional mortgage market into the reverse mortgage market with little adaptation. This bias towards fixed interest rates may be doing consumers a disservice when it comes to reverse mortgages, however.[245]

Unlike in the traditional mortgage market, adjustable-rate reverse mortgages do not carry the risk of payment shock, as there are no mortgage payments required on a reverse mortgage. Moreover, the higher initial interest rates, coupled with the fact that fixed-rate loans require borrowers to take all of their available proceeds upfront as a lump-sum, may well mean that consumers stand to lose more of their home equity to compounded interest with a fixed-rate loan than with an adjustable-rate loan. Finally, the credit-line growth feature of the adjustable-rate, line-of-credit product in some ways compensates for the interest rate risk that adjustable-rate borrowers bear. If rates rise, borrowers' home equity is depleted more quickly as interest accrues on the loan balance. However, because the growth rate of the remaining credit line is equal to the current interest rate plus the mortgage insurance premium, if interest rates rise, the amount of additional funds that the borrower can access increases at a greater rate as well. See Section 2.4.1a for more discussion of the credit line growth feature.

4.5.3. Challenges in the Market to Offering Adjustable-Rate Loans

As discussed in Section 4.4.3a, adjustable-rate HECMs pose a unique capital requirement on issuers: the need to fund future draws, which are unpredictable in both timing and dollar size. Both the need for capital itself and the uncertainty around the timing and size of future draws are particularly problematic for smaller nondepositary and/or lightly capitalized issuers relying on warehouse lines of credit.[u]

Since the market turmoil in 2008 and the switch to the Ginnie Mae securitization model in 2009, warehouse lenders have been generally unwilling to allow HECM issuers to use their warehouse lines of credit to fund future draws on adjustable rate loans.[v] Thus, nonbank issuers without access to a bank's liquidity and resources (or a well-capitalized parent company) have been largely unable to issue adjustable-rate securities because they have no way to fund the future draws.[246]

Because of these risks, in the first two years of the Ginnie Mae program, Ginnie Mae was generally *not* approving nonbank mortgage companies to issue adjustable-rate HMBS securities. From the inception of the Ginnie Mae program through early 2011, Generation Mortgage and Urban Financial Group, the two largest issuers today, had approval for fixed-rate issuance only.[247]

This dynamic limited the potential outlet for adjustable-rate loans in the recent past. Prior to their exit, Bank of America, Wells Fargo, and MetLife were the primary issuers of adjustable-rate securities. Having now received Ginnie Mae approval, Urban Financial Group and Generation Mortgage stepped in (along with MetLife, until its exit) to help fill the gap in adjustable-rate issuer capacity left by the departure of Wells Fargo and Bank of America, but they do not have the liquidity that the big banks had.

With the departure of MetLife, internal funding constraints on the nonbank issuers could again limit the potential outlet for adjustable-rate loans. Reverse Mortgage Solutions, the third-largest issuer today, is still only issuing fixed-rate HECM securities. Industry participants report, however, that warehouse lenders may soon begin offering credit lines that permit the funding of future draws.

4.5.4. Pricing in the Secondary Market Favors Fixed-Rate Loans

As discussed in Section 4.3.5, issuers earn a premium when they securitize loans and sell them into the secondary market. That premium is structured as a percentage of the loan balance at closing, and the percentage rate is higher for fixed-rate loans than for adjustable-rate loans. As of early 2012, secondary market investors paid a premium of between 10 and

[u] In mortgage finance, nonbank mortgage companies typically negotiate revolving credit lines, known as warehouse lines, with commercial banks. These warehouse lines are used to fund the mortgage company's working capital needs, but they are subject to specific terms and conditions governing how the money can be used.

[v] In contrast, using warehouse credit lines to fund the initial advance to the borrower is permitted under the warehouse credit agreements currently in use by nonbank lenders and issuers. Industry experts have indicated concerns that the Ginnie Mae HMBS participation structure inhibits warehouse lending because the issuers are not able to pledge to the warehouse lender the participations created by the warehouse lending as collateral subject to repurchase.

12 percent of the loan balance on fixed-rate loans, and a premium of between 6 and 9 percent of the loan balance on adjustable-rate loans. There are three primary reasons for this.

First, the FHA floor, coupled with low underlying market interest rates and consumers who value loan proceeds more than other factors, has resulted in above-market interest rates for fixed-rate HECMs in recent years. Secondary market investors pay higher prices for higher interest rates, relative to alternative securities. While there is some evidence that the floor may be boosting the interest rates of adjustable-rate HECMs in recent months, the impact is not as large as on the fixed-rate side.[248]

Second, the secondary market values HECM securities in part because of the stable rate of HECM prepayments.[249] Unlike traditional mortgage borrowers, HECM borrowers do not generally refinance when rates fall. Investors are concerned that adjustable-rate borrowers may prepay at faster rates than fixed-rate borrowers.[250] Thus, investors are not willing to pay quite as high a premium for adjustable-rate HECM securities as for fixed-rate HECMs. As more data on adjustable-rate borrowers becomes available, the difference in premium may change depending on whether the data confirms or dispels this concern.

Third, there is a chicken-and-egg problem with loan volume. The loan volume of adjustable-rate HECMs is low compared to fixed-rate HECMs, and some institutional investors are unwilling to invest in securities unless they can buy large, steady quantities. If adjustable-rate loan volume increases, secondary market premiums may drop initially as supply outpaces demand, but may rise in the long term relative to fixed-rate premiums as more buyers enter the market.

4.5.4a. Loan originators may have an incentive to recommend fixed-rate loans

Issuers earn their upfront revenues based on the *loan balance* at time of securitization, not the total authorized *proceeds* available to the borrower. Fixed-rate, lump-sum loans typically have a higher initial loan balance than adjustable-rate, line-of-credit loans. The higher balance, coupled with the higher *percentage* paid on that balance (as discussed above), mean that fixed-rate loans generate more revenue at time of origination. The secondary market premium *at origination* is not the only component of loan profitability, however.

Large lender-issuers will earn premiums from the secondary market as they securitize and sell each subsequent draw of an adjustable-rate loan. However, these future revenues are subject to more risk than the upfront revenues of a fixed-rate loan. For example, changing market conditions could alter the pricing that issuers receive from the secondary market. Alternatively, borrowers could move, die, or otherwise repay the loan without ever using much of their available credit lines. Nevertheless, lender-issuers can factor the future secondary market revenue of adjustable-rate loans, discounted for risk, into their profitability calculations.

Retail lender-issuers do appear to be taking a long view of the profitability of adjustable-rate loans. They are adopting policies designed to ensure that their retail loan officers have no incentive to favor fixed-rate loans over adjustable-rate loans. Several large lender-issuers report that they compensate their company-branded, retail loan officers the same amount regardless of whether the loan is a fixed-rate, lump-sum loan or an adjustable-rate, line-of-credit or monthly disbursement loan. These lenders typically charge an origination fee on adjustable-rate loans, but the fee is paid to the corporate lender rather than to the retail loan officer. Retail loan officers at these lender-issuers earn a fixed percentage of either the initial principal limit or the maximum claim amount (depending on the lender), neither of which varies based on the consumer's choice of product.[251]

Non-issuer lenders and brokers face a different set of circumstances. Once a correspondent lender or broker sells or places a loan with an issuer, its involvement with the loan is finished. Thus, for a correspondent lender or broker, the amount of the loan balance at time of closing and the premium it earns on the basis of that loan balance is very important to profitability. Today, aggregator-issuers' pricing policies for correspondent lenders and compensation policies for brokers typically mirror the revenues that aggregator-issuers earn in the secondary market. Correspondent lenders and brokers earn a percentage of the funded loan balance at closing. Adjustable-rate loans not only have lower *balances* at closing, but the *percentage rate* applied to that balance is lower.[252] As a result, most correspondent lenders and brokers charge origination fees for adjustable-rate loans. The potential impact of this pricing difference is discussed in the next section.

Even with an origination fee, in some cases broker or correspondent loan originators may still earn lower revenues on adjustable-rate loans than on the comparable fixed-rate product. According to industry rate sheets obtained by the CFPB, the percentage rate that brokers are paid on fixed-rate loan balances is nearly twice that of adjustable-rate loans.[253] Accordingly, some originators may be recommending the fixed-rate product more strongly than – or even to the exclusion of – the adjustable-rate product to prospective borrowers. Anecdotally, multiple HECM counselors interviewed for this study reported that some clients reported having *only* been presented with the fixed-rate product by their loan originator.

With the exit of Wells Fargo, Bank of America, and MetLife, the remaining issuers are all nonbank mortgage companies relying heavily on wholesale and correspondent channels, where the financial incentives for loan originators are more heavily tilted towards fixed-rate loans. Figure 40 illustrates the stark difference between the large retail players that have now left the market (shown in orange) and the remaining top 10 originators in terms of the balance between fixed-rate and adjustable-rate loans.

In theory, large aggregator-issuers could estimate their future revenues from adjustable-rate loans and pay their suppliers (correspondent lenders and brokers) higher upfront premiums based on the initial principal limit (or other metric) rather than the loan balance at time of closing. Prior to its exit, MetLife had begun to experiment with various methods of raising the amount paid to brokers and correspondents on low-balance, adjustable-rate loans.[254] However, given that correspondents and brokers have a choice as to which issuers they work with on a loan-by-loan basis, in the short term, issuers following this strategy are at risk of adverse selection.[255]

4.5.4b. Consumer-facing pricing structures are different for fixed-rate versus adjustable-rate loans

The high secondary market premiums have allowed originators to reduce or even eliminate the origination fees they charge borrowers. In some cases, originators have even begun paying third-party closing costs and/or FHA's upfront mortgage insurance premium (MIP) on behalf of the borrower.[256]

In most cases, originators charge lower upfront fees for fixed-rate loans than for adjustable rate loans. Fixed-rate, fully drawn loans not only earn a higher percentage premium in the secondary market, but they earn that premium on a higher loan balance. Thus, there is more money in the equation for fixed-rate loans, making it easier to return more of that money to consumers in the form of waived origination fees and lender-paid discounts on closing costs and/or MIP.

Originator	Q4 2010 Fixed	Q4 2010 Adjustable	Q4 2011 Fixed	Q4 2011 Adjustable
METLIFE BANK, NATIONAL ASSOCIATION	44%	56%	39%	61%
BANK OF AMERICA NA CHARLOTTE	56%	44%	-	-
WELLS FARGO BANK NA	35%	65%	46%	54%
GENERATION MORTGAGE COMPANY	89%	11%	76%	24%
URBAN FINANCIAL GROUP	86%	14%	90%	10%
AMERICAN ADVISORS GROUP	79%	21%	77%	23%
GENWORTH FINANCIAL HM EQUITY ACCESS INC	76%	24%	67%	33%
SECURITY ONE LENDING	90%	10%	74%	26%
ONE REVERSE MORTGAGE LLC	86%	14%	66%	34%
THE FIRST NATIONAL BANK LAYTON	-	-	89%	11%

Source: CFPB analysis of FHA data.

Figure 40. Adjustable and fixed-rate market share, by originator, Q4 2010 & Q4 2011.

Fixed-rate loans are also subject to a different regulatory regime than adjustable-rate loans. This regulatory difference tends to encourage zero origination fees for fixed-rate loans. As explained in Section 5.1.1b, under the mortgage loan originator (MLO) compensation rules under the Truth in Lending Act (TILA) that became effective in April 2011, brokers can receive compensation from only one source (consumer or lender) for closed-end loans.[257] In today's reverse mortgage market, closed-end loans are synonymous with fixed-rate loans.[w] In the wholesale channel, brokers and lenders have universally opted for the lender-paid model. Under the lender-paid model, the lender controls the pricing of the loan, any origination fee is paid to the lender and not to the broker, and the lender compensates the broker based on a fixed percentage of the loan balance.[258] Retail and correspondent lenders typically have a similar arrangement, in which the origination fee is paid to the lender and the lender compensates its loan officers separately. In today's market, consumers will typically encounter a zero origination fee fixed-rate loan no matter where they shop. Some lenders also offer additional lender credits to cover a portion of the loan's closing costs.

In contrast, adjustable-rate loans, which are open-end loans, are not subject to the MLO rule's prohibition on compensation from more than one source.[259] Thus, brokers are permitted to receive compensation from two sources on adjustable-rate loans – a small premium from the lender based on the typically smaller balance at closing, and an origination fee from the borrower. Individual brokers choose how much of an origination fee to charge (within HECM guidelines). Some brokers report charging an origination fee on adjustable-rate HECMs at all times, while others report waiving or discounting that fee if the balance at closing is high enough for the broker to make sufficient revenue from the premium.[260]

In the retail and correspondent channels, the lender sets the origination fee on both fixed-rate and adjustable-rate loans. Generally, adjustable-rate loans will carry an origination fee while fixed-rate loans will not.

[w] Adjustable-rate loans, in contrast, are open-end loans. Open end loans (e.g., a line of credit) allow additional amounts to be borrowed after closing, subject to the conditions of the loan. Closed-end means that the loan is for a fixed amount and additional principal amounts cannot be borrowed after closing. The fixed-rate, closed-end / adjustable-rate, open-end categorization is market-driven rather than regulatory. In theory, fixed-rate loans could be open-end, and adjustable-rate loans could be closed-end, but such combinations are not present in the market today.

There is some evidence to suggest that the presence of an origination fee on adjustable-rate products could impact borrower decisions. On fixed-rate products, most lenders offer a few different combinations of interest rate and origination fee (a lower rate is available with a higher origination fee). Industry participants interviewed for this study report that the vast majority of consumers choose the zero-fee loan with the higher rate. Thus, it seems possible that when faced with a choice between a zero-fee fixed-rate loan and a several thousand dollar origination fee for the adjustable-rate loan, borrowers might opt for the zero-fee fixed-rate loan.

Moreover, higher upfront fees for adjustable-rate loans introduce a slight difference in *net* proceeds between fixed-rate and adjustable-rate loans. Origination fees, closing costs, and upfront MIP (in the case of HECM Standard loans) are typically financed into the loan and thus reduce the *net* proceeds available to the borrower. As borrowers have historically displayed a strong sensitivity to loan proceeds, this slight difference in net proceeds could prompt some borrowers to choose the fixed-rate product.

5. Regulatory Structure

The regulatory structure that applies to the reverse mortgage industry is very different from that of most other consumer financial products because of the dominance of the FHA-insured HECM products in the marketplace. FHA program regulations apply only to FHA-insured HECM products – which means they cover almost all, but not quite all, of the market.

Several states have adopted laws and regulations that extend HECM-style protections to proprietary products and/or require lenders to submit proprietary products to state regulators for approval. A few states have gone above and beyond the FHA rules to place additional requirements on HECM and proprietary products alike.

Federal banking regulators have been involved in the regulation of reverse mortgages through implementation of federal consumer financial protection laws applicable to consumer credit generally. As explained below, federal regulations implementing the Truth in Lending Act (TILA) and the Real Estate Settlement Procedures Act (RESPA) set forth protections applicable to reverse mortgages. Most recently, the Federal Financial Institutions Examinations Council (FFIEC) issued guidance in 2010 encouraging supervised entities offering proprietary reverse mortgage products to adopt HECM-style consumer protections as a best practice.

With the exit of Wells Fargo, Bank of America, OneWest (the current parent company of Financial Freedom), and MetLife from reverse mortgage lending, the market share subject to oversight by federal banking regulators has substantially decreased. Most of the remaining large reverse mortgage lenders are nonbank financial companies. In the past, these companies would have been supervised only at the state level. The CFPB now has the authority to supervise these nonbank reverse mortgage companies for the first time at the federal level.

The broad federal consumer protection statutes that apply to reverse mortgages are rarely tailored to the particular features of these products. Thus, some of these protections are of limited use to reverse mortgage borrowers and prospective borrowers. In 2010, the Board of Governors of the Federal Reserve System (the Board) issued a proposed rule that would have extended several HECM-style consumer protections to the proprietary market, and improved the usefulness of reverse mortgage disclosures to potential borrowers. Authority and responsibility for this proposed rule transferred from the Board to the CFPB on July 21, 2011.

5.1. Federal Consumer Protection Regulation

Like traditional mortgages, reverse mortgages are subject to federal laws governing mortgage lending, including TILA, RESPA and fair lending laws such as the Equal Credit Opportunity Act (ECOA).[261] These laws and their implementing regulations set forth important protections for all mortgage borrowers, including reverse mortgage borrowers. However, many of the protections are not tailored to the unique needs of reverse mortgage consumers. In the Dodd-Frank Act, Congress granted the CFPB the authority to implement TILA and RESPA, as well as other federal consumer financial protection laws and fair lending laws applicable to reverse mortgages.

5.1.1. Truth in Lending Act

TILA and its implementing regulation, Regulation Z, set forth rules regarding disclosure of information, finance costs, and borrower rights in connection with reverse mortgage transactions. Only some of the disclosures are specific to reverse mortgages.

Reverse mortgage consumers receive different documents at the time an application is provided. The specific disclosure documents depend on whether a reverse mortgage is open- or closed-end. Generally, fixed-rate reverse mortgages are structured as closed-end loans, while adjustable-rate reverse mortgages are structured as open-end loans, though future product innovation could produce other combinations. Figure 41 explains the different disclosures.

Because TILA applies provisions and regulations designed for traditional mortgages to reverse mortgages, many of the documents required by TILA are not tailored to reverse mortgages. For instance, the HELOC brochure required for open-end reverse mortgages does not contain information specific to reverse mortgages.[266]

5.1.1a. Reverse-mortgage specific provisions

TILA establishes additional requirements applicable specifically to reverse mortgage transactions. These requirements state that reverse mortgage consumers shall receive disclosures substantially similar to the model form included in the appendix to Regulation Z at least three business days before obtaining the reverse mortgage.[267] The disclosure must:

1. State that the consumer is not obligated to complete a reverse mortgage transaction even though the consumer received disclosures or signed a reverse mortgage loan application;
2. Include itemized loan terms, charges, age of the youngest borrower, and the appraised property value;
3. Set forth a good faith projection of the total cost of credit expressed as a table of “total annual loan cost” (TALC) rates; and
4. Provide an explanation of the TALC table.[268]

All reverse mortgage creditors must provide the TALC disclosure. The TALC table is designed to show consumers how the cost of the reverse mortgage varies over time and with house price appreciation. Generally, the longer the consumer keeps a reverse mortgage the lower the relative cost will be because the upfront costs of the reverse mortgage will be amortized over a longer period of time. Thus, the TALC rates usually will decline over time even though the total dollar cost of the reverse mortgage rises over time due to interest and fees being charged on an increasing loan balance.

Disclosure Requirements	Loan Type	
	Closed-end	Open-end
Typical rate type*	Fixed rate	Adjustable rate
Pre-application disclosures	None for fixed-rate loans. In the event an adjustable-rate, closed-end product were to be developed, the lender would be required to provide the consumer with a booklet entitled "Consumer Handbook on Adjustable Rate Mortgages" (CHARM Booklet).[262]	Standardized HELOC brochure, or a suitable substitute.[263] Disclosures that contain information about the creditor's open-end reverse mortgage plans.[264] These disclosures do not include consumer-specific information.
Post-application disclosures	Early TILA disclosure within three business days after application (but no less than seven business days before closing, and before the consumer has paid any fee other than for obtaining a credit history).	None.
Pre-closing disclosures	Reverse mortgage-specific disclosure provided at least three business days before closing, to include information on the loan terms, itemized charges, and a total annual loan cost (TALC table). (See discussion below).	Reverse mortgage-specific disclosure provided at least three business days before account opening, to include information on the loan terms, itemized charges, and a total annual loan cost (TALC table). (See discussion below).
Closing disclosures	None required.	Disclosure of transaction-specific costs and terms at the time that an open-end reverse mortgage plan is opened.[265]

*Note: According to FHA Mortgagee Letter 2008-08, fixed-rate reverse mortgages can be open-end or closed-end, though in practice the CFPB is not aware of any lenders making open-end, fixed-rate HECMs. HECM regulations do not specifically permit nor prohibit closed-end, adjustable-rate loans, though in practice the CFPB is not aware of any lenders making these loans.

Figure 41. TILA disclosures by loan type.

The Board tested the TALC rate disclosure with consumers prior to proposing new reverse mortgage disclosures.[269] Participants were shown a disclosure with the TALC table as currently required by Regulation Z. According to the Board, very few consumers understood the TALC table, and some could not even attempt to explain what it was showing. The Board found that most participants "thought the TALC rates shown were interest rates, and interpreted the table as showing that their interest rate would decrease if they held their reverse mortgage for a longer period of time."[270] Consumers indicated a preference for a disclosure that set forth the costs of a reverse mortgage as a dollar amount rather than as a percentage of costs incurred over the duration of the mortgage. [271]

In 2010, the Board published for public comment a proposed rule, which is discussed in detail in Section 5.5, to address many of the issues identified here. The CFPB now has the responsibility for any further rulemaking activity.

5.1.1b. Mortgage loan originator compensation

On September 24, 2010, the Board finalized a rule amending Regulation Z to implement TILA with respect to mortgage loan originator compensation for all closed-end mortgages, including both traditional mortgages and closed-end reverse mortgages.[272] The rule sets forth the manner in which mortgage loan originators may be compensated.[273] For closed-end reverse mortgages, which in today's market are synonymous with fixed-rate, lump-sum reverse mortgages, a mortgage loan originator may not receive compensation based on the reverse mortgage transaction's terms and conditions.[274] For example, an originator of a closed-end reverse mortgage may be compensated based on a fixed percentage of the credit extended, but not on a term or condition of the mortgage, such as the interest rate.[275] Further, mortgage brokers may receive compensation from only one source – either the consumer or the lender --for closed-end loans.[276]

In contrast, open-end reverse mortgage loans, which in today's market are synonymous with adjustable-rate loans, are not subject to the mortgage loan originator compensation rules. Thus, for an open-end reverse mortgage, a mortgage loan originator is not barred by the rule from receiving compensation from more than one source or from receiving compensation that is based on the terms or conditions of the open-end reverse mortgage.[277]

5.1.2. Real Estate Settlement Procedures Act

RESPA and its implementing regulation, Regulation X, set forth, among other things, rules regarding the disclosure of settlement costs and fees and the servicing of mortgage transactions.

The rules set forth in RESPA and Regulation X apply to reverse mortgage transactions. RESPA and Regulation X require that a lender provide a Good Faith Estimate (GFE) to a reverse mortgage consumer within three business days after a lender receives an application.[278] Further, settlement agents are required to use the HUD-1 settlement statement for reverse mortgage transactions.[279] The Department of Housing and Urban Development (HUD), which had authority to implement RESPA prior to the transfer of this authority to the CFPB under the Dodd-Frank Act, published "New RESPA Rule FAQs" in 2010 that provided guidance to reverse mortgage lenders on adapting these forms for use in reverse mortgage transactions.[280]

Rules in RESPA and Regulation X with respect to mortgage loan servicing also apply to reverse mortgages.[281] Further, like other mortgage lenders, reverse mortgage lenders may neither pay nor accept any fee or other thing of value in exchange for the referral of business related to a reverse mortgage transaction.[282]

In accordance with the Dodd-Frank Act, the CFPB plans to issue a proposal in July 2012 to integrate the separate disclosures required by TILA and RESPA into a new combined disclosure statement. Though the integrated disclosure statement currently contemplated by the CFPB will not apply to reverse mortgages, the CFPB expects separately to undertake a project to integrate TILA and RESPA disclosure requirements with respect to reverse mortgage transactions.

5.1.3. Equal Credit Opportunity Act

ECOA and its implementing regulation, Regulation B, set forth rules prohibiting discrimination by a creditor on the basis of age (or race, color, religion, national origin, sex or marital status) with respect to any aspect of a credit transaction. ECOA covers both intentional discrimination (disparate treatment) and also facially neutral practices that have a disparate impact on a prohibited basis, including age. Regulation B also prohibits creditors from making statements to applicants or prospective applicants discouraging – on a prohibited basis – a reasonable person from making or pursuing an application.

Reverse mortgages are available only to consumers 62 years of age and older. As discussed in Section 2.4.1a, the amount that a consumer can borrow is partly a function of the consumer's age. This is permissible under Regulation B.[283] However, fair lending concerns can still arise in the reverse mortgage context. For example, if a lender that offers a range of lending products including reverse mortgages were to discourage creditworthy applicants over age 62 from applying for alternatives to a reverse mortgage, the lender could risk violating Regulation B.

5.2. FHA Regulation of Reverse Mortgages through the HECM Program

Because the vast majority of reverse mortgages are insured under the HECM program, regulations implementing the HECM program have a substantial impact on the reverse mortgage market. However, HECM program regulations are narrower in scope than consumer protection regulations in two important ways. First, HECM program regulations are applicable only to FHA-insured loans and do not directly impact the smaller proprietary market. Second, HECM program regulations exist primarily to establish the conditions under which FHA will accept HECM mortgages for insurance. HECM borrowers have been unsuccessful in enforcing HECM program requirements against lenders in private litigation.[284]

Congress established the HECM program as a pilot program in the Housing and Community Development Act of 1987.[285] In 1998, Congress made the HECM program permanent and expanded FHA's authority to insure reverse mortgages to 150,000 total loans.[286]The cap has since been raised to 275,000.[287] However, as of November 2011, there were nearly 550,000 HECMs outstanding. For the past several years, the HECM program has been operating under a series of waivers exempting the program from the loan volume cap that were passed during the appropriations process. The most recent waiver expires on December 31, 2012.[288]

HUD, through FHA, administers the HECM program and is authorized to implement the program through regulations.[289] HUD further supplements the regulations through interpretative guidance. These interpretations are provided in HUD's HECM Handbook and through a series of "Mortgagee Letters" directed to private lenders participating in the HECM program. The HECM Statute, the HECM Regulations, the HECM Handbook and the Mortgagee Letters all serve to guide the reverse mortgage market.

5.2.1. Conditions of the HECM Program

The HECM Statute states that the Secretary of HUD may insure any HECM eligible for insurance to the extent such mortgages "(1) have promise for improving the financial situation or otherwise meeting the special needs of elderly homeowners; (2) will include appropriate safeguards for borrowers to offset the special risks of such mortgages; and (3) have a potential for acceptance in the mortgage market."[290] To be eligible for insurance as a HECM, a reverse mortgage must meet certain eligibility requirements and satisfy certain consumer protections as explained in Section 2.3.

The Housing and Economic Recovery Act of 2008 (HERA) made several amendments to the HECM Statute. Among other things, HERA authorized HUD to insure reverse mortgages for cooperatives and reverse mortgages used to purchase property.[291] HERA also prohibited reverse mortgage lenders or any other party from requiring the borrower to purchase insurance, an annuity, or other similar product as a condition of obtaining a HECM.[292] Moreover, HERA requires that reverse mortgage lenders and any other party that participates in the origination of a HECM must either:

1. Refrain from participating in, being associated with, or employing any party that participates in or is associated with any other financial or insurance activity; or
2. Demonstrate that appropriate safeguards are in place to ensure that (a) personnel involved in the reverse mortgage transaction have no involvement with or incentive to provide any other financial or insurance product and (b) a borrower will not be required to purchase any other financial or insurance product as a condition of obtaining a HECM.[293]

5.3. State-Level Regulation & Oversight

State regulation of reverse mortgages generally takes a three-prong approach focusing on licensing, supervision, and enforcement. State banking regulators, insurance regulators, and other state agencies may be involved. Over half of all states have regulations specific to reverse mortgages. There was an increase in state regulation after the enactment of HERA in 2008, the Secure and Fair Enforcement for Mortgage Licensing Act of 2008 (SAFE Act), and the Dodd-Frank Act. Many states have consumer protections that expand upon those provided by federal law.

5.3.1. State Legislation

State legislation has focused on deceptive marketing techniques, the adequacy of disclosures and counseling, and the dangers of cross-selling unsuitable financial or insurance products with a reverse mortgage. Specific provisions are discussed in greater detail in the *Consumer Protection Concerns* chapter. Recent state legislative proposals have considered strengthening consumer protections for reverse mortgage borrowers by extending a consumer's right of rescission and calling for the imposition of a fiduciary duty on those who offer, sell, or arrange the sale of a reverse mortgage.[294]

5.3.2. State Oversight

State oversight of reverse mortgage lenders and brokers includes licensing, examination, and enforcement actions. Many state enforcement actions have focused on deceptive marketing techniques. These actions are discussed in greater detail in Section 6.2. Meanwhile, concern over lending practices has led some states to expand oversight to include prior approval of the specific reverse mortgage lending programs offered, in addition to licensing requirements.

5.3.2a. Lender & product licensing

In 2008, Congress enacted the SAFE Act, which is implemented by the CFPB's Regulation H. As a result, states have established uniform methods for registering and licensing mortgage loan originators, including reverse mortgage loan originators and brokers.[295] Some states have sought to expand consumer protections by requiring the licensing not only of entities and individuals but of reverse mortgage lending programs as well. In Iowa, a financial institution must submit to regulators a prototype plan for offering reverse mortgages before making reverse mortgage loans.[296] In Massachusetts, the Commissioner of Banks must review and approve reverse mortgage lending programs, and cannot approve a program that does not provide for specific disclosures and protections.[297] Washington requires proprietary reverse mortgage loan products to be preapproved by the state banking department.[298]

Some state regulations have effectively banned proprietary products. Vermont, for example, provides that only FHA-approved lenders may issue reverse mortgage loans, and those loans must comply with all requirements for participation in the HECM program and be insured by the FHA.[299] Texas did not allow reverse mortgage lending of any kind until 1995, and its homestead law prevents the offering of the HECM for Purchase program until 2013.[300] Other states have adopted, or recommended that licensees adopt, guidance from federal regulators advising entities and individuals to follow HECM requirements such as mandatory counseling and cross-selling restrictions when offering proprietary products.[301]

5.4. Prudential Regulator Guidance

In August 2010, the Office of the Comptroller of the Currency, the Board of Governors of the Federal Reserve System (the Board), the Federal Deposit Insurance Corporation, the Office of Thrift Supervision and the National Credit Union Administration, through the FFIEC, adopted guidance regarding reverse mortgage lending. FFIEC published the guidance to assist their supervised financial institutions in managing compliance and reputation risk with respect to reverse mortgages.[302] Importantly, this guidance is primarily directed at depositary financial institutions supervised by the FFIEC agencies. With the exit of Wells Fargo, Bank of America, and MetLife, today's reverse mortgage market is dominated by nonbank financial companies not subject to supervision by these regulators.

The guidance directed financial institutions to voluntarily adopt relevant HECM program requirements for any proprietary reverse mortgages the financial institution may offer. Those requirements include mandatory independent counseling and restrictions on cross-selling. The guidance also directs institutions to provide clear information about the costs and risks of reverse mortgage products, and take appropriate steps to determine that consumers will be able to pay required property taxes and homeowner's insurance. Finally, the guidance directs institutions to adopt clear compensation policies to guard against inappropriate incentives to make reverse mortgage loans and to develop effective internal controls to ensure that policies and procedures are followed.

5.5. Federal Reserve Board's Proposal

On September 24, 2010, the Board published a proposed rule to amend Regulation Z as part of a comprehensive review of TILA's rules for home-secured credit.[303] Among other subjects, the proposed rule addressed disclosures and other consumer protections for reverse mortgages. Authority for any future rulemaking under TILA was transferred to the CFPB on July 21, 2011.

5.5.1. Reverse Mortgage Disclosures

The Board proposed revised disclosure forms to create a new unified disclosure system for all reverse mortgages (HECMs and proprietary products).[304] The proposal would have exempted reverse mortgages from existing TILA disclosure requirements and would have required the following new forms of disclosure:[305]

- A two-page disclosure entitled "Key Questions to Ask About Reverse Mortgage Loans," provided before a consumer applies for a reverse mortgage.
- For open-end reverse mortgages, an "early" open-end reverse mortgages disclosure provided within three business days after application, and an account-opening disclosure provided at least three business days before account opening.
- For closed-end reverse mortgages, a closed-end reverse mortgage disclosure provided within three business days after application and again at least three business days before closing.

The proposed rule also would have replaced the table of TALC rates with a table that demonstrated how the reverse mortgage loan balance grows over time expressed through dollar amounts.[306] Using a total dollar cost demonstrates how a reverse mortgage balance will grow over time and eliminates confusion from TALC rates that may decline over time as the initial costs of a reverse mortgage are amortized over a longer period.

5.5.2. Additional Consumer Protections

The Board's proposed rule also would have provided important consumer protections for all reverse mortgage consumers, not just HECMs subject to regulation by HUD. The protections in the proposed rule included:

- Reverse-mortgage consumers would have been required to receive mandatory counseling prior to obtaining a reverse mortgage.
- Nonrefundable fees would have been barred until the third business day following a consumer's completion of counseling.

- Lenders would have been prohibited from steering consumers to a particular counselor or counseling agency.
- Lenders would have been prohibited from requiring the purchase of another financial or insurance product as a condition of the reverse mortgage.
- Certain advertising statements that may mislead reverse mortgage borrowers would have triggered clarifying statements. These provisions are discussed in further detail in the Section 6.2.

6. Consumer Protection Concerns

Reverse mortgages have long been the subject of consumer protection scrutiny. As a product targeted specifically at an elderly, vulnerable population, the risk of fraud, scams, discrimination, and poor financial decisions is particularly acute.[307] So, too, is the potential harm of misleading advertising, aggressive sales tactics, and discriminatory practices. Consumer advocates have long documented cases of seniors who did not fully understand what they were getting into and who were rushed into a decision.[308] Mandatory counseling, which has been a part of the HECM program since its inception, is intended to counter these concerns. However, the counseling itself has not always been fully effective. In 2009, the U.S. Government Accountability Office (GAO) published a study highlighting concerns about deceptive advertising and ineffective counseling (2009 GAO report).[309]

As with any financial product, reverse mortgages have costs, risks, and benefits. Individual consumers have to decide whether the benefits outweigh the costs and the risks in their particular situation. Historically, reverse mortgages have had very high costs and fees relative to traditional home loans, and advocates have been concerned that for many borrowers, the benefits might not outweigh the costs. With recent changes to product offerings, consumers now have more options for lower-cost products. However, the resulting array of choices present prospective borrowers with complex decisions that they may find challenging to make. One new and very popular choice, the fixed-rate, lump-sum product, raises particular concerns about its suitability for borrowers.

Reverse mortgages pose several risks to prospective borrowers and their families. Borrowers who live for many years after taking on the reverse mortgage may ultimately need to move due to health or other reasons. These borrowers risk having no equity left in their homes with which to finance that move. This risk is greater for the recent wave of borrowers who are taking out reverse mortgages at an early age. Borrowers who fail to pay their property taxes and homeowner's insurance are at risk of losing their homes to foreclosure.

Spouses of reverse mortgage borrowers who are not themselves named as borrowers are often unaware that they are at risk of losing their homes. If the borrowing spouse dies or needs to move, the non-borrowing spouse must sell the home or otherwise pay off the reverse mortgage at that time. Other family members (children, grandchildren, etc.) who live with reverse mortgage borrowers also are at risk of needing to find other living arrangements when the borrower dies or needs to move.

Reverse mortgages also provide several benefits to the prospective borrower, which in some cases will outweigh the costs and risks. Reverse mortgages allow borrowers to access the equity in their homes knowing that their credit lines will not be cut and they are not required to pay back more than the value of the home. These loans require no monthly mortgage payments and are typically easier to qualify for than a traditional mortgage refinance or home equity loan. A reverse mortgage can also provide an annuity-like stream of income for as long as the borrower remains in the home, although most borrowers do not choose this option.

6.1. Everse Mortgages Are Complex Products That Are Difficult for Consumers to Understand

The costs, risks, and benefits of reverse mortgages are complex. Consumers struggle to understand the product and make good decisions about tradeoffs on two levels. First, they may have difficulty deciding between a reverse mortgage and an alternate course of action, such as downsizing, refinancing with a traditional mortgage, or using a traditional home equity loan or line of credit. Second, consumers may have difficulty assessing costs and making tradeoffs between the different types of reverse mortgage products and options in the marketplace today.

A 2006 AARP survey found that certain aspects of reverse mortgage loans were challenging for most respondents, even after counseling.[310] In general, survey respondents found it difficult to assess monthly loan costs, the "rising balance, falling equity" nature of the loans, and the cost impact of interest rate and home value changes. The AARP study also found that consumer confusion was particularly pronounced among women, nonwhites, consumers age 85 and over, and consumers in poor health.

There are several reasons why consumers may not be well equipped to fully assess the long-term cost of reverse mortgages. Given that borrowers do not make monthly payments for a reverse mortgage, costs accrue throughout the life of the loan. Borrowers may have trouble understanding the extent of accruing servicing, interest, insurance, and financed upfront costs because they can delay payment until the loan becomes due.[311] Research has found that consumers often focus on short-term costs and underestimate long-term costs.[312] This consumer bias, coupled with the sheer complexity of the product's pricing, may result in an inaccurate perception of how much it costs to take out a reverse mortgage.[313] To the extent that consumers underestimate the costs of a reverse mortgage, they are at risk of choosing to pursue a reverse mortgage when another option might be a better financial choice.[314] Borrowers who underestimate the effects of compounded interest may also be more likely to choose a reverse mortgage product option that is poorly suited to their situation.

6.1.1. Consumer Education Challenges

The CFPB interviewed HECM counselors from counseling agencies around the country for this study. The counselors identified five main challenges they encounter in working to educate and assist prospective borrowers. These challenges, explored more fully below, highlight the need for more effective counseling as well as the need for other consumer protections discussed in the remainder of this chapter.

6.1.1a. A reverse mortgage is a complex product

The overarching message among counselors is that reverse mortgages are difficult to understand, even among sophisticated borrowers. Counselors noted that borrowers often come to counseling sessions with misperceptions about the product.

6.1.1b. A reverse mortgage is a loan

The most common misperception counselors reported was the presumption that a reverse mortgage is a government entitlement program similar to Medicare. Counselors often find themselves explaining to clients that a reverse mortgage is in fact *a loan*. This confusion echoes concerns expressed in the 2009 GAO report about advertising suggesting that a reverse mortgage is a government benefit. Counselors recommended that misleading marketing should remain a focus for regulators. Other HECM clients come to counseling with fears that a reverse mortgage will allow the federal government to confiscate their homes.

6.1.1c. Rising balance, falling equity

Counselors unanimously reported that the concept of a home loan with a rising balance and falling equity is the most difficult concept to teach. Reverse mortgage consumers struggle to understand how interest gets compounded on a loan that does not involve monthly payments on interest and principal. A HECM counselor in the Midwest echoed other counselors when he reported, "We spend a lot of time on this in our agency. People don't understand how this loan works, and because of that, they don't understand how expensive it can be."

6.1.1d. Loan disbursement options

As described in Section 2.4.3, HECMs provide a number of loan disbursement options (lump sum, line of credit, term, and tenure) and interest rate options (fixed and adjustable). Counselors report that many borrowers are confused about the options available to them. Many borrowers also did not make the product choices that the counselor believed was best for the borrower based upon the information provided by the borrower about their health, finances, family, and expected remaining time in the home.

As detailed in the *Market* chapter, the fixed-rate, lump-sum payment option remains the most popular payment choice among borrowers, even though it may not be an optimal choice for many of them. As one counselor reported, "Many seniors do not trust an adjustable rate even when it will benefit them. It confuses them even after it is explained, and most of them come in wanting the fixed rate from the beginning."

Most counselors interviewed for this study presumed that prevailing wisdom from the traditional mortgage market (where adjustable rates create a risk of payment shock if the adjustment results in an increase in the interest rate) is influencing borrowers to choose the fixed-rate lump-sum option. "We can't tell them not to do it [take a lump-sum draw]," said one counselor. "But for some who use a lump sum, they could be at risk later if their homes require a large repair, or a major medical expense arises and they don't have enough equity or cash left to draw on."

6.1.1e. Aging in the home

Another challenge for HECM counselors is to ensure that borrowers have a reasonable chance of remaining in their homes as they age. Most counselors reported confidence in the

FHA-provided Financial Interview Tool (FIT) as a means to discuss physical needs and health concerns with clients. However, counselors also expressed doubt in borrowers' ability to accurately project their needs 10 years or more into the future. In some cases, counselors observe dependent spouses who will be poorly equipped to manage alone in their home if widowed. As one counselor put it, "No matter how you ask them, many borrowers are unable to imagine what life will be like after a spouse dies or a health crisis limits mobility. Many do not realize how dependent they are on another person."

6.2. Advertising

Numerous state and federal agencies have expressed concerns about how reverse mortgage products are advertised. Reverse mortgages are inherently complex products, which can make it difficult for consumers to recognize inaccurate or misleading statements.

6.2.1. Risks to Consumers

False or misleading advertising poses a serious risk to consumers. If consumers misunderstand the features, risks, and obligations of a reverse mortgage, they are more likely to make poor decisions. They may take out a reverse mortgage when an alternative product would better suit their needs or when selling the home and downsizing would be a wiser financial choice. They may not choose the best set of mortgage features for their situation. They may also be more likely to fail to meet their mortgage-related obligations, such as payment of taxes and insurance.

In connection with its 2009 report, the GAO reviewed marketing materials for major HECM lenders.[315] The GAO's study included a review of Internet marketing materials for 12 major HECM lenders, as well as mailed materials from 11 of the 12 lenders. The GAO further reviewed DVDs and other materials from HECM lenders that advertise on television, conducted Internet searches for materials with potentially misleading statements, and collected materials distributed at reverse mortgage information seminars.[316]

In its study, the GAO identified six potentially misleading claims:[317]

1. A borrower will "never owe more than the value of your home."
2. A reverse mortgage is a "government benefit" or otherwise not a loan.
3. A reverse mortgage is a "lifetime loan" or a borrower "can't outlive the loan."
4. Borrowers can "never lose" their home.
5. Implied or misrepresented government affiliation.
6. Implied time limits or geographic limits on the availability of reverse mortgages.

6.2.2. Policy and Enforcement Response

In response to the risks posed by misleading advertising for reverse mortgage consumers, state regulators have introduced more specific regulations and taken enforcement actions against individual companies. The Board of Governors of the Federal Reserve System (the Board) also issued a proposed rule that would have imposed new restrictions at the federal level.

6.2.2a. State regulation and enforcement actions

Most of the state regulation against deceptive marketing has focused on how information is disseminated to the consumer and the information required to be in the disclosures. Several states require the loan agreement to specifically state that the deed or mortgage "secures a reverse mortgage loan."[318] Some states also require explicit descriptions of fees and costs,[319] with many states requiring the inclusion of interest and fees to be charged when the loan becomes due and payable.[320] Arizona requires an originator to disclose in writing all costs being charged and clearly identify which charges are for items not required to obtain the reverse mortgage.[321] Other states have focused on the disclosure of events that could trigger the loan to become due and payable.[322]

State regulators have taken enforcement actions to combat unfair and deceptive marketing of reverse mortgages. Recent actions have centered not only on individuals and entities that make unfair or deceptive statements about reverse mortgages, but also those that misrepresent their ability and qualifications to offer reverse mortgages to consumers.

Between 2008 and 2010, regulators in Florida, Illinois, Maryland, Massachusetts, Virginia and Washington brought allegations of deceptive marketing or consumer fraud against American Advisors Group of Irvine, California (AAG). The allegations centered on multiple direct-mail solicitations marked "Notice of 2008 Government Benefits"[323] or "2009 Economic Stimulus Plan – HECM Program"[324] that could have created the impression that the product being offered was a benefit and not a reverse mortgage loan. The marketing also contained the Equal Housing Opportunity logo, identified "Administrative Offices" as the sender of the mailing, and told consumers that they had been "pre-selected" and that they would have to make "NO MONTHLY PAYMENTS of any kind on proceeds."[325]

To resolve the administrative action and allegations in Massachusetts, AAG entered into a Consent Order with the Massachusetts Commissioner of Banks agreeing, among other things, to (1) revise its advertising practices and procedures; (2) to issue a written clarification notice to consumers stating that it was not affiliated with a government entity; and (3) pay an administrative penalty.[326] To resolve the suit and allegations by the Attorney General in Illinois, AAG agreed to enter an Agreed Order and Consent Decree that, among other things, required the payment of an administrative penalty and enjoined American Advisors Group from making certain statements in connection with the marketing and sale of reverse mortgages.[327] The types of statements AAG is permanently enjoined from making include any that represent, expressly or by implication, that: (1) a reverse mortgage is a government benefit; (2) President Obama's stimulus plan created the HECM; and (3) AAG is affiliated with a government agency.[328]

State regulators have also taken action against individuals and entities that misrepresent their ability to offer reverse mortgages to consumers.[329] In 2011, the Massachusetts Commissioner of Banks took action against several Internet-based entities that were not licensed in the Commonwealth as mortgage brokers, lenders, or originators. The Commissioner issued Cease Directives to these entities for misrepresenting themselves as being licensed to transact business, collecting personal information from consumers, and offering quotes to consumers.[330] One entity offered consumers a "Lender's Pledge" claiming: "We at Reverse Mortgage Page are committed to bringing you together with the best, most reputable reverse mortgage lenders. Our reverse mortgage lenders pledge to: 1) be registered and in good standing with all appropriate government regulators…7) completely follow all federal, state, and administrative laws..."[331] Another entity referred consumers from its "Find a Lender" webpage to entities not authorized to conduct mortgage business in Massachusetts and further claimed, "You won't lose your home through a reverse mortgage. Your lender does not ever gain ownership."[332]

Similar concerns about how individuals and entities represent themselves have been noted by other regulators, who as early as 2007 took note of aggressive marketing campaigns targeted at seniors utilizing purported credentials or designations that implied a level of expertise or special training in advising senior citizen investors.[333] Securities regulators in the Commonwealth of Massachusetts and other states made it a dishonest or unethical practice for individuals (broker-dealers, agents, and investment adviser representatives) to use these so-called senior designations unless the regulator has somehow recognized the use of the designation and the accrediting organization conferring it.[334] State insurance regulators have also issued similar regulations.[335] Community groups have noted the rise of the use of the similar so-called senior designations, including the "Certified Senior Adviser" title, in the marketing and sale of reverse mortgages.[336]

As recently as late 2011, consumers reported to the CFPB that they had received direct-mail solicitations from reverse mortgage lenders claiming to offer government benefits and displaying the seal of a federal agency.[337]

6.2.2b. The Federal Reserve Board's proposal

On September 24, 2010, the Board proposed a rule that would have imposed new restrictions on reverse mortgage advertisements. The Board's proposed rule would have required advertisements to disclose clarifying information if the advertisement used statements similar to those identified as potentially misleading by the GAO or other problematic statements identified by the Board.

The Board's proposed rule would have required clarifying disclosures for the following types of statements: [338]

1. **A reverse mortgage is a "government benefit."**
   Clarification: A reverse mortgage is a loan that must be repaid.
2. **A reverse mortgage provides payments "for life" or a consumer need not repay a reverse mortgage "during your lifetime."**
   Clarification: Explain the circumstances under which payments or access to a line of credit may end or a consumer would be required to repay a reverse mortgage during the consumer's life (e.g., the borrower sells the home).
3. **A consumer "cannot lose his or her home" or there is "no risk" to a consumer's home with a reverse mortgage.**
   Clarification: Foreclosure may occur if the consumer (1) lives somewhere other than the home longer than allowed by the loan agreement; or (2) does not pay property taxes or insurance premiums.
4. **Payments are not required for a reverse mortgage.**
   Clarification: Consumers must make payments for taxes and insurance during the term of the reverse mortgage.
5. **Government fee limits apply to a reverse mortgage.**
   Clarification: Reverse mortgage costs may vary among creditors and loan types. Less expensive options may be available.

6. **A reverse mortgage does not affect a consumer's eligibility for, or benefits under, a government program.**
   Clarification: A reverse mortgage may affect eligibility for some government programs. Specifically, SSI and Medicaid may be affected.
7. **A consumer or a consumer's heirs "cannot owe" or will "never repay" more than the value of the consumer's home.**
   Clarification: In order to retain the home when the reverse mortgage becomes due, (1) the consumer or the consumer's heirs or estate must pay the entire loan balance and (2) the balance may be greater than the value of the consumer's home.[x]

The advertising provisions of the Board's proposed rule were designed to assist consumers in understanding potential risks associated with taking out a reverse mortgage. The authority for future rulemaking on reverse mortgage advertising under the Truth in Lending Act (TILA) transferred to the CFPB on July 21, 2011.

6.2.3. Conclusions

Given the complex nature of reverse mortgages, consumers may be particularly susceptible to misleading advertisements. Such statements can create confusion about fundamental features of reverse mortgages, leading consumers to make poor product choices.

The CFPB remains concerned about the consumer harm caused by misleading advertisements. The CFPB plans to consider the Board's 2010 proposal and other potential means of combating misleading advertisements in this area. Additionally, the CFPB currently has authority to take supervisory and enforcement actions against deceptive practices.[339]

6.3. Cross-Selling

The fundamental purpose of a reverse mortgage – to generate cash for the borrower – has the inevitable side effect of making reverse mortgage borrowers especially susceptible to unscrupulous or aggressive salespeople selling investment and/or insurance products. Egregious stories of seniors who were convinced to take out lump-sum reverse mortgages and use the proceeds to purchase deferred annuities have made headlines and formed the basis of several consumer advocacy campaigns.[340] These annuities typically accrued interest at less than the interest rate on the loan and often did not provide any cash flow to the senior for 10 years or more.

In response, numerous prohibitions against cross-selling have been enacted. Cross-selling occurs when a lender (a) requires the consumer to purchase financial or insurance products with the proceeds from a reverse mortgage, or (b) convinces a consumer to make such a purchase with the proceeds.[341] In general, cross-selling is prohibited for the HECM program.[342] Some state laws also address this issue with respect to proprietary reverse mortgages.[343] As in any industry, however, bad actors willing to violate the law still persist.

[x] These types of advertising statements may be less problematic today as a result of HUD's rescission of FHA Mortgagee Letter 2008-38, which required the borrower's estate to pay off the entire reverse mortgage loan balance in order to retain ownership of the home. See Section 6.7.2.

6.3.1. Risks to Consumers

Cross-selling can harm consumers if they are required or persuaded to purchase products that are overly expensive or otherwise inappropriate for their needs. Cross-selling can not only result in consumers being persuaded to purchase a product they do not need, but also in consumers paying far more for the product than they would if they purchased it outside of a reverse mortgage context. When a borrower uses reverse mortgage proceeds to purchase another financial product, the fees for the products compound. Consumers pay fees and interest to take out a reverse mortgage and then pay fees to purchase the other product.

The cross-selling of annuities is particularly harmful to consumers because an annuity-like monthly payment stream is one of the payment options available with a reverse mortgage. A consumer who uses a reverse mortgage to purchase an annuity pays a hefty fee for the annuity and receives no additional benefit, since the reverse mortgage itself could have been set up to provide an annuity-like stream of payments. Cross-selling can also be particularly harmful when borrowers are tapping a large portion of their home equity with a lump-sum draw. If borrowers then funnel most or all of their proceeds into an illiquid investment or insurance policy, borrowers lose the flexibility of being able to access the equity in their home when they need it.

Numerous government investigations of the reverse mortgage market, as well as consumer advocacy groups, have identified the inappropriate cross-selling of financial and insurance products with reverse mortgage loans as an important consumer protection concern.[344]

6.3.2. Policy Response

In response to widespread concern about harmful cross-selling, prohibitions on cross-selling have been enacted at both the federal and state levels.

6.3.2a. HERA prohibitions on cross-selling

In the Housing and Economic Recovery Act of 2008 (HERA), Congress adopted rules restricting the sale of other products or services with a HECM mortgage. HERA prohibits a reverse mortgage lender from requiring a borrower or any other party to purchase an insurance annuity or other similar product as a condition of obtaining a HECM mortgage.[345] HERA also generally prohibits a HECM mortgage originator or any other party that participates in the origination of a HECM mortgage from participating in, being associated with, or employing any party that participates in or is associated with any other financial or insurance activity. However, an exception to this general provision applies if the originator establishes "firewalls and other safeguards" designed to ensure that "(i) individuals participating in the origination of a HECM mortgage have no involvement with, or incentive to provide the mortgagor with, any other financial or insurance product; and (ii) the mortgagor shall not be required, directly or indirectly, as a condition of obtaining a mortgage under this section, to purchase any other financial or insurance product."[346]

6.3.2b. State regulation

Patterns of aggressive and abusive sales tactics led states to pass laws and issue guidance restricting cross-selling with respect to all reverse mortgages, not just HECMs.[347] These laws and restrictions are designed to both ban business practices that would make senior citizens purchase unsuitable products and provide recourse for reverse mortgage borrowers against individuals and entities employing aggressive and unfair, deceptive or abusive acts or practices.

Some states have gone beyond the provisions in HERA that require appropriate firewalls between reverse mortgage originators and company divisions selling other products. Maryland, Rhode Island, Vermont, and Washington have further separated the reverse mortgage transaction from the sale of other financial products by prohibiting lenders from referring consumers to anyone for the purchase of an annuity or other financial or insurance product within certain time periods of the reverse mortgage transaction.[348]

6.3.2c. FFIEC guidance to prohibit cross-selling

As discussed in Section 5.4, the federal banking agencies, through the FFIEC, issued guidance on cross-selling and other issues to institutions offering reverse mortgages. The FFIEC guidance provides that institutions should avoid any appearance of a conflict of interest by (1) adopting clear written policies prohibiting cross-sales of products that appear to be linked to the decision to provide a reverse mortgage, and (2) adopting clear compensation policies to guard against inappropriate incentives to make a reverse mortgage loan. This guidance applies equally to HECMs and proprietary reverse mortgages.

6.3.2d. Anti-tying laws that bar cross-selling by depository institutions

Certain laws applicable to banks and other depository institutions contain anti-tying rules that would bar tying a reverse mortgage loan to the borrower's purchase of certain other types of financial products. Specifically, the Bank Holding Company Act and the Home Owners' Loan Act generally prohibit banks, savings associations, and savings and loan associations from conditioning the price or availability of a product, including a reverse mortgage, on the borrower's purchase of insurance or an annuity from the bank or its affiliate.[349] Further, the Gramm-Leach-Bliley Act required the federal banking agencies to prescribe regulations prohibiting "a depository institution from engaging in any practice that would lead a customer to believe an extension of credit is conditional upon— (1) the purchase of an insurance product from the institution or any of its affiliates; or (2) an agreement by the consumer not to obtain, or a prohibition on the consumer from obtaining, an insurance product from an unaffiliated entity."[350]

6.3.2e The Board's proposed rule barring cross-selling

Importantly, the cross-selling prohibitions in HERA only apply to HECMs and the anti-tying provisions only apply to reverse mortgages originated by depository institutions. There are no express federal rules currently prohibiting cross-selling of other financial and insurance products with proprietary reverse mortgages originated by nonbanks.

Because of this regulatory gap, the Board's 2010 proposed rule included a provision to bar creditors or loan originators from cross-selling certain other financial and insurance products with *all* reverse mortgages, including both HECMs and proprietary products.[351]

Notably, the Board's proposed rule included a regulatory safe harbor. The Board's proposed safe harbor provided that if (a) a consumer received a copy of a disclosure (provided in the proposed rule) regarding key questions to ask about a reverse mortgage and (b) the reverse mortgage was obtained at least ten calendar days before the consumer purchased the financial or insurance product, a creditor or loan originator will not be found to have violated the prohibition against cross-selling. While industry groups supported this safe harbor,[352] several consumer groups commented that the Board should eliminate the safe-harbor provision prior to finalizing the proposed rule.[353]

6.3.3. Conclusions

The current combination of state and federal regulations provides significant consumer protections against inappropriate cross-selling for most types of reverse mortgages. The only reverse mortgages not subject to rules prohibiting cross-selling are proprietary products originated by nonbanks. Today, this segment constitutes only a handful of loans, but nearly all of the remaining large reverse mortgage originators are nonbanks, and the proprietary market could expand again in the future. The CFPB will consider this regulatory gap in its future efforts in this area.

Given the prohibitions already in place, protecting consumers from inappropriate cross-selling is largely a matter of appropriate supervision and enforcement. The CFPB has identified cross-selling as an issue in its supervision manual, and will work to ensure that reverse mortgage lenders and related companies are complying with existing laws. Consumer advocates interviewed for this study indicated that they have not encountered many cases of cross-selling since the passage of HERA.

However, there is some anecdotal evidence that some annuity salespeople are still targeting reverse mortgage borrowers as a method for generating clients. Multiple HECM counselors interviewed for this study reported occasionally encountering clients who had decided to use a reverse mortgage to purchase an annuity after having attended an information seminar co-hosted by a reverse mortgage loan originator and an annuity salesperson.

6.4. Counseling

When the HECM program was created, the statute included a mandate to provide information about loan details and costs to borrowers prior to their obtaining a HECM.[354] To meet this objective, HUD developed a counselor training program in collaboration with AARP and other nonprofit organizations. The training program eventually developed into a national network of HUD-approved HECM counselors.

The HECM counseling session is composed of a series of modules designed by HUD and contained in the HUD HECM Counseling Protocol. Under the Protocol, a counseling session may be in person or over the telephone. Counselors are required to send information packets to clients in advance of the session for their review. Agencies are required to set counseling fees at a "reasonable and customary" level, and must waive fees for clients whose incomes are less than twice the poverty level.[355] The counseling component of the HECM product is critical to ensure product understanding, alternatives, and compatibility between potential borrowers and loans.

HUD's HECM Counseling Protocol currently requires counselors to cover the following general topics in depth for each session: [356]

1. Reverse Mortgage Basics
2. HECM Costs and Benefits
3. Alternatives to a Reverse Mortgage
4. Financial Interview Tool (FIT)

6.4.1. Risks to Consumers

Reverse mortgage counseling should be effective, impartial, and accessible. Anything that threatens the effectiveness, impartiality, or accessibility of counseling can put consumers at risk.

- **Counselor efficacy:** Ineffective counseling may be a result of counselor noncompliance with the established HUD protocol. However, as discussed in Section 6.1.1, consumer research and interviews with counselors suggest that consumers may struggle to understand reverse mortgages even if counselors follow the HECM protocols. The increased variety of product options may also be overwhelming borrowers with information, making decision-making more difficult.
- **Counselor impartiality and accessibility:** Maintaining an adequate cadre of well-trained, impartial, and accessible counselors often comes down to funding. Without an adequate and stable funding source, accessibility to counselors becomes more limited. Counseling agencies may have to start charging fees, which can deter seniors in need of counseling. Agencies that defer the fee until closing may struggle to maintain impartiality.

Borrowers reported to the CFPB frustration that certain topics either were not addressed in the counseling process, not adequately explained, or not understood.[357] Borrowers commonly cited issues surrounding when the loan becomes due and payable, taxes and insurance, costs and fees, and whether family members would be able to pay off the mortgage after the borrower passed away. Family members of prospective reverse mortgage borrowers reported that prospective borrowers who were hard of hearing had received counseling over the phone and were physically incapable of processing the information and understanding the product.[358]

6.4.1a. Counselor noncompliance

The 2009 GAO report raised concerns over counselor compliance with the HUD Protocol.[359] GAO staff posed as prospective HECM borrowers for 15 counseling sessions at 11 separate agencies. The evaluation found that none of the counselors consistently complied with HECM counseling requirements. The GAO concluded that HUD should tighten controls over the HECM Protocol so that noncompliance does not diminish counseling efficacy.

The information most frequently omitted from the counseling sessions was:

- **Alternative financial options.** Many counselors did not discuss financial options beyond the HECM, such as alternative living arrangements, meal programs, or other social services that might be available to help meet financial needs.
- **Alternative home equity products.** Many counselors neglected to discuss alternative ways to access home equity, such as state or local government-sponsored home equity loans.
- **Financial implications.** Most counselors only partially met the requirement to fully explain the financial implications of entering into a HECM loan.
- **Impact on eligibility for assistance.** Many counselors did not adequately explain how a HECM may affect eligibility for federal or state assistance programs. A

borrower can become ineligible for Supplemental Security Income, for example, by depositing too much money from a HECM loan into a bank account.

- **Estate planning.** Most counselors did not explicitly ask if the borrower had signed a contract or agreement with an estate-planning service. Such third-party services may take advantage of borrowers by charging for arranging a meeting with HECM counselors.

Based on its findings, the GAO recommended that HUD implement the following:[360]

- Checks to verify length and content of HECM counseling sessions
- Guidance to counselors for accurately recording counseling time
- Procedures for counseling providers to assess counselee's ability to pay

6.4.1b. Other challenges to counselor efficacy

Counselors interviewed for this study reported that many prospective borrowers did not take the sessions seriously. According to counselors, these prospective borrowers viewed counseling not as an opportunity to learn about the product and make a better decision, but as a hurdle between them and their goal. Counselors stressed that prospective borrowers needed to allow themselves the time to learn about the product and the options without rushing toward a desired conclusion.

HUD's HECM protocol contains prohibitions against counselors recommending one product option over another.[361] While this prohibition is designed to ensure that counselors remain unbiased, the sheer number of options available and factors to consider in making a decision means that prospective borrowers may struggle to sort through all of the relevant information and may make decisions based more on gut feelings than on careful evaluation of tradeoffs.[362]

Some consumer groups have raised concerns about the prevalence of telephone counseling and the possibility that telephone counseling may be less effective than face-to-face counseling. In particular, consumer groups have claimed that many telephone-based counselors spend less than an hour per session on the material.[363] The issues of impaired hearing in the older population must also be considered.

6.4.1c. Counselor impartiality and access

While impartiality and access are separate issues, they both relate to counselor funding. Without adequate and stable funding, it is more difficult for counseling agencies to maintain high quality, impartial counseling and to offer their services to the widest range of clients.

In the absence of appropriated funds for the counseling program, many counseling agencies have begun to charge their clients.[364] However, HUD regulations state that counseling agencies may not turn clients away because of an inability to pay.[365] HUD also allows the cost of counseling to be paid using the reverse mortgage proceeds.[366] The ability to defer the fee until closing may increase access to counseling. If it becomes the counseling agency's standard business practice, however, the agency will only be able to collect fees if the loan actually closes. This could create an incentive for the counselor to encourage counselees to take out loans.

The issue of telephone versus face-to-face counseling has potential implications for access to counseling as well. While face-to-face counseling could improve the effectiveness of counseling, requiring all counseling sessions to be conducted face-to-face would make it difficult for consumers in rural areas to get counseling without having to travel long distances. Such requirements could also increase the cost of providing counseling, which could reduce the number of agencies that are able to offer the service under the current fee structure.

6.4.2. Policy Response

In response to the concerns raised by the GAO report, HUD has increased its oversight of the HECM counseling program and introduced additional content. Some states have also passed legislation requiring face-to-face counseling and/or additional information.

6.4.2a. Increased compliance effort & expanded HUD protocol

In response to the 2009 GAO report, the FHA redoubled its efforts to ensure that HUD-approved HECM counselors are knowledgeable about program requirements and comply with the HECM protocol.

Effective October 2, 2009, HUD adopted testing standards for certifying HECM counselors.[367] Counselors must pass the exam to be included on a national HECM Counseling Roster and must be retested every three years.[368]

Subsequently, HUD implemented an addition to the HECM protocol known as the Financial Interview Tool (FIT) in 2010.[369] The FIT is a 25-question instrument designed to help clients discuss their income, debt and expenses, health status, and future plans with counselors. This discussion helps clients and counselors assess how the mortgage might assist borrowers in meeting their needs and goals.

6.4.2b. State regulations

State regulation of reverse mortgage counseling includes requirements for additional information to be provided to the consumer and, in some cases, requirements about the form of the counseling. California and Maryland require lenders to give consumers a checklist of items they should discuss with the housing counselor prior to completion of an application.[370] Illinois, New York, South Carolina, and other states require a statement to be given to all consumers at the time of the inquiry about the advisability and availability of independent counseling.[371]

Some states have passed additional regulations recommending or requiring counseling for prospective borrowers of proprietary reverse mortgages. Colorado requires counseling unless the prospective proprietary borrower waives it in writing.[372] Louisiana requires that a mortgage lender seeking to pay a prospective proprietary borrower's counseling fees must disclose, in writing, that this may create a conflict of interest and also disclose any other payment arrangements or business affiliations between the lender and counseling agency.[373]

While many states and consumer groups recommend face-to-face counseling, Massachusetts, North Carolina, and Vermont are the only states to have passed statutes requiring it.[374] North Carolina has required in-person counseling for all borrowers since 1991.[375] Vermont does allow borrowers who cannot or choose not to travel to a counselor and cannot be visited by one in their home to receive counseling by phone.[376] Effective August 1, 2012, the Massachusetts in-person counseling requirement will apply to borrowers making less than 50 percent of the area median income and have assets worth less than $120,000 outside of their home.[377] California and other states have also proposed legislation requiring in-person counseling.[378]

6.4.3. Conclusions

The existing concerns related to HECM counseling can be reduced to three essential topics: (1) compliance and efficacy, (2) impartiality, and (3) access. Any changes to the counseling program should carefully weigh potential tradeoffs in each of these areas.

6.4.3a. Continued need for improvements in counseling practice

Counseling remains a critical tool for helping borrowers understand reverse mortgages. Counselors provide a line of defense, dispelling misconceptions and explaining fundamental concepts underpinning these products. Their services become increasingly important as borrowers face more complex choices as a result of new product offerings, such as the HECM Saver and the fixed-rate, lump-sum product.

On the other hand, research indicates that confusion on certain topics persists even after counseling. With the increased array of products to choose from, consumers may find themselves having *too much* information at their disposal. While it is unclear just how much counseling can do to alleviate these difficulties, there appears to be room for improvement. Continued innovation and enhanced counseling tools should focus on areas that remain difficult for consumers to understand.

The CFPB will continue to learn from stakeholders and counselors to better understand the primary obstacles to good consumer decision-making regarding reverse mortgages. The CFPB will explore improved methods and approaches for helping consumers compare products, understand costs and risks, and evaluate tradeoffs.

6.4.3b. Funding

The unpredictability of counselor funding remains a concern. Ideally, funding mechanisms would provide a stable, predictable source of sufficient funding for counseling without creating misaligned incentives. If such a funding method could be devised, it would benefit counseling agencies and borrowers. Counseling agencies would benefit from the added workforce stability. At the same time, they could potentially offer their clients increased access to counselors. Borrowers would also benefit if new funding mechanisms enabled ways for counselors to improve efficacy.

One possible funding mechanism worth considering is a lender-funded pool. Lenders could contribute funds to a central pool, which would then be disbursed to counseling agencies according to need or client volume. The pool could be administered either by HUD or by a neutral third party. A mechanism of this sort has the potential to provide a more stable funding source for counseling while mitigating any conflict of interest. However, this type of funding mechanism currently appears to be prohibited by HERA, which prohibits lenders from funding counseling directly or indirectly.[379]

6.5. Costs & Fees

As discussed in Section 2.6, reverse mortgages include several different types of upfront and ongoing costs and fees. These costs and fees may be difficult for consumers to effectively evaluate and in many cases may be higher than alternative products.

6.5.1. Risks to Consumers

Costs and fees reduce the principal amount initially available to HECM borrowers, and can increase the amount owed throughout the life of the loan. Upfront costs include origination, closing, and insurance fees, some of which may be financed into the loan. Monthly servicing and insurance fees are added to the loan balance as they accrue. These fees compensate mortgage professionals for services they provide, and also help FHA offset the risk it takes on when insuring HECM loans. However, the high fees may incentivize loan originators to steer seniors into reverse mortgages even when lower fee alternatives, such as HELOCs or home equity loans, may be more appropriate credit products.

Consumer groups and personal finance commentators have expressed concern that reverse mortgages are high-cost products.[380] A 2006 survey conducted by the AARP found that the main reason consumers decided against taking out a reverse mortgage was because of high costs.[381] In the same survey, nearly 70 percent of consumers who did opt for a reverse mortgage did so despite believing that the costs and fees were high.[382] One consumer reported to the CFPB believing that origination and interest fees must be fraudulent because they were so high.[383]

6.5.2. Policy and Market Response

HERA placed a $6,000 limit on origination fees in 2008, which helped reduce costs for owners of higher value homes.[384] During 2010, both market pricing and FHA policies further reduced HECM costs and fees. Lenders first began waiving origination fees on fixed-rate products in April 2010.[385] Some lenders have also begun offering discounted origination fees on adjustable-rate products. These waivers or discounts are offered with slightly higher interest rates than the rates paid by the few borrowers who choose to pay the origination fee upfront. Lenders have also incorporated servicing fees into the interest rate. Doing so eliminates the upfront reduction in a borrower's net proceeds, but it does not actually eliminate the fee.[386]

On September 21, 2010, FHA responded to consumer concerns about high costs by releasing the HECM Saver option.[387] The HECM Saver charges a significantly lower upfront insurance fee of 0.01 percent of appraised home value (or FHA loan limit, whichever is less).[388] FHA offset this lower fee by lowering the amount of funds available under HECM Saver in comparison to HECM Standard loans.[389] However, the same Mortgagee Letter increased monthly HECM insurance premiums from 0.5 percent to 1.25 percent of the outstanding loan balance in an effort to improve the sustainability of the insurance fund.[390] This policy change reduced upfront fees for consumers choosing the Saver product (6.0 percent in FY 2011) but increased ongoing fees for all consumers.

Both the market reduction in fees and the HECM Saver option have helped ease concerns that upfront costs and fees are too high.[391] However, at least some of these upfront fees have been converted into ongoing monthly fees in the form of higher ongoing mortgage insurance premiums and higher interest rates than would otherwise be the case. The HECM Saver is emerging as a comparable alternative to other home equity products such as a home equity line of credit (HELOC). HELOCs have been much less costly than reverse mortgages in the past because they require minimal closing costs, no insurance premiums, and no servicing fees. However, HELOCs may not be a viable alternative for some borrowers because they require monthly interest payments and do not provide nonrecourse protection. The HECM

Saver option and reduced lender fees make reverse mortgages a relatively more competitive home equity product than it has been in the past.

6.5.3. Future Concerns

Market conditions enabled the elimination or reduction of reverse mortgage origination fees. However, lenders may need to bring back these fees if market conditions change. FHA has also expressed concern that the HECM program cannot support the current level of defaults within its existing book of business.[392] As FHA continues to look toward the sustainability of the HECM program and its threat to the Mutual Mortgage Insurance Fund, it may need to further increase insurance fees.

6.6. Tax and Insurance Defaults

As discussed in the *Product* chapter, HECM loans require borrowers to remain current on all property taxes and homeowner's insurance.[393] This requirement protects FHA's collateral interest in the property and ensures that borrowers are fulfilling their mortgage obligations. If borrowers fail to pay these property-related charges, the servicer may pay the charges using any remaining available proceeds from the loan. In these instances, servicers pay the outstanding charges directly, add them to the borrower's loan balance, and notify the borrower.[394] This option is not available to fixed-rate borrowers, because fixed-rate HECMs require borrowers to withdraw all of their proceeds upfront as a lump-sum payment.

As of the end of February 2012, 9.4 percent of active HECM loans were in default on taxes and/or insurance.[395] This proportion has increased from 8.1 percent in July 2011.[396]

6.6.1. Risks to Consumers

Tax and insurance defaults can lead to foreclosure, though in practice both FHA and HECM lenders and servicers would prefer to avoid foreclosing on elderly borrowers.[397]

Tax and insurance defaults are more likely in reverse mortgages than in traditional mortgages for several reasons. Unlike traditional mortgages, HECM borrowers do not have the option of an escrow account maintained by the lender or servicer where they can pay taxes and insurance premiums on a monthly basis. HECM borrowers may opt to set aside funds for payment of taxes and insurance, but few borrowers use this option because it reduces the amount of principal available.[398] Therefore, instead of having a small monthly payment that is automatically set aside, borrowers must plan for tax and insurance payments that may only come due once a year.

With a traditional mortgage, underwriting rules are used to determine whether a borrower can be expected to make the mortgage payments. Since reverse mortgages do not require payments for the mortgage itself, lenders are not required to assess a borrower's income or creditworthiness. However, this also means that lenders do not assess a borrower's ability to pay taxes and insurance when they underwrite the loan.[399] Therefore, borrowers may be able to take out a reverse mortgage even if they are unlikely to be able to pay the associated taxes and insurance on the property.

Finally, reverse mortgages require no payments for the mortgage itself. Therefore, borrowers are more likely to forget that tax and insurance payments are required, or they may not fully understand the implications of failing to pay these charges. Borrowers have reported confusion about the need to pay taxes and insurance to the CFPB. Some borrowers report that they did not understand the need to make the payments or the potential consequences of not making the payments. Several borrowers expressed frustration and distress after having difficulty receiving clarification about the tax and insurance bills.[400] In one instance, the borrower reported that the loan had gone into technical default by the time the borrower received clarifying information. The Federal Trade Commission received three complaints in which consumers acknowledged that they had not paid taxes and insurance but did not understand that this nonpayment was grounds for foreclosure.[401]

6.6.2. Guidance from FHA

HECM regulations state that if a loan becomes due and payable because the borrower failed to pay taxes or insurance, the servicer must request permission from FHA's National Servicing Center before the loan can progress to the default phase.[402] Property charge defaults leave a servicer in a vulnerable position. These "due and payable" regulations are ambiguous as to how the servicer must handle the outstanding property charges before it submits an insurance claim to FHA. If a servicer allows a property to stay uninsured or delinquent on taxes, it risks losing the mortgage collateral. If a servicer pays these property charges on behalf of the borrower, it risks incurring charges that might not be reimbursed by FHA.[403]

Between 2007 and April 30, 2009, FHA informally instructed servicers to defer foreclosure on borrowers with property charge defaults.[404] Servicers paid the property charges for these mortgages despite the fact that borrowers had already withdrawn their entire authorized loan proceeds and did not have any mortgage loan funds left. These payments are known as "corporate advances." Servicers continued to service the loans but did not proceed with foreclosure unless some other due-and-payable event occurred (e.g., the borrower died or sold the home). The servicers expected to be reimbursed for these corporate advances through the claim filing process with FHA.

On May 20, 2009, FHA informed HECM servicers that it would no longer accept foreclosure deferral requests for mortgages in default due to nonpayment of property charges.[405] This guidance was issued through an informal email and stated that the denial policy would be effective retroactively starting April 30, 2009.[406] Some servicers interpreted this limited guidance to mean that FHA was waiving the requirement to report property charge defaults.[407] Accordingly, servicers continued to make corporate advances to pay the property charges associated with the loans but did not notify FHA of these defaults.[408] The informal 2009 guidance resulted in servicers continuing the same practice as before, except that they no longer asked FHA for permission to delay foreclosure.

This ambiguous guidance and concern about increasing property charge defaults prompted the HUD Office of the Inspector General (OIG) to conduct an internal audit of the HECM program in 2010.[409] The OIG contacted four out of the 16 HECM servicers and discovered that they were holding approximately 13,000 loans in default due to nonpayment of property charges.[410] These four servicers alone had paid over $35 million in corporate advances to cover unpaid property charges between May 2009 and March 2010.[411] These advances were added to the principal balance on the loans, even though the loans had already reached the principal limit.[412] The OIG concluded that the foreclosure delay on these properties, accumulating corporate advances, and increasing number of mortgages in default for property charges threatened the FHA's Mutual Mortgage Insurance Fund.[413]

6.6.3. Corrective Action

FHA issued formal guidance on property charge defaults in a January 3, 2011 Mortgagee Letter.[414] The Letter clarified the servicer's obligations to pay outstanding property charges, to use loss mitigation to help bring the loan out of default, and to pursue foreclosure if loss mitigation proved unsuccessful.[415]

Under this Letter, a borrower's nonpayment of property charges triggers several servicer obligations.[416] Servicers must send delinquent borrowers a "Property Charge Delinquency Letter" that provides a 30-day period to cure the delinquency.[417] They must report such cases to FHA within five calendar days prior to the end of the month in which the delinquencies occur. In order to protect FHA's collateral interest in the property, servicers are required to pay the outstanding property charges on the borrower's behalf. The servicer can seek reimbursement on these advances from the borrower.[418]

In addition to contacting the borrower, reporting the delinquency, and paying the outstanding charges, servicers must try to cure the borrower's default through loss mitigation strategies.[419] These strategies may include: (a) establishing a repayment plan for the outstanding property charges; (b) contacting a HUD-approved counseling agency for free assistance to the borrower; and (c) refinancing the delinquent HECM into a new HECM if there is sufficient equity remaining in the property.[420] The Letter provides a table of repayment plans, with no plans exceeding 24 months.[421] Borrowers who repay the servicer's advances and become current on property charges will become compliant with their mortgage terms.[422]

After all loss mitigation options have proved unsuccessful, the servicer may submit a due-and-payable request to FHA.[423] Servicers have to attach documentation of their loss mitigation efforts to these requests. If the request is denied, the servicer must continue attempts at loss mitigation.[424] If the request is approved, the servicer must proceed with foreclosure.[425]

FHA has developed a network of specialized HECM counselors to work with delinquent borrowers and identify ways to help the borrowers become current on their obligations and avoid foreclosure.[426] A pilot program is also being developed in Philadelphia that will assist the most distressed borrowers – those whose mortgages have been declared due and payable and are facing imminent foreclosure – in resolving their situation. The program will help borrowers evaluate options for avoiding foreclosure and, if the foreclosure cannot be averted, attempt to find alternative housing.[427]

6.6.4. Conclusions

As of February 2012, approximately 54,000 borrowers are at risk of losing their homes due to property charge defaults.[428] These default cases account for 9.4 percent of active HECM loans.[429] Some borrowers may not realize that they risk losing their home if they cannot make payments for taxes and insurance.[430] Borrowers who take most or all of their available funds upfront at closing are particularly at risk. Stricter underwriting requirements and increased emphasis on property charge obligations during HECM counseling sessions would help ensure that borrowers are prepared for the obligations that come with the reverse mortgage loan and help avoid foreclosures. Other options, such as monthly escrow payments or a tax and insurance "set aside" from loan funds, could also reduce the likelihood that borrowers fall into default.

Voluntary efforts to introduce underwriting standards have so far proved unsuccessful. The industry has asked FHA to provide a baseline underwriting requirement, and FHA is working on new policy. FHA has indicated that it is evaluating all policy options, including underwriting, escrow requirements, and tax and insurance set asides, and it expects to publish a proposal in the fourth quarter of 2012.[431] The CFPB supports FHA and the industry in this effort.

6.6.4a. Stricter underwriting criteria and enhanced counseling

More thorough underwriting requirements and an increased focus on property charge obligations during counseling could help ensure that borrowers are able to meet their obligation to pay property charges. For example, underwriting requirements could compare borrowers' monthly income with monthly property charges. Although this practice may prevent some borrowers from obtaining a HECM loan, initial disqualification may be a better outcome than getting a HECM only to be foreclosed upon later.

Acting FHA Commissioner Carol Galante issued a letter on October 5, 2011 explaining that the HECM regulations do not prohibit lenders from conducting more thorough financial and credit assessments of borrowers.[432] Given that individual lenders may suffer a competitive disadvantage if they implement a stricter financial assessment, market practices are unlikely to change without a mandate that applies to all providers. For example, MetLife implemented a financial assessment in November 2011 but stopped after other industry originators failed to adopt a similar policy.[433] These stricter assessment requirements could be coupled with an emphasis on property charge obligations during HECM counseling sessions and closing.[434]

Many borrowers may not be used to paying their taxes and insurance themselves because they paid them through an escrow arrangement with their traditional mortgage. Monthly escrow payments are another option that could help reverse mortgage borrowers remember and budget for these expenses. However, escrow arrangements could increase the costs of servicing the loan.

6.6.4b. Risks of fixed-rate, lump-sum product

The number of HECM borrowers at risk for property charge default appears to be increasing. Borrowers with higher initial draws are more likely to default on property charges.[435] Currently, about 70 percent of borrowers choose a fixed-rate, lump-sum product. Borrowers who choose a fixed-rate, lump-sum product by definition do not have any additional reverse mortgage funds available to use to pay the property charges. Without remaining available funds, borrowers who do not pay their property charges will be immediately placed in default. Therefore, options such as a limited tax and insurance set aside – to be used only in the event of a default – may offer protection against foreclosure, particularly for lump-sum borrowers.

6.7. Non-Borrower Protections

Consumer advocates have expressed concerns regarding whether the interests of non-borrower spouses and other family members are properly protected in connection with HECM reverse mortgage loans. Spouses of reverse mortgage borrowers who are not themselves named as borrowers are often unaware that they are at risk of losing their homes. If the borrowing spouse dies or needs to move, the non-borrowing spouse must sell the home or otherwise pay off the reverse mortgage at that time. Other family members (children, grandchildren, etc.) who live with reverse-mortgage borrowers also are at risk of needing to find other living arrangements when the borrower dies or needs to move.

6.7.1. Risks to Non-Borrowers

Typically, couples will include both spouses/partners as borrowers on a reverse mortgage. Therefore, if one spouse dies, the other spouse can continue to live in the home as long as no other circumstances prompt repayment. Sometimes, however, the reverse mortgage is taken out in the name of only one spouse. This may happen because (1) the other spouse was younger than 62 when the reverse mortgage was originated and therefore could not qualify as a borrower; (2) the younger spouse was left off the reverse mortgage contract so that the older borrower could receive higher proceeds from the loan; or (3) the couple married after the reverse mortgage was originated.

In these cases, the non-borrower spouse is at risk of needing to sell the home to pay off the reverse mortgage when the borrowing spouse dies or needs to move. A reverse mortgage can jeopardize the living situation of any other non-borrowers living in the home, such as children, grandchildren, or other relatives.

Several borrowers reported to the CFPB that they did not understand the consequences of not having a spouse on the deed and the reverse mortgage. Borrowers reported that brokers promised lower rates, additional funds, or a more favorable deal if spouse's names were not on the deed or reverse mortgage, and promised that borrowers would be able to add a spouse or family member when they reached a certain age. Instead, when borrowers later reached out to lenders, they reported that the lender did not allow them to add the name to the mortgage, causing frustration and difficulties when the spouse passed away. In particular, consumers reported an inability to pay off the loans in full, which resulted in foreclosure. Family members reported trying to refinance or seek other means of modifying the reverse mortgage into another type of loan without success. Others believed the borrower would not have taken out the loan if they knew it meant relatives could not keep the home.[436]

6.7.1a. Legal response

Consumer advocates and HUD are currently engaged in a legal dispute regarding whether non-borrower spouses must be considered "borrowers" in connection with HECM reverse mortgage transactions. The AARP is assisting three non-borrower spouses of reverse mortgage borrowers to assert claims on the basis that HUD has insured mortgage loans that do not provide required protections to non-borrower spouses of reverse mortgage borrowers.[437]

The HECM Statute states that HUD "may not insure a [HECM] . . . unless such mortgage provides that the Homeowner's obligation to satisfy the loan obligation is deferred until the homeowner's death, the sale of the home, or the occurrence of other events specified in regulation of the Secretary" and that "[f]or purposes of this subsection, the term homeowner includes the spouse of the homeowner."[438]

HUD's regulations that implement this provision refer to the *borrower* rather than the homeowner. Essentially, HUD, through FHA, will insure reverse mortgages so long as the payment obligation is deferred until a due and payable event occurs with respect to the *borrower* without regard to any non-borrower spouse.[439]

HUD stated that any interpretation of the HECM Statute that deferred repayment of a reverse mortgage to the length of a non-borrower spouse's life would eviscerate the actuarial soundness of the HECM program. HUD fears a borrower "could even marry a much younger person after taking out the mortgage, thus requiring the lender to wait decades more than anticipated for repayment while interest continues to accrue beyond the value of the house." The losses then could be passed on to HUD as an insurance claim.[440] In at least one case, reverse mortgage borrowers have attempted to circumvent HECM restrictions in an attempt to obtain a reverse mortgage and preserve ownership of the property by a non-borrower spouse that does not meet the age requirements.[441]

Courts have not directly addressed the meaning of the HECM Statute. The AARP-supported action was dismissed on the basis that HUD's rules for insuring HECMs would not impact the challenged foreclosures affecting the plaintiffs. One court, however, has allowed a plaintiff to assert a claim for reformation of a contract based upon the borrower's understanding of the HECM Statute.[442] The court observed that "[t]he statute suggests that HECM loans, by default, apply to both spouses and that any reference to homeowner is, again, by default, a reference to the couple,"[443] and could be a factor in favor or reforming the contract to match the party's understanding.

6.7.1b. Policy response

On August 26, 2011, HUD issued new guidance stating that all spouses of prospective borrowers and all co-owners of the property *must* receive reverse mortgage counseling in addition to the borrower.[444]

6.7.1c. Conclusions

Consumers and counselors should be aware of the risks reverse mortgages pose to non-borrower spouses. Consumers can be harmed if they are told (or otherwise assume) that non-borrowers will be allowed to stay in the home for the length of the non-borrower's life. The new guidance requiring non-borrower spouses and co-owners to attend counseling is an important step forward. However, some consumers considering borrowing in one name only may not share these plans with their counselor. Thus, counselors must be certain to emphasize the importance of including both spouses on the mortgage to *all* couples. Additional consumer education regarding the impacts of a reverse mortgage on a non-borrower spouse or other family member may still be needed. The CFPB is considering this issue and will work with HUD to explore additional ways to strengthen consumer protection.

6.7.2. Risk of Owing More Than the Value of the Home

Recently, there has been uncertainty regarding the extent to which borrowers and their heirs are responsible for repaying reverse mortgage loan amounts that exceed the value of the property encumbered by the mortgage.

Consumer advocates allege that in 2008, FHA fundamentally changed the protections applicable to reverse mortgages by issuing Mortgagee Letter 2008-38. The Letter stated that in the event a consumer or a consumer's heirs wished to *retain* a property when a reverse mortgage became due and payable, they were required to pay the outstanding balance of the reverse mortgage in full, even when that balance exceeded the value of the property. This requirement changed the prior rule that a borrower or the borrower's estate could sell the secured property to anyone for the lesser of the unpaid mortgage balance or 95 percent of the appraised value. As a result of FHA Mortgagee Letter 2008-38, the property could be sold for the lesser of the unpaid mortgage balance or 95 percent of appraised value *only* in an arm's length transaction.

6.7.2a. Policy response

FHA Mortgagee Letter 2008-38 was rescinded by FHA Mortgagee Letter 2011-16 on April 5, 2011.[445]

6.7.2b. Conclusions

FHA has rescinded the guidance that indicated that a borrower or the borrower's heirs would have to pay the entirety of the loan balance in order to retain the property. However, it has not yet provided new guidance in its place. FHA's current position is that properties subject to a reverse mortgage may be sold anyone, including a borrower's heir, for the lesser of the unpaid mortgage balance or 95 percent of the appraised value.

6.8. Fraud

Fraud is especially troublesome in the reverse mortgage context given the vulnerability of senior borrowers. Victims of reverse mortgage fraud are at risk of losing their home and may have few other financial resources.

6.8.1. Risks to Consumers

Reverse mortgage fraud includes bad actors who target reverse mortgage consumers.[446] Unsuspecting consumers are at risk of losing their home equity in several ways. A trusted adviser or imposter can take out a reverse mortgage without their knowledge, or the borrower can be drawn into a property-flipping scheme. Reverse mortgage borrowers are further at risk of losing their home equity to fraud perpetrators who manipulate the loan application and closing process to inflate appraisals and siphon off the borrower's funds.

6.8.1a. Power of attorney and third-party imposters

Some scams involve taking out a HECM without the borrower's knowledge. Individuals could use power of attorney to close the HECM loan, or third parties may target senior homeowners and take out a HECM in their name. Some borrowers reported to CFPB that they never intended to take out a reverse mortgage themselves, or reported a "cash-out theft" by a family member or other person with power of attorney who took out the reverse mortgage in their names and then absconded with the proceeds.[447] In a recent Brooklyn, New York case, the victim responded to a television advertisement for debt assistance.[448] The defendant worked for the marketing company and collected the victim's information. The defendant had another individual pose as the borrower during closing and took out a HECM in the victim's name. Age is a protected status in New York, and this case is being charged as a hate crime.

6.8.1b. Property flipping

Another common type of reverse mortgage fraud targeting unsuspecting consumers involves straw buyers and property flipping.[449] Fraud perpetrators convince a borrower to take out a reverse mortgage to buy a lower-cost, often uninhabitable home. After introduction of the HECM for Purchase program, schemes using fake down payments appeared. For example, a group of fraud perpetrators in Georgia gave a conspiring attorney down payments so that borrowers would qualify to buy a new home through HECM for Purchase.[450] Seniors were often led to believe that they were getting the new properties for free through a government program. The borrowers were sold low-value properties at up to 16 times the true acquisition costs. The fake down payments were then returned to the fraud participants along with the reverse mortgage proceeds.

6.8.1c. Inflated appraisals

Inflated appraisals allow fraud perpetrators to increase the amount of funds available to the deceived reverse mortgage borrower, ultimately allowing more money to be stolen. They also create a false appearance of high equity, allowing borrowers to obtain HECMs who otherwise would not qualify. An organized group in Florida falsified the amount of equity borrowers had in a property.[451] Two participants worked as loan officers in order to solicit borrowers, while another altered the appraisals to reflect inflated property values. This appearance of increased equity qualified the borrowers for HECMs. The group then submitted these HECMs to the unknowing lender and FHA, resulting in over $2.5 million in fraudulent reverse mortgage loans. The group took the money on the loans without paying off the borrowers' first mortgages, and provided borrowers with false statements that those mortgages had been paid off.

6.8.1d. Cash-out theft and investment scams

Fraud perpetrators may target borrowers who take all of their HECM proceeds out at closing. A borrower may give the proceeds check to a family member or loan officer, who co-endorses the payment and places it in a personal account.[452] The borrower then must rely on this individual in order to receive payments. After receiving several payments, the borrower may be told that all funds have been exhausted. The perpetrator keeps the remaining HECM funds. In a Michigan case, a loan officer was accused of directing a closing agent to write one check for $42,667 to himself, and another for $61,325 to the borrower.[453] The loan officer allegedly cashed the $42,667 check and kept the money, while the borrower was left with a loan balance of over $131,000.[454] Other perpetrators may convince borrowers to invest their HECM proceeds in scam investments. These schemes involve the borrower turning over the loan proceeds to fraudulent investment pools promising sweepstakes "winnings," partnership in property developments, and investments in gold and silver.[455]

6.8.2. Policy Response

A number of enforcement initiatives and regulatory changes have improved reverse mortgage fraud prevention and prosecution. These changes include new state and federal laws that have broadened enforcement abilities, mortgage fraud task forces that include several federal agencies, and collaborations among federal and state enforcement agencies.

6.8.2a. Federal and state legislation

Fraud involving reverse mortgages may be prosecuted at the federal level under 18 USC § 2314, which prohibits the transfer of something worth $5,000 or more that is known to have been taken by fraud, or from fraudulently obtaining or attempting to obtain a value of $5,000 or more through fraud.[456]

Reverse mortgage cases may also qualify as federal bank fraud.[457] On May 20, 2009, President Obama signed the Fraud Enforcement and Recovery Act of 2009 (FERA). FERA changed the definition of "financial institution" to including "mortgage lending business."[458] This broader definition allows the Department of Justice (DOJ) to prosecute mortgage fraud cases as bank fraud, which allows severe penalties in addition to a longer statute of limitations.[459] FERA also expands the definition of false statements in a mortgage application that can be prosecuted as fraud. Previously, false statements could only be prosecuted by DOJ if they were intended to influence federal agencies, banks, or credit associations. FERA applies to false statements that are intended to influence action by a mortgage lending business.

States have also enacted new fraud laws for mortgage lending activity. Georgia passed the Georgia Residential Mortgage Fraud Act in 2010, which prohibits individuals from making any "misstatement, misrepresentation, or omission during the mortgage lending process" with the intent to defraud the mortgage lender, borrower, or any other affiliated party.[460] Michigan made mortgage fraud a crime in 2012, punishable with up to 20 years in prison and a $500,000 fine.[461] Other state initiatives include the establishment of a "mortgage lending fraud prosecution account" in Washington State. This account is funded by a surcharge on deed-of-trust recordings.[462]

6.8.2b. Initiatives

The federal government has several ongoing initiatives to centralize enforcement and monitoring of mortgage fraud. The Financial Crimes Enforcement Network (FinCEN) is a bureau of the U.S. Department of Treasury that seeks to detect and deter financial crime.[463] FinCEN collects information on suspicious mortgage activity by requiring lenders to submit Suspicious Activity Reports (SARs). Realizing the threat that reverse mortgage fraud poses to borrowers, FinCEN has reached out to lenders with guidance on identifying and reporting HECM fraud.[464]

Improved reporting may help enforcement agencies identify fraudulent activity before the perpetrator disappears with HECM proceeds and may help target repeat players. FinCEN recently published a final rule that requires nonbank mortgage lenders and originators to create anti-money laundering programs and file SARs.[465] Bank mortgage lenders are already required to file SARs with FinCEN under the Bank Secrecy Act.[466] This expansion will help improve fraud reporting and will contribute to the centralized database of fraudulent activity. The effective date of the rule is April 16, 2012, and the nonbank lenders must comply by August 13, 2012.[467]

FinCEN issued proposed regulations in November 2011 that would also require Fannie Mae, Freddie Mac, and the Federal Home Loan Banks to file SARs directly with FinCEN.[468] These government-sponsored enterprises already file SARs with the Federal Housing Finance Agency, which passes the reports along to FinCEN. Direct reporting will allow FinCEN to access the data more quickly and allow it to immediately track any fraudulent activity within the network.

Other initiatives include the FBI/ HUD-Office of Inspector General National Mortgage Fraud Team, the Financial Fraud Enforcement Task Force (FFETF), and a Mortgage Fraud

Working Group within FFETF. Operation Stolen Dreams was a 2010 multi-agency effort to combat mortgage fraud that resulted in more than 500 arrests.[469]

6.8.2c. Enforcement actions

State and federal reverse mortgage fraud investigations may stem from victims and their relatives, prosecutors, self-reporting by lenders and originators, the Federal Housing Administration, HUD Office of the Inspector General audits and data mining, community liaison offices, and adult protective services.[470] Although there is limited data on the national prevalence of HECM fraud, instances appear to be significant. In 2010, the FBI/ HUD Mortgage Fraud Team spent approximately 25 percent of their time on reverse mortgage fraud investigations.[471] The team has approximately 1,500 ongoing mortgage fraud investigations nationwide.[472] Between 2011 and March 2012, Region 2 of the HUD Office of Inspector General presented 45 cases involving reverse mortgage fraud in the New York and New Jersey area.[473]

6.8.3. Emerging Concerns

The shift toward fixed-rate, lump-sum HECMs places more borrowers at risk of losing their loan proceeds shortly after closing. Borrowers holding a large amount of funds may attract fraudsters simply because they are more lucrative targets. In a Houston case, a caretaker was accused of having the borrower sign what appeared to be checks for bill payments.[474] She allegedly made these checks out to herself in order take over $18,000 in the borrower's lump sum reverse mortgage proceeds.[475] A caretaker in Miami was accused of making ATM withdrawals to take more than $35,000 from the victim, including $26,000 in reverse mortgage proceeds.[476]

Reverse mortgage counselors need to be aware that lump-sum payments increase the vulnerability of a borrower to fraud. They should consider asking who has access to the borrower's financial accounts. Counselors may be able to identify vulnerabilities in the borrower's financial security. They could refuse to issue a HECM counseling completion certificate when they have concerns that the borrower plans to provide funds to a fraud perpetrator.[477]

6.8.4. Conclusions

Vigorous enforcement is necessary to ensure that older homeowners are not defrauded of a lifetime of home equity. Federal and state working groups may consider focusing on state prosecutions in some HECM fraud cases. Given strict financial harm requirements and limited resources at the federal level, state enforcement actions often may be more effective.[478] The recent hate crime charge in New York demonstrates how state laws allow more flexibility in reverse mortgage fraud prosecutions. The shift to fixed-rate products and the heightened risks these products pose is an important consideration in the development of additional reverse mortgage consumer protections.

6.9. Emerging Concerns

The CFPB has identified two emerging consumer protection concerns that pose considerable risks to consumers. These are the prevalence of fixed-rate, lump-sum products and the business practices of lead generators.

6.9.1. Prevalence of Fixed-Rate, Lump-Sum Products

As discussed in both the *Product* and *Market* chapters, the market share of fixed-rate, lump-sum products has increased dramatically, from less than 3 percent in 2008 to an average of 68 percent from mid-2009 through the end of 2011. In the first quarter of 2012, fixed-rate, lump-sum market share stood at 67.7 percent.[479]

The market, policy, and consumer behavior forces that combined to produce this shift are complex and interconnected, as explained in detail in Section 4.5. While there is no one cause of the sudden prevalence of fixed-rate, lump-sum products, there are several reasons to be concerned that consumers may not be acting in their own best interest when taking these loans.

6.9.1a Risks to consumers

Fixed-rate, lump-sum loans require borrowers to withdraw the entire available proceeds at the time of closing – whether or not they actually need all of the funds upfront. As several consumer advocacy groups have noted, this requirement introduces several possible risks to consumers.[480] As discussed in Section 3.4.1, some borrowers are refinancing existing traditional mortgages with their lump-sum loans, while others are taking large sums in cash. Both types of borrowers face additional risks.

Risks to borrowers who do not need most of the funds immediately

HEIGHTENED RISK OF SCAMS, ELDER ABUSE, AND UNSUITABLE INVESTMENTS

Seniors who take out large lump sums all at once are naturally more at risk of being convinced to part with these funds by scam artists, family members or acquaintances, or insurance and annuities salesmen than seniors who do not take out large lump sums all at once. According to the National Consumer Law Center, some lenders may even be selling lists of recent fixed-rate, lump-sum borrowers to insurance and f inancial products firms.[481]

BORROWING HIGH, SAVING LOW

Seniors who take out more loan proceeds than they need immediately must do something with that money. If they put it in a standard savings account or other liquid, safe asset, it cannot possibly earn more than the loan is accruing in interest. In contrast, if the borrower were to choose an adjustable-rate, line-of-credit plan instead of a fixed-rate, lump-sum product, the borrower would not pay interest on the unused funds. Moreover, the unused credit line available to the borrower would grow at the same rate (interest + mortgage insurance premium) as the loan.

UNWISE SPENDING

While any reverse mortgage borrower can make unwise spending choices, withdrawing money from a bank account is psychologically different than requesting a draw on a loan. It is possible that lump-sum borrowers may be more tempted to spend their proceeds less wisely than line-of-credit or monthly payment plan borrowers.[482]

Risks to borrowers paying off a traditional mortgage

The majority of fixed-rate borrowers use at least a portion of their proceeds to pay off a traditional mortgage.[483] If the amount of that mortgage is low, most borrowers would be better served by choosing an adjustable-rate product for the reasons discussed above. If the amount of that mortgage is only slightly less than the borrower's maximum available proceeds, however, a fixed-rate product may make more sense. Borrowers trade a higher interest rate at origination for interest rate certainty over the life of the loan. An adjustable-rate product may still make more sense for some borrowers, depending on the borrower's time horizon and interest rate expectations, but a fixed-rate product is not necessarily a poor choice in this case.

The more troubling risk in this case is the risk that the overall financial transaction – using a reverse mortgage to pay off a sizeable traditional mortgage – may be an easy way to deal with financial difficulties in the short term but a poor choice in the long term. If the only way a borrower can afford to keep the home is to deplete their equity, that borrower may want to reconsider moving or downsizing instead of refinancing their traditional mortgage with a reverse mortgage.

Risks to all fixed-rate borrowers, regardless of how they use the funds

HEIGHTENED RISK OF TAX & INSURANCE DEFAULTS

As noted in Section 6.6.4b, FHA and major lenders alike have indicated that the incidence of tax and insurance defaults are higher among fixed-rate borrowers. When adjustable-rate borrowers fail to pay taxes and insurance, lenders can pay these expenses on the borrower's behalf using the borrower's available credit line. Fixed-rate borrowers, by definition, do not have any available credit line. Any financial shortfall that prevents a fixed-rate borrower from paying taxes or insurance is more likely to result in a default and potential foreclosure than an adjustable-rate borrower suffering a similar financial shortfall.

HEIGHTENED RISK OF FINANCIAL VULNERABILITY LATER IN LIFE

Seniors who access the entirety of their available equity upfront have fewer resources to draw upon in the future to pay for everyday expenses and unexpected major expenses, such as home repairs or medical expenses.

6.9.1b. Policy proposals

Consumer advocates have proposed restrictions on fixed-rate, lump-sum reverse mortgages. One proposal would require the loan originator to apply a suitability standard to borrowers requesting lump sum draws greater than 50 percent of maximum loan proceeds.[484] The proposal would refrain from requiring loan originators to apply the suitability standard if a housing counselor certifies that the withdrawal is necessary for (a) keeping the home; (b) medical expenses; or (c) another valid reason other than financial planning.[485]

6.9.1c. Conclusions

This is an area in need of further monitoring and research. Currently, there are no published analyses or datasets available on what consumers do with the proceeds of their reverse mortgages. The CFPB has obtained limited data from one lender on the amounts of reverse mortgage proceeds used to pay off traditional mortgages and the amounts paid in cash to the borrower. Data from additional lenders is needed to ensure that the information is representative of the entire market. Moreover, this data does not provide insight as to what consumers who receive their upfront proceeds in cash do with these funds. More research is also needed on the behavioral reasons consumers gravitate so heavily towards fixed-rate reverse mortgages and on what types of information and tools would enable them to make better decisions.

6.9.2. Lead Generators

Lead generators collect information from consumers directly, such as when they visit a website to find a lender, and indirectly through mailing lists and similar sources. Lead generators provide lenders and brokers with consumers' contact information for a fee. Lenders or brokers then pursue the consumers with solicitations for reverse mortgages. The solicitations range from direct mail marketing campaigns and phone calls to door-to-door sales pitches.

Lead generation can be very lucrative. For "cold leads," which generally consist of a consumer's name and address, lenders and brokers have been willing to pay between $15 and $45 per lead.[486] Cold leads include consumers that may not have expressed any interest in a reverse mortgage. "Hot leads" generally include the name, address, age, phone number, home value, and mortgage balance of a consumer who has expressed an interest in obtaining a reverse mortgage, and can cost between $100 and $200 per lead.[487] A lead generator can sell the contact and personal information for each consumer to multiple lenders and brokers. Some lenders have even purchased lead generator companies in order to control access to and save on the costs of obtaining consumer information.[488]

6.9.2a. Risks to consumers

The purchase and sale of consumer information by lead generators can result in consumers receiving aggressive marketing solicitations. Some targeted consumers may not be interested at all in reverse mortgages. Faulty lead generators may state that unknowing consumers have consented to receiving more information about reverse mortgages, when they actually have never been asked for consent. Several loan originators complained to the FTC about fake leads where the consumers had not agreed to receiving solicitations about reverse mortgages.[489] These consumers may be unwillingly subjected to in-person visits about entering into a reverse mortgage.

Other consumers initially may be interested in receiving information about reverse mortgages but subsequently receive harassing and repeated solicitations. Several complaints submitted to the FTC involve consumers who report that they are receiving multiple calls a day for reverse mortgage solicitations.[490] One consumer called a company about a reverse mortgage but decided to take one with another company. She continued to receive calls even after she explained that she had already taken out a reverse mortgage. Another consumer called for information about reverse mortgages and received constant phone calls for over eight months.

6.9.2b. Policy environment

Lead generation is classified as a mortgage origination activity, and entities are required to be licensed by the SAFE Act. The CFPB, FTC, DOJ, and state attorneys general, among others, have regulatory and enforcement authority over lead generators. In particular, the FTC's Telemarketing Sales rule[491] and the Mortgage Assistance Relief Services Rule (MARS Rule) apply to lead generators.[492] Lead sales activities can also trigger RESPA provisions and prohibitions on unfair, deceptive, or abusive acts or practices. The Commonwealth of Massachusetts and several other states have brought enforcement actions against lead generators for doing business without licenses, deceptive practices, and misuse of personal information.[493] The FTC has also taken action against lead generators for deceptive advertising.[494]

6.9.2c. Industry concerns

Industry participants may also be taken advantage of by lead generators. Loan originators have reported paying for leads they never received, refusals to give refunds, and receiving leads that did not meet the terms of the contract signed with the lead generator. The FTC received seven complaints regarding deficient reverse mortgage "leads," all of which involved fake leads and refusal to return funds.[495]

6.9.2d. Conclusions

This is an area in need of further monitoring and research. Additionally, if the CPFB determines that the federal consumer protection laws are being violated, it could exercise its supervision and enforcement authorities.

CONCLUSION

Reverse mortgages are inherently complicated products that are not easy for the average consumer to understand. Consumers particularly struggle with the rising balance, falling equity nature of the loan. Recent innovation and policy changes have increased the complexity of the choices and tradeoffs consumers have to make when deciding to take out a reverse mortgage loan.

Prior to 2009, all but a handful of reverse mortgages were adjustable-rate loans in which borrowers could choose a line of credit, monthly disbursements, or a combination of the two. Since mid-2009, fixed-rate, lump-sum reverse mortgages, which require borrowers to take out all their available proceeds at closing, have become the dominant product in the marketplace with around 70 percent market share. A complex combination of market forces helps to explain this shift. Since October 2010, borrowers have also had a choice between the original HECM Standard loan, which provides maximum loan proceeds but carries a high upfront mortgage insurance premium, and the new HECM Saver product, which provides lower proceeds at a lower upfront cost.

The choice between a fixed-rate, lump-sum loan or an adjustable-rate loan with a line of credit and/or monthly disbursements requires consumers not only to have a firm understanding of how they plan to use the funds from their loan, but also to make complex economic tradeoffs between costs and risks. The same is true for the choice between the HECM Standard, with higher upfront fees and higher proceeds, and the new HECM Saver, with lower upfront fees and lower proceeds.

Today's prospective reverse mortgage consumers are ill-equipped to make these tradeoffs. Revisions to the existing disclosures are needed to make the costs and risks of different products more transparent and more easily understandable to the consumer. Reverse mortgage counseling could also be improved to help consumers think more carefully about tradeoffs between product options.

Reverse mortgages are designed to give older homeowners access to the wealth stored in their homes so that they can live more comfortably in retirement. However, because reverse mortgages do not require monthly mortgage payments, the accrued interest and ongoing mortgage insurance premium are added to the loan balance each month. Over time, the compounded interest and mortgage insurance can consume a large part of the borrower's home equity. There is a risk – especially in periods of low home price appreciation – that there will be little to no equity left when the home is sold.

For borrowers who live in their homes for the rest of their lives, this may be an acceptable risk. But most borrowers ultimately sell their homes while they are still alive. These borrowers may face increased financial difficulties later in life if they use all their home equity while living in the home and have none left to help finance their next living arrangement. This risk is especially troubling for younger borrowers, who receive less in loan proceeds yet have a longer life expectancy.

Borrowers who take out all their loan proceeds upfront also face increased risks. There are good reasons that borrowers might want to take out a *portion* of the loan proceeds upfront as a lump sum – such as paying off a traditional mortgage or making needed repairs to the home. But borrowers who take *all* of their funds upfront lose the ability to access additional funds in the future when emergencies or other pressing financial needs arise. Borrowers who do not have an immediate need for all of their proceeds are generally better off taking only what they need upfront. The unused amount available to the borrower will actually increase in value over time. Borrowers who do have an immediate need for all (or almost all) of their loan proceeds should carefully consider how they will handle future financial needs and whether an alternative course of action might be a better choice.

Overall, borrowers appear to be using reverse mortgages in very different ways and for very different purposes than was originally intended when the product was first developed. This departure in borrower behavior warrants more research on how loan proceeds are used and what happens at the end of the loan. Are borrowers downsizing, moving to assisted living, or moving in with family? Do they have enough financial resources to make those transitions, or do they face financial difficulties? Did they derive enough benefit from the reverse mortgage to offset the lost home equity? Or do they wish that they had made the hard decision to downsize or explore other alternatives instead of taking out the loan?

The CFPB is tasked with protecting American consumers and empowering them to lead better financial lives. In fulfilling this mission, we have three main goals. First, consumers need the best possible information – in a form that they can readily understand – to enable them to make the best possible decisions for their specific situation. Second, when there are incentives in the marketplace or predatory practices that create the potential for exploitation of consumers, these practices need to be addressed. Third, when consumer decisions, market dynamics, or product designs create unintended consequences that contribute to bad outcomes for consumers, these factors also need to be addressed.

The CFPB has identified five key findings from this study that are relevant to our work protecting American consumers in the area of reverse mortgages.

7.1. Key Findings

1. **Reverse mortgages are complex products and difficult for consumers to understand.**
    - Lessons learned from the traditional mortgage market do not always serve consumers well in the reverse mortgage market. The rising balance, falling equity nature of reverse mortgages is particularly difficult for consumers to grasp.
    - Recent innovation and policy changes have created more choices for consumers, including options with lower upfront costs. However, these changes have also increased the complexity of the choices and tradeoffs consumers have to make.
    - The tools – including federally required disclosures – available to consumers to help them understand prices and risks are insufficient to ensure that consumers are making good tradeoffs and decisions.
2. **Reverse mortgage borrowers are using the loans in different ways than in the past, which increase risks to consumers.**
    - Reverse mortgage borrowers are taking out loans at younger ages than in the past. In FY2011, nearly half of borrowers were under age 70. Taking out a reverse mortgage early in retirement, or even before reaching retirement, increases risks to consumers. By tapping their home equity early, these borrowers may find themselves without the financial resources to finance a future move – whether due to health or other reasons.
    - Reverse mortgage borrowers are withdrawing more of their money upfront than in the past. In FY2011, 73 percent of borrowers took all or almost all of their available funds upfront at closing. This proportion has increased by 30 percentage points since 2008. Borrowers who withdraw all of their available home equity upfront will have fewer resources to draw upon to pay for everyday and major expenses later in life. Borrowers who take all of their money upfront are also at greater risk of becoming delinquent on taxes and/or insurance and ultimately losing their homes to foreclosure.
    - Fixed-rate, lump-sum loans now account for about 70 percent of the market. The availability of this product may encourage some borrowers to take out all of their funds upfront even though they do not have an immediate need for the funds. In addition to having fewer resources to draw upon later in life, these borrowers face other increased risks. Borrowers who save or invest the proceeds may be earning less on the savings than they are paying in interest on the loan, or they

may be exposing their savings to risky investment choices. These borrowers also face increased risks of being targeted for fraud or other scams.

- Reverse mortgage borrowers appear to be increasingly using their loans as a method of refinancing traditional mortgages rather than as a way to pay for everyday or major expenses. Some borrowers may simply be prolonging an unsustainable financial situation.

3. **Product features, market dynamics, and industry practices also create risks for consumers.**
   - A surprisingly large proportion of reverse mortgage borrowers (9.4 percent as of February 2012) are at risk of foreclosure due to nonpayment of taxes and insurance. This proportion is continuing to increase.
   - Misleading advertising remains a problem in the industry and increases risks to consumers. This advertising contributes to consumer misperceptions about reverse mortgages, increasing the likelihood of poor consumer decision-making.
   - Spouses of reverse mortgage borrowers who are not themselves named as co-borrowers are often unaware that they are at risk of losing their homes. If the borrowing spouse dies or needs to move, the non-borrowing spouse must sell the home or otherwise pay off the reverse mortgage at that time. Other family members (children, grandchildren, etc.) who live with reverse mortgage borrowers are also at risk of needing to find other living arrangements when the borrower dies or needs to move.
   - The reverse mortgage market is increasingly dominated by small originators, most of which are not depository institutions. The changing economic and regulatory landscape faced by these small originators creates new risks for consumers.
4. **Counseling, while designed to help consumers understand the risks associated with reverse mortgages, needs improvement in order to be able to meet these challenges.**
   - Reverse mortgages are inherently complicated, and the new array of product choices makes the counselor's job much more difficult. Counselors need improved methods to help consumers better understand the complex tradeoffs they face in deciding whether to get a reverse mortgage.
   - Funding for housing counseling is under pressure, making access to high-quality counseling more difficult. Some counselors may frequently omit some of the required information or speed through the material.
   - Some counseling agencies only receive payment if and when the reverse mortgage is closed (the counseling fee is paid with loan proceeds), which could undermine counselors' impartiality.
   - Some borrowers may not take the counseling sessions seriously. Additional consumer awareness and education may be necessary.
   - Counseling may be insufficient to counter the effects of misleading advertising, aggressive sales tactics, or questionable business practices. Stronger regulation, supervision of reverse mortgage companies, and enforcement of existing laws may also be necessary.

5. **Some risks to consumers appear to have been adequately addressed by regulation, but remain a matter for supervision and enforcement, while other risks still require regulatory attention.**
   - Cross-selling, previously a top consumer protection concern, appears to have been considerably dampened as a result of federal legislation, though some risks remain. Strong supervision and enforcement is necessary to ensure that industry participants abide by existing laws.
   - The risk of fraud and other scams is heightened for this population. Vigorous enforcement is necessary to ensure that older homeowners are not defrauded of a lifetime of home equity.
   - Special disclosures are required for reverse mortgages, but existing disclosures are quite difficult for consumers to understand.
   - There are general prohibitions against deceptive advertising, but there are no specific federal rules governing deceptive advertising with respect to reverse mortgages.

7.2. The CFPB's Role

Under the Dodd-Frank Act, rulemaking and interpretive authority for consumer protection laws and regulations that apply to mortgages transferred to the CFPB on July 21, 2011.[496] The Dodd-Frank Act authorizes the CFPB to issue regulations it determines, as a result of this reverse mortgage study, are necessary or appropriate to accomplish the purposes of the Act. These regulations may include providing integrated disclosures and identifying practices as unfair, deceptive, or abusive.[497] The CFPB also has authority to supervise nonbank reverse mortgage companies and larger depository institutions and credit unions for compliance with federal consumer financial protection laws.

The findings of the study reveal several areas where the CFPB can play a role to protect consumers from risks posed by reverse mortgages and to help consumers make better decisions about reverse mortgages.

1. The CFPB can **issue regulations** under the federal consumer protection laws addressed specifically to protecting consumers considering a reverse mortgage.
   - The CFPB expects to undertake a project to improve and integrate TILA and RESPA disclosure requirements for reverse mortgages so that consumers can know before they owe when considering a reverse mortgage.
   - As part of this project, the CFPB will consider the 2010 proposal by the Board of Governors of the Federal Reserve System regarding reverse mortgages. The proposal would have placed limits on misleading advertising, improved disclosures, and closed regulatory gaps related to cross-selling, among other things.[498]
   - The CFPB will also consider whether other regulations are necessary and appropriate to protect consumers in the reverse mortgage market.
2. The CFPB can **develop improved approaches** to **engage** consumers considering a reverse mortgage and **empower** them to make better informed decisions.
   - The CFPB will continue to learn from stakeholders and counselors to better understand the primary obstacles to good consumer decision-making about reverse mortgages.

- The CFPB will explore improved methods and approaches for helping consumers compare products, understand costs and risks, and evaluate tradeoffs.

3. The CFPB can **monitor the market** for unfair, deceptive, or abusive practices and compliance with existing laws.
   - The CFPB will take enforcement and supervisory actions if necessary.
4. The CFPB can **accept complaints** from consumers and work to **resolve** those complaints.
   - The CFPB is currently accepting reverse mortgage complaints through the web at www.consumerfinance.gov, phone at 1-855-411-CFPB, and mail.
   - The CFPB's Consumer Response team works with lenders, servicers, and other related companies to resolve consumer complaints and answer consumer inquiries.
5. The CFPB can **work with the Department of Housing and Urban Development (HUD)**, the parent agency of the FHA, to develop solutions to issues identified in this report over which HUD has influence.
   - The CFPB welcomes the opportunity to strengthen its partnership with HUD and improve outcomes for consumers.

7.3. Areas for Further Research

The findings of the study have revealed several areas where additional research would help determine if additional consumer education or regulatory action is needed.

1. The factors influencing consumer decisions, particularly the choice between fixed-rate and adjustable-rate products.
2. Consumer use of reverse mortgage proceeds, particularly the ways they are using large upfront cash draws.
3. The longer-term outcomes of reverse mortgages, particularly the reasons why borrowers typically pay off the loans before they die and the level of satisfaction among later-stage or former borrowers.
4. The differences in market dynamics and business practices among the broker, correspondent, and retail channels, particularly how these differences affect the choices presented to consumers.

APPENDIX I. THE PROPRIETARY MARKET

A.1. Proprietary Reverse Mortgage Products

Reverse mortgages that are not government-insured are known collectively as proprietary reverse mortgages. Proprietary reverse mortgages have existed for decades, but the market has never been large. In the product's early days, proprietary products may have enjoyed sizeable market share, but the overall market volume was extremely small. By the mid-2000s, when the HECM program achieved moderate scale, proprietary market share had fallen to around 5 to 10 percent.[499] Today the proprietary market has all but disappeared.

In the 1970s and 1980s, before the HECM program was authorized, private lenders as well as state and local agencies were working to develop viable reverse mortgage products. The first proprietary reverse mortgages offered a fixed interest rate and monthly disbursements to the borrower for as long as the borrower remained in the home. This product was similar to the "tenure" disbursement option that would ultimately be incorporated into the HECM program.[500]

As the HECM program slowly expanded throughout the 1990s from a few hundred to a few thousand loans per year, private lenders continued to experiment outside the HECM program with new product variations. In 1994, Household Finance introduced a line-of-credit product known as Ever Yours, which had limited reach.[501] In 1997, Transamerica HomeFirst introduced an adjustable-rate, line-of-credit proprietary product known as the "Cash Account," among others. Financial Freedom purchased Transamerica in 1999 and went on to develop the "Cash Account" brand name (albeit with a substantially revised product structure) into one of the most widely originated proprietary products.[502]

In 1996, Fannie Mae developed its own proprietary Home Keeper reverse mortgage as an alternative to a HECM.[503] The Home Keeper was designed to address needs unmet by the HECM program at the time. It provided options to seniors who wanted to purchase a home through the Home Keeper for Home Purchase product, to condominium owners, and to individuals with high property values in areas where FHA lending limits were low.[504] As of 2005, borrowers could choose from three payment plans: a tenure option, line-of-credit option, and a modified tenure plan. The Home Keeper had similar counseling, age, and equity requirements to the HECM.[505] Fannie Mae discontinued the Home Keeper in 2008 when the Housing and Economic Recovery Act (HERA) increased loan limits for the HECM product, eliminating the need for Home Keeper.[506]

In 2005, Seattle Mortgage introduced the Independence Plan, which sought to offer lower rates and fees than other proprietary products. In 2007, Bank of America acquired Seattle Mortgage and with it the Independence Plan product. Bank of America's Independence Plan was the second most widely originated product after Financial Freedom's Cash Account.[507]

During the heyday of the housing boom, a number of lenders introduced new proprietary products. Some were available for as little as six months before the crisis or, in some cases, regulatory action forced lenders to cease offering the products. Despite the marked increase in proprietary activity, proprietary products' market share actually fell to around 5 to 10 percent during the boom because HECM loan production was increasing even more rapidly.

Today, Generation Mortgage is the only lender currently offering a proprietary product. Its Generation Plus loan has a minimum borrower age of 62 and a loan limit of $6 million.[508] The product is available only as a fixed-rate, lump-sum loan with an 8.875 percent interest rate and an origination fee of 1.5 percent of the initial principal balance.[509] In comparison, fixed-rate HECMs are currently available with interest rates ranging from 4.5 to 5.0 percent and a low or zero origination fee.[510]

The Generation Plus loan offers considerably lower proceeds than the HECM as a percentage of home value because it is uninsured and carries a higher interest rate than HECMs. Of course, due to FHA's loan limit of $625,000, homeowners with multi-million dollar homes may still be able to receive a higher dollar amount with the Generation Plus than with the HECM. At today's rates, a 62-year-old borrower could get 62 percent of their home's value (or the product's loan limit, whichever is less) with a HECM standard, 52 percent with a HECM Saver, and only 26 percent with a Generation Plus. A 90-year old borrower could get 78 percent with a HECM Standard, 61 percent with a HECM Saver, and only 49 percent with a Generation Plus. Only 51 loans totaling about $48 million have been originated since this product was created in July 2010.[511]

A.2. Product Features

Proprietary products came in many different forms but nearly all retained the same basic structure of a nonrecourse loan in which the amount borrowers qualified for varied based on age, home value, and prevailing interest rates. Most line-of-credit products also offered some type of guaranteed line-of-credit growth, though the precise way of calculating that growth varied by product.

However, because proprietary loans were not insured, lenders had to be very conservative in underwriting them. Proprietary products typically carried higher interest rates and used lower proceeds-to-home value ratios than HECM loans.[512] As a result, the dollar amount a typical borrower could qualify for with a proprietary product was usually substantially lower than the amount the same borrower could qualify for under the HECM program.

The primary exception to this pattern was borrowers with high home values. Under the HECM program, borrowers' loan proceeds are determined by their home value or the applicable FHA loan limit, whichever is less. Borrowers whose home values substantially exceeded the FHA loan limits (which were much lower in the 1990s and the early to mid-2000s than they are today) could sometimes receive higher loan proceeds with a proprietary loan despite the lower proceeds-to-home value ratios used by proprietary products. Thus, proprietary products catered primarily to borrowers seeking "jumbo" reverse mortgages.

Proprietary products may also have been attractive to borrowers who needed only a small amount of cash and/or borrowers looking to use a reverse mortgage as a short-term financing strategy rather than a long-term plan to provide income in retirement. The HECM program historically was structured with a 2.0 percent upfront mortgage insurance premium calculated based on the home value (or applicable FHA loan limit, whichever is less) rather than on the amount drawn. This structure resulted in particularly high upfront fees for borrowers who did not need all of their authorized proceeds and/or borrowers who intended to pay off the loan quickly. Proprietary products, which did not charge an upfront insurance premium, may have offered a better value to this particular segment of reverse mortgage borrowers.

Most proprietary products used the same minimum age threshold (62) as the HECM program, though a few offered minimum ages as low as 60. Some proprietary products offered fewer property restrictions when compared to HECMs, such as the ability to take out a reverse mortgage on a second home or condo. Figure A-1 illustrates the key differences between HECMs and most proprietary products.

A.3. Product Risks

Compared to HECMs, the primary additional risk for the proprietary reverse mortgage borrower is the risk that the lender does not fulfill its obligations to make payments to the borrower as agreed. This risk may be mitigated somewhat in states where state legislation imposes stiff penalties on lenders that fail to honor their obligations.[513] In practice, even bankrupt lender/investors such as Lehman Brothers and Financial Freedom (which went through FDIC receivership while it was owned by failed IndyMac bank) have continued to honor payment obligations to proprietary reverse mortgage borrowers.[514]

Perhaps the greater risk to consumers with proprietary products is simply the fact that borrowers may not realize that the consumer protections built into the HECM program may not be required for proprietary products. Thus, there may be important differences in terms between a particular proprietary product and the more familiar HECM products. While most proprietary products in practice did mimic most of the key features and protections of the HECM program, future products could develop in different ways. A proprietary lender could conceivably, for example, slightly change the conditions under which the loan may be declared due and payable.

With FHA lending limits currently set at $625,500 and private-label mortgage securities still dormant, an explosion of proprietary product variations seems a distant future. When the proprietary market does rebound, however, regulators will want to monitor the market closely.

A.4. Secondary Market

In 1999, Lehman Brothers introduced the first private-label reverse mortgage securitization. Lehman set standardized terms for the loans included in the securitization pool and aggregated the loans. The majority of the loans for the pool were originated or aggregated by Financial Freedom or its predecessors. The $317.4 million issuance constituted perhaps as much as 25 percent of the reverse mortgage market that year.[515] Lehman later purchased Financial Freedom in October 2000. Between 2002 and 2007, Lehman issued four more proprietary reverse mortgage securitizations, comprised primarily of Financial Freedom loans. A sixth securitization was in progress in 2008 when the housing crisis drove Lehman into bankruptcy.[516]

In 2004, IndyMac Bank purchased Financial Freedom from Lehman Brothers. Some of the proprietary loans originated during that time were never securitized and remained on IndyMac's balance sheet. Those loans are believed to have since passed to One West bank, which purchased the bankrupt IndyMac Bank from FDIC receivership.[517] As noted earlier, OneWest announced in 2011 that it was winding down Financial Freedom and its participation in the reverse mortgage industry.

Bank of America invested heavily in proprietary reverse mortgage loans, primarily during the heady year of 2007 with the acquisition of Seattle Mortgage and its Independence Plan product. Bank of America has also exited the reverse mortgage business but it still holds $1.1 billion in proprietary reverse mortgages.[518]

The proprietary market today is virtually non-existent. Generation Mortgage is the only originator offering a proprietary product, and those loans are held by a private investor. The exit of the major banks (which are able to hold loans on balance sheet) and major proprietary originators of the past (such as Financial Freedom) means there are few players in the market with the ability to offer a proprietary product. It is hard to imagine that the secondary market for proprietary reverse mortgage securitizations will revive before the much larger and more mainstream market for private-label, traditional mortgage-backed securities. Despite rumors in the trade press, it seems unlikely that we will see many new proprietary products in the near future without a ready secondary market for them.

	HECM	Proprietary
Eligibility age	Borrower (or youngest co-borrower) must be at least 62 years old.	Some products offered a minimum age as low as 60, but most products used 62.
Authorized loan proceeds	Generally, a substantially **higher** percentage of the value of the home as compared to proprietary products.	Generally, a substantially **lower** percentage of the value of the home as compared to HECM.
Loan limits	All homeowners are eligible, but FHA loan limits cap proceeds on homes valued more than $625,000 (prior to 2009, the FHA cap was lower).	Some products may cap proceeds for homes valued in excess of a certain threshold.
Insurance premium	Upfront insurance premium (2.0% or 0.1% of home value*, depending on product choice) plus ongoing monthly insurance premium (1.25% of loan balance).	No insurance premium, but generally higher interest rates.
Guarantee to borrowers	FHA guarantees borrowers that if the lender fails to make payments to the borrower as agreed, the FHA will make those payments on behalf of the lender.	No protection from insolvent lenders, though to date, even bankrupt entities have honored all payments to reverse mortgage borrowers.
Consumer protections	Mandatory pre-loan counseling; limits on costs and fees.	No federal counseling mandate although counseling may be mandated in some states; no federal limits on costs and fees, although some states have limits.
Protection for lenders/investors	FHA insurance guarantees that lenders/investors will receive repayment of the loan in full, subject to certain conditions.	Lenders/investors must self-insure through conservative underwriting and potentially higher interest rates.

* Or FHA loan limit (currently $625,000), whichever is less.

Figure A-1. Key differences between HECM and proprietary reverse mortgages.

APPENDIX II. DISCLOSURE FORMS

SAMPLE TALC DISCLOSURE
(Current Law: Appendix K to Regulation Z)

TOTAL ANNUAL LOAN COST RATE				
Loan Terms			**Monthly Loan Charges**	
Age of youngest borrower:	75		Service fee:	None
Appraised property value:	$100,000			
Interest rate:	9%		**Other Charges**	
Monthly advance:	$301.80		Mortgage insurance:	None
Initial draw:	$1,000		Shared appreciation:	None
Line of credit:	$4,000		**Repayment Limits**	
Initial Loan Charges			Net proceeds estimated at 93% of projected home sale	
Closing costs:	$5,000			
Mortgage insurance premium:	None			
Annuity cost:	None			
Assumed Annual Appreciation	**2-year loan term**	**[6-year loan term]**	**12-year loan term**	**17-year loan term**
0%	39.00%	[14.94%]	9.86%	3.87%
4%	39.00%	[14.94%]	11.03%	10.14%
8%	39.00%	[14.94%]	11.03%	10.20%

The cost of any reverse mortgage loan depends on how long you keep the loan and how much your house appreciates in value. Generally, the longer you keep a reverse mortgage, the lower the total annual loan cost rate will be.

The table above shows the estimated cost of your reverse mortgage loan, expressed as an annual rate. It illustrates the cost for three [four] loan terms: two years, [half of life expectancy for someone your age], that life expectancy, and 1.4 times that life expectancy. The table also shows the cost of the loan, assuming the value of your house appreciates at three different rates: 0 percent, 4 percent, and 8 percent.

The total annual loan cost rates in this table are based on the total charges associated with this loan. These charges typically include principal, interest, closing costs, mortgage insurance premiums, annuity costs, and servicing costs (but not disposition costs--costs when you sell the home).

The rates in this table are estimates. Your actual cost may differ if, for example, the amount of your loan advances varies or the interest rate on your mortgage changes.

SIGNING AN APPLICATION OR RECEIVING THESE DISCLOSURES DOES NOT REQUIRE YOU TO COMPLETE THIS LOAN.

Figure A-2. Sample TALC Disclosure (Current Law: Appendix K to Regulation Z).

FEDERAL RESERVE BOARD CONSUMER PROTECTION RESOURCES

Key Questions to Ask about Reverse Mortgage Loans

When you are shopping for a reverse mortgage loan, consider the questions below. Ask your lender about other loan products, such as a traditional home equity loan or home equity line of credit. For more information, go to: www.frb.gov.

1) What is a Reverse Mortgage Loan?

A reverse mortgage loan is available to seniors (usually age 62 and older) who own all or almost all of the equity in their home. This loan allows you to exchange equity in your home for cash. With a reverse mortgage loan, you typically don't pay back the loan for as long as you live in your home. Instead, the loan must be repaid in full when the last living borrower dies, sells the home, or moves out of the home for 12 months or more. Repaying the loan in full includes the amount of the original loan plus all interest and any other fees and charges. Most borrowers (or their heirs) repay a reverse mortgage by selling the home.

2) How is a reverse mortgage loan different from a traditional mortgage?

- **Traditional mortgages** are loans generally used to buy a home or to borrow against your home equity for bills or other expenses. When you take out a traditional mortgage, typically the lender owns most of the equity in your home. As you pay back the loan over time (usually through monthly payments), you get that equity back from the lender. Once the traditional mortgage is paid off, you own all the equity in your home—the lender owns nothing.
- With a **reverse mortgage loan,** you already own all or most of the equity in your home, and you exchange this equity for cash from a lender. Because you do not pay back this money gradually over time, you do not earn equity back from the lender. Instead, the equity you own decreases and the amount you owe increases as interest and other fees and charges are added to the amount of the original loan.

3) Is a reverse mortgage loan right for me?

The advantage of a reverse mortgage is that you can exchange your home equity for cash and do not have to make monthly payments. **But reverse mortgages have risks:**

- ***Loan amount increases over time***
  The amount you owe increases every month. The younger you are when you take out a reverse mortgage, the more time there will be for the interest to grow and the more you will owe.
- ***Less cushion for emergencies***
  By taking out a reverse mortgage now, you will have less home equity later when you may need it more, for example, to pay for future emergencies, health care needs, home repairs, or everyday living expenses. If you are not facing a financial emergency now, consider postponing taking out a reverse mortgage.
- ***Costs more than other loan options***
  Reverse mortgages are generally more expensive than other home loans, so consider other options before taking a reverse mortgage. Reverse mortgages may also have tax consequences or may affect your eligibility for federal or state assistance. Talk with a HUD-approved reverse mortgage counselor or financial advisor to learn more.

Figure A-3. (Continued)

4) What fees and charges are added to a reverse mortgage loan?

Fees and charges can vary in amount and type from one reverse mortgage loan to another. Most borrowers choose to have these costs added to their loan balance. If you choose to add these costs to your loan balance, you will be charged interest on these costs each month in addition to the interest charged on the cash you receive. Reverse mortgage loan fees and charges typically include:

- **Closing costs**, which are charged once, at closing
- **Reverse mortgage insurance premium**, which is charged in two parts: once at closing and each month as a percent of your outstanding loan balance
- **Interest**, which is charged on your outstanding loan balance each month
- **Servicing fee**, which is charged each month.

5) What if my lender wants me to use money from my reverse mortgage to buy an annuity or make another investment?

Under federal law, you cannot be required to use your reverse mortgage money to purchase any other financial or insurance product (such as an annuity, long-term care insurance, or life insurance). If another product is offered to you, make sure you understand: (1) how the product works and what its benefits are, (2) how much it costs, (3) whether you need it, and (4) how much money the person selling the product makes if you purchase it. Talk with a HUD-approved reverse mortgage counselor or financial advisor before you decide.

6) Does the lender take the title to my home while I have a reverse mortgage?

No. You continue to own your home while you have a reverse mortgage loan. This means that you must still pay for property taxes, insurance, and repairs.

7) Can I lose my home while I have a reverse mortgage?

Yes. You could lose your home if you do not pay for property taxes, insurance, and repairs. For example, if you don't pay your taxes, the lender could demand that you repay the loan in full. You may have to sell your home to repay the loan. Or the lender could take your home through foreclosure. Also, if you don't live in your home for 12 straight months or more (for example, if you are in the hospital or a nursing home), the lender could demand that you repay the loan in full, and you may have to sell your home to repay the loan.

8) What happens at the end of the loan? What if I owe more than my home is worth when the loan comes due?

A reverse mortgage loan is usually repaid by selling the home. If the money earned through selling the home isn't enough to repay the reverse mortgage, almost all lenders will absorb the difference. These lenders will not be able to sue you or your heirs for more money. If the reverse mortgage is insured by the federal government, the government will absorb the difference instead of the lender. However, if you or your heirs want to keep your home, the loan must be repaid in full. Ask your lender if this applies to your loan.

9) What happens if there is money left over after the home is sold?

Almost all reverse mortgage loans let the homeowner (or the homeowner's heirs) keep any money left over after the loan is repaid in full. Ask your lender if this applies to your loan.

Figure A-3. Federal Reserve Board proposed consumer information sheet to be provided at application.

REVERSE MORTGAGE LOAN SUMMARY

LENDER ABC Bank
LOAN OFFICER 12345 1234

DATE April 30, 2010

Borrower & Property Information	
Borrowers' Names & Ages	John Doe (84); Jane Doe (82)
Property Address	123 Ward Street, Jingle Bells, TX 12345
Appraised Value	$275,000

About this Loan

- You are applying for a reverse mortgage loan on your home that you do not have to repay for as long as you live there.
- You may get money from this loan paid to you all at once, as a regular monthly advance, or at times and in amounts that you choose.
- You will continue to own your home so you must pay your property taxes and insurance, and keep the home in good repair (see the Risks section).
- If the loan balance eventually is greater than the value of the home, you will continue to receive monthly payments and have access to your loan funds as long as you remain in the home.
- The amount of the loan, plus interest and fees, must be paid back in full if the home is sold **or** when the last surviving borrower dies or does not live in the house for 12 consecutive months.

Payment of Loan Funds

You may receive your funds as follows:

Line of Credit	**$186,974** available to you at any time while you remain in your home
You may choose to change the type of payments you receive. Your other choices are:	
Initial Advance	paid to you after you accept the loan
Monthly Advance	paid to you each month while you remain in your home

Annual Percentage Rate	
Annual Percentage Rate (APR)	**2.93%.** This is a variable rate that will change annually based on the Treasury rate plus 2.5%. Each year, your rate can increase by up to 2.0%.
Maximum APR	**7.93%**
Historical Changes to Treasury Rate	Over the past 15 years, the Treasury rate plus 2.5% has varied between 2.77% and 8.90%.

Interest charges will be added to your loan balance each month and collected when the loan is due.

Fees

We will refund all fees you paid if you tell us that you do not want to open an account:

- for any reason within three business days after you receive this statement; or
- for any reason within three business days after you receive reverse mortgage counseling; or
- any time before your account is opened if any of these terms (other than the APR) change.

Account Opening Fees	
Loan Origination	$ 4,735
Inspection	$ 500
Title Search & Title Insurance	$ 595
Appraisal	$ 295
Reverse Mortgage Insurance Premium	$ 5,500
TOTAL Account Opening Fees	**$11,625**

Figure A-4. (Continued)

Monthly Fees *(added to your loan balance each month but not collected until the loan is due)*	
Servicing Fee	**$35 per month** ($420 annually)
Reverse Mortgage Insurance Premium	**0.042%** monthly (0.5% annually)
Monthly Interest Charges	**Starts at 2.93%** annually but this rate can change.
Other Fees	
Other fees may apply. Ask us for additional information about these fees.	

How the Loan Balance Grows

The table shows an example of how your loan balance might grow if:

- You borrow $186,974 after you accept the loan and do not borrow any more money, *and*
- The APR stays at 2.93%.

	After 1 Year	After 5 Years	After 10 Years
How much money will you have received?	$186,974	$186,974	$186,974
How much will be owed for interest + fees?	$18,972	$51,015	$97,764
How much will be owed altogether?	**$205,946**	**$237,989**	**$255,750**

Repayment Options

At the end of the loan, you or your heirs may either:

- Pay the loan balance in full and keep the home, or
- Sell the home and use the proceeds to pay off the loan. If your home sells for less than you owe, you will not be required to pay the difference. If your home sells for more than you owe, the difference will be given to you or your heirs.

Risks

Your reverse mortgage loan will be secured by your home. If you default on your reverse mortgage loan by:

- Allowing the property to deteriorate beyond reasonable wear and tear; or
- Failing to pay property taxes or insurance; or
- Failing to live in the house for 12 consecutive months; or
- Failing to meet any other obligation

then we may take any or all of the following actions:

• Foreclose On Your Home	We could foreclose on your property and require that you leave the home.
• Stop Giving You Money	We may stop making payments to you and not allow you to borrow any more money from your line of credit, even if you have borrowed less than your credit limit.
• Terminate Your Loan	We may terminate your loan, make you pay the outstanding loan balance in one payment, and charge you fees on termination.

We may also make other changes to your loan.

➔ **You have no obligation to accept these terms. These terms could change before we open your account.**

➔ **You may be entitled to a refund of all fees paid if you decide not to open an account.** See "Fees" section above for more details.

➔ **Ask questions if you do not understand any part of this form.**

➔ **For more information, go to** *www.frb.gov/reverse_mortgages/*.

By signing below, I acknowledge receipt of this form.

Borrower's Signature **Date**

Figure A-4. Federal Reserve Board proposed application disclosure for open-end reverse mortgages.

REVERSE MORTGAGE LOAN SUMMARY

LENDER ABC Bank
LOAN OFFICER 12345 1234

DATE April 30, 2010
LOAN NUMBER 123-12-1234-567

Borrower & Property Information	
Borrowers' Names & Ages	John Doe (84); Jane Doe (82)
Property Address	123 Ward Street, Jingle Bells, TX 12345
Appraised Value	$275,000

About this Loan

- You are applying for a reverse mortgage loan on your home that you do not have to repay for as long as you live there.
- You may get money from this loan paid to you all at once, as a regular monthly advance, or at times and in amounts that you choose.
- You will continue to own your home so you must pay your property taxes and insurance, and keep the home in good repair (see the Risks section).
- If the loan balance eventually becomes greater than the value of the home, you will continue to receive monthly payments and have access to your loan funds as long as you remain in the home.
- The amount of the loan, plus interest and fees, must be paid back in full if the home is sold **or** when the last surviving borrower dies or does not live in the house for 12 consecutive months.

Payment of Loan Funds

You have chosen to receive your funds as follows:

Initial Advance	**$12,000**	will be paid to you after you accept the loan
Monthly Advance	**$ 1,287**	will be paid to you each month while you remain in your home
Line of Credit	**$15,000**	will be available to you at any time while you remain in your home

You may choose to change the type of payments you receive.

Annual Percentage Rate	
Annual Percentage Rate (APR)	**2.93%.** This is a variable rate that will change annually based on the Treasury rate plus 2.5%. Each year, your rate can increase by up to 2.0%.
Maximum APR	**7.93%**
Historical Changes to Treasury Rate	Over the past 15 years, the Treasury rate plus 2.5% has varied between 2.77% and 8.90%.

Interest charges will be added to your loan balance each month and collected when the loan is due.

Fees

Account Opening Fees	
Loan Origination	$ 4,735
Inspection	$ 500
Title Search & Title Insurance	$ 595
Appraisal	$ 295
Reverse Mortgage Insurance Premium	$ 5,500
TOTAL Account Opening Fees	**$11,625**

Monthly Fees *(added to your loan balance each month but not collected until the loan is due)*	
Servicing Fee	**$35 per month** ($420 annually)
Reverse Mortgage Insurance Premium	**0.042%** monthly (0.5% annually)

Figure A-5. (Continued)

Interest Charges	**Starts at 2.93%** annually but this rate can change.
Other Fees	
Other fees may apply; see your account agreement for details. Ask us for additional information about these fees.	

How the Loan Balance Grows

The table shows an example of how your loan balance might grow if:

- You never borrow from the Line of Credit, only receiving the *initial* and *monthly* advances listed on page 1, *and*
- The APR stays at 2.93%.

	After 1 Year	After 5 Years	After 10 Years
How much money will you have received?	$27,443.00	$80,208.00	$166,434.00
How much will be owed for interest + fees?	$13,166.00	$23,023.00	$56,300.00
How much will be owed altogether?	**$40,609.00**	**$103,232.00**	**$222,733.00**

Repayment Options

At the end of the loan, you or your heirs may either:

- Pay the loan balance in full and keep the home, or
- Sell the home and use the proceeds to pay off the loan. If your home sells for less than you owe, you will not be required to pay the difference. If your home sells for more than you owe, the difference will be given to you or your heirs.

Risks

Your reverse mortgage loan will be secured by your home. If you default on your reverse mortgage loan by:

- Allowing the property to deteriorate beyond reasonable wear and tear; or
- Failing to pay property taxes or insurance; or
- Failing to live in the house for 12 consecutive months; or
- Failing to meet any other obligation

...then we may take any or all of the following actions:

• Foreclose On Your Home	We could foreclose on your property and require that you leave the home.
• Stop Giving You Money	We may stop making payments to you and not allow you to borrow any more money from your line of credit, even if you have borrowed less than your credit limit.
• Terminate Your Loan	We may terminate your loan, make you pay the outstanding loan balance in one payment, and charge you fees on termination.

We may also make other changes to your loan.

Billing Rights: Information on your rights to dispute transactions and how to exercise those rights is provided in your account agreement.

→ **You have no obligation to accept these terms.** Use this statement to confirm that these are the terms for which you applied.

→ **Ask questions if you do not understand any part of this form.**

→ **For more information, go to** *www.frb.gov/reverse_mortgages/*.

By signing below, I acknowledge receipt of this form.

Borrower's Signature **Date**

Figure A-5. Federal Reserve Board proposed account-opening disclosure for open-end reverse mortgages.

REVERSE MORTGAGE LOAN SUMMARY

LENDER:	ABC Bank	DATE:	April 30, 2010
LOAN OFFICER NO.:	12345-1234		

Borrower & Property Information

Borrowers' Names & Ages	John Marsh (62)
Borrowers' Account Number	123456789
Property Address	123 Ward Street, Jingle Bells, TX 12345
Appraised Value	$120,000

About this Loan

- You are applying for a reverse mortgage loan on your home that you do not have to repay for as long as you remain in the home.
- You will continue to own your home so you must pay your property taxes and insurance, and keep the home in good repair (see the Risks section).
- The amount of the loan, plus interest and fees, must be paid back in full if the home is sold **or** when the last surviving borrower dies or does not live in the house for 12 consecutive months.

Payment of Loan Funds

You will receive your funds as follows:

Initial Advance	**$55,242** will be paid to you after you accept the loan

Annual Percentage Rate (APR)

Overall cost of this loan including interest and settlement charges	**7.16 % APR**
Rate Type	This is a fixed rate

Interest charges will be added to your loan balance each month and collected when the loan is due.

Fees

Account Opening Fees

Loan Origination	$ 2,500
Inspection	$ 500
Title Search & Title Insurance	$ 590
Appraisal	$ 298
Settlement Fee	$ 415
Counseling Fee	$ 125
Reverse Mortgage Insurance Premium	$ 2,400
TOTAL Account Opening Fees	**$6,828**

Monthly Fees *(added to your loan balance each month but not collected until the loan is due)*

Servicing Fee	**$30 per month** ($360 annually).
Reverse Mortgage Insurance Premium	**0.042%** monthly (0.5% annually).
Interest Charges	**5.56%** annually.

Figure A-6. (Continued)

How the Loan Balance Grows

The table shows how your loan balance will grow.

	After 1 Year	After 5 Years	After 10 Years
How much money will you have received?	$55,242.00	$55,242.00	$55,242.00
How much will be owed for interest + fees?	$11,068.00	$30,838.00	$63,321.00
How much will be owed altogether?	**$66,310.00**	**$86,080.00**	**$111,600.00**

Total Payments	If your loan lasted 21 years, you would make one payment totaling $236,165.31. Of this amount, $180,923.50 would go to interest and settlement charges. This amount, and your amount financed of $55,241.81, is used to calculate your APR.

Repayment Options

At the end of the loan, you or your heirs may either:

- Pay the loan balance in full and keep the home, or
- Sell the home and use the proceeds to pay off the loan. If your home sells for less than you owe, you will not be required to pay the difference. If your home sells for more than you owe, the difference will be given to you or your heirs.

Risks

Your reverse mortgage loan will be secured by your home. If you default on your reverse mortgage loan by:

- Allowing the property to deteriorate beyond reasonable wear and tear; or
- Failing to pay property taxes or insurance; or
- Failing to live in the house for 12 consecutive months; or
- Failing to meet any other obligation;

then we may take any or all of the following actions:

• Foreclose On Your Home	We could foreclose on your property and require that you leave the home.
• Terminate Your Loan	We may terminate your loan, make you pay the outstanding loan balance in a single payment, and charge you fees on termination.

➔ **You have no obligation to accept these terms.**

➔ **Ask questions if you do not understand any part of this form.**

➔ **For more information, go to** www.frb.gov/reverse_mortgages/.

By signing below I acknowledge receipt of this form.

Borrower's Signature **Date**

Figure A-6. Federal Reserve Board proposed disclosure for closed-end reverse mortgages.

APPENDIX III. METHODOLOGY

The Bureau had three objectives in designing this study: (1) provide an authoritative resource on reverse mortgage products, consumers, and markets; (2) identify and assess consumer protection concerns; and (3) explore critical unanswered questions and update the public body of knowledge to reflect new market realities.

The Bureau took a comprehensive approach to its research. We reviewed consumer protection laws and regulations applicable to the reverse mortgage market. We also reviewed the laws, regulations, FHA Mortgagee Letters, and other guidance that governs the HECM program. We read many published reports and articles produced by academics, consumer advocacy groups, industry, mainstream journalists, and the trade press.

We conducted extensive original analyses of the public-use, loan-level HECM dataset maintained by FHA. This dataset contains detailed information on all HECM loans from the inception of the program through November 2011. We also conducted original analyses of Survey of Consumer Finances microdata, and consulted published tables of Census, American Housing Survey, and other datasets.

To gain insight into the market dynamics of the industry, the factors driving recent market changes, and current business practices, we attended two industry conferences and conducted extensive interviews with industry participants. We spoke with more than 30 people from at least 15 companies involved in reverse mortgages. We spoke with lenders, brokers, Ginnie Mae issuers, servicers, consultants, and capital market traders. Many of these individuals had been in the industry for many years, often at several different companies in different roles, and provided excellent historical background in addition to insights on current market conditions. Several lenders provided us with rate sheets. We also spoke with staff at Ginnie Mae and FHA, as well as former Fannie Mae staff.

To gather information on the challenges consumers face in deciding whether to take out a reverse mortgage, we interviewed six HECM counselors from different counseling agencies and parts of the country. Counselors were selected according to recommendations from policy experts, consumer advocates, and HECM counseling agency staff. A selection of counselors considered most highly recommended for their subject matter expertise was finalized. The counselors were asked about borrower comprehension of loan details, borrower ability to assess long-term planning, and suggestions for improving HECM counseling in general.

In order to further understand the challenges and concerns faced by reverse mortgage consumers, we reviewed consumer submissions to the CFPB as well as consumer complaints submitted to the Federal Trade Commission. We utilized raw consumer narratives, which provided an insight into consumers' understanding and perspectives that informed various aspects of the report. All information reviewed was received by either the CFPB or Federal Trade Commission in 2011 and 2012, and was identified as containing discussions of reverse mortgages.

In addition, we interviewed five external consumer advocates for their depth of knowledge in the reverse mortgage market. These advocates possessed particular expertise in counseling, legislation, and mortgage policy. The consumer advocates were asked about consumer protection issues, policy developments, and their overall concerns for future reverse mortgage borrowers. We also spoke with several consumer advocacy organizations about their overall concerns about the reverse mortgage market.

Appendix IV. Reverse Mortgage Consumer Guide

The attached consumer guide provides plain language guidance to consumers considering reverse mortgages. The guide includes an explanation of how reverse mortgages work, important questions to ask if you are considering a reverse mortgage, and information about several alternatives to reverse mortgages that seniors may want to consider. It will be available on the ConsumerFinance.gov website and will be offered to government agencies, nonprofit organizations, and housing counselors throughout the country that work with seniors.

To order copies, please contact the Office for Older Americans at CFPB_SeniorsInput@cfpb.gov.

CONSIDERING A **REVERSE MORTGAGE?**

PROCEED WITH CAUTION

1. Don't sign the loan documents unless you **understand how a reverse mortgage works**.
2. **Know your options** – you may have a better choice.
3. Have a serious **talk with a counselor** before you make any decisions.

WHAT IS A REVERSE MORTGAGE?

IT IS A LOAN

A reverse mortgage is a special type of home equity loan sold to homeowners aged 62 and older. The loan allows homeowners to access a portion of their home equity as cash. In a reverse mortgage, interest is added to the loan balance each month, and the balance grows.

The loan must be repaid when the borrower sells the home, moves out of the home, or dies. Most reverse mortgages today are called Home Equity Conversion Mortgages (HECMs). HECMs are federally insured. If you are interested in a reverse mortgage, you must first see a HECM counselor.

HOW DOES A REVERSE MORTGAGE WORK?

After years of paying off your mortgage, you have built up value in your home in the form of equity. With a reverse mortgage, you borrow against your equity.

The loan balance grows over time. You don't have to pay the loan while you live in the home.

When you move out, sell your home, or die, your loan must be paid off. Most people will need to sell their home to pay off the loan. But, you won't have to pay back more than your home is worth.

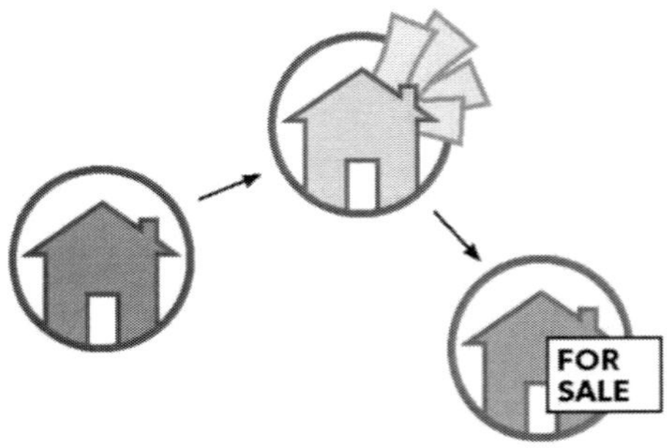

cfpb Consumer Financial Protection Bureau

Figure A-7. (Continued)

CONSIDERING A **REVERSE MORTGAGE?** 2

IMPORTANT QUESTIONS

Are the borrowers the only people who live in the home?

Yes ⊕ You can remain in the home until you move out or die.

No ⊖ If your partner is at least 62, consider whether she or he should be a co-borrower. Children and other dependents should be prepared to move when you die or move out of the home.

Can I afford my living expenses, property taxes, and insurance?

Yes ⊕ A reverse mortgage can help, but it is important to have other retirement resources too.

No ⊖ You could face foreclosure if you run out of money to pay property taxes, insurance, or other expenses in the future.

Do I plan to remain in my home for a long time?

Yes ⊕ A reverse mortgage usually makes more sense the longer you live in your home.

No ⊖ If a health issue or other event may cause you to move out soon, a reverse mortgage is an expensive way to cover short term cash needs.

Can I wait until I am older?

Yes ⊕ It is usually best to wait, especially if you are in your 60s.

No ⊖ Borrowing too soon can leave you without resources later in life. Remember to look at all your options first.

Figure A-7. (Continued)

CONSIDER ALTERNATIVES

Wait

If you take out a reverse mortgage when you are too young, you may run out of money when you're older and need it more. The older a borrower is, the more money he or she can borrow.

Other Home Equity Options

A home equity loan or a home equity line of credit might be a cheaper way to borrow cash against your equity. However, these loans carry their own risks and usually have monthly payments. These also depend on your income and credit.

Lower Your Expenses

There are state and local programs that may help you defer property taxes, lower your heating costs, or save on other bills. Consider selling your current home and moving to a more affordable home.

> By refinancing your current mortgage, you may be able to lower your monthly expenses.

IF YOU DECIDE ON A REVERSE MORTGAGE

Know your payout options

Line of Credit

With a line of credit, you only pay interest on money you use. The amount of money available to you grows over time.

Monthly Payout

This can be a good choice if you need additional monthly income to cover daily living expenses. The amount of money available to you grows over time.

Lump Sum

Borrowing a lot of money at once has risks. If you borrow more than you need, you will pay interest on all of it even if you don't need it.

Know your product options

Standard

This allows you to borrow more, but you pay higher fees and costs.

Saver

This reverse mortgage allows you to borrow less, and pay lower fees and costs.

HECM for Purchase

This reverse mortgage allows you to borrow for the purpose of buying a new home.

Figure A-7. (Continued)

CONSIDERING A **REVERSE MORTGAGE?** 4

BEFORE YOU MAKE ANY DECISIONS ABOUT A LOAN USING YOUR HOME

Considering a lump-sum payout reverse mortgage?

If you take out a line of credit instead, the amount of money you can borrow will grow over time.

If you take all the money upfront, you won't be able to get money from your house later in life.

Be sure you need all of the money now.

If you are considering a lump-sum to pay off your current mortgage, make sure you look into refinancing or downsizing first.

You are required to go to housing counseling before you decide on a federally insured reverse mortgage.

Tell your counselor everything about your situation. Only a serious discussion with a counselor will give you the information you need to make a good decision about your home.

Counseling before any decision involving your home is a good idea.

Visit HUD's website (http://go.usa.gov/v2H) or call HUD's housing counselor referral line (1-800-569-4287) to find a qualified reverse mortgage counselor near you.

Figure A-7. Reverse mortgage consumer guide.

End Notes

[1] CFPB analysis of 2009 Survey of Consumer Finances public use microdata, available at http://federalreserve.gov/econresdata/scf/scfindex.htm. [CFPB Analysis of SCF 2009 Data]

[2] As of the 2010 Census, there were about 24 million eligible homeowner households. As of November 2011, there were about 582,000 HECM loans outstanding. Homeowner population: CFPB estimate derived from 2010 U.S. Census Bureau data, Tables QT-H2 and QT-P2, available at http://factfinder2.census.gov/main.html. HECM loans outstanding: CFPB analysis of FHA public use loan-level HECM data, available at http://portal.hud.gov/hudportal/HUD?src=/program_offices/housing/rmra/oe/rpts/hecmdata/hecmdatamenu. [CFPB Analysis of FHA Loan-Level HECM Data] Loan volume figures in this report are based on the closing date of the loan and may differ from other published sources that use the FHA insurance endorsement date, which lags behind the closing date. The FHA endorsement date is not available in the FHA public-use dataset used to prepare this report.

[3] The U.S. Census Bureau defines the baby boom cohort as people born between 1946 and 1964. CFPB estimate derived from 2010 U.S. Census Bureau data, Tables QT-H2 and QT-P2, available at http://factfinder2.census.gov/main.html.

[4] *See* CFPB Analysis of SCF 2009 Data, endnote 1. Note: Baby Boomers were age 45 to 63 in 2009.

[5] Dodd-Frank Wall Street Reform and Consumer Protection Act, Pub. L. No. 111-203 § 1076, 124 Stat. 2075 (2010) (codified at 12 U.S.C. § 1076).

[6] 12 U.S.C. § 1061.

[7] 12 U.S.C. § 1076(b).

[8] 75 Fed. Reg. 58539 (2010).

[9] This provision is discussed in more detail in Sections 2.3 and 6.7.

[10] *See* CFPB Analysis of SCF 2009 Data, endnote 1.

[11] A more detailed comparison between reverse mortgages and HELOCs is found in Section 2.7.1.

[12] Proprietary (non-government insured) reverse mortgages have all but disappeared today, but a range of products existed in the past and could return in the future.

[13] As of the 2010 Census, there were about 24 million eligible homeowner households. As of November 2011, there were about 582,000 HECM loans outstanding. Homeowner population: CFPB estimate derived from 2010 U.S. Census Bureau data, Tables QT-H2 and QT-P2, available at http://factfinder2.census.gov/main.html. HECM loans outstanding: *see* CFPB Analysis of FHA Loan-Level HECM Data, endnote 2.

[14] HECM outstandings: *see* CFPB Analysis of FHA Loan-Level HECM Data, endnote 2. Traditional mortgage and home equity outstandings: Moody's Analytics data, available with subscription at www.economy.com.

[15] The U.S. Census Bureau defines the baby boom cohort as people born between 1946 and 1964. CFPB estimate derived from 2010 U.S. Census Bureau data, Tables QT-H2 and QT-P2, available at http://factfinder2.census.gov/main.html.

[16] *See* CFPB Analysis of SCF 2009 Data, endnote 1. Note: Baby Boomers were age 45 to 63 in 2009.

[17] Dodd-Frank Wall Street Reform and Consumer Protection Act, Pub. L. No. 111-203 § 1076, 124 Stat. 2075 (2010) (codified at 12 U.S.C. § 1076).

[18] Peter Passell, *Tapping Home Equity to Cushion Old Age*, New York Times (Jan. 30, 1994), available at http://www.nytimes.com/1994/01/30/realestate/tapping-home-equity-to-cushion-old-age.html?pagewanted=all &src=pm.

[19] *See* Deborah Scholar, *Reverse Mortgages: Growing Older and Richer by Cashing in the House*, Government Law Center of Albany Law School, pp. 7-8 (1996) (discussing development of Reverse Annuity Mortgages), available at http://www.governmentlaw.org/ files/ReverseMortgages.pdf; Opportunities in Home Equity Conversion for the Elderly: Hearing Before the Senate Special Subcommittee on Aging (July 20, 1982) (statement of Kenneth Scholen, National Center for Home Equity Conversion) (reviewing efforts by lenders in San Francisco, New Jersey, and Buffalo to develop a reverse mortgage product), available at http://aging.senate.gov/publications/7201982.pdf; Jack Guttentag, *Creating a New Financial Instrument: The Case of Reverse Mortgages*, Wharton School Working Paper No. 19-73 (1975) (discussing why reverse mortgages have not been widely adopted despite consumer need), available at http://finance.wharton.upenn.edu/~rlwctr/papers/7319. PDF; Economics of Aging: Hearing Before the Senate Special Committee on Aging (Aug. 1, 1969) (statement of Yung Ping Chen, University of California), available at http://aging. senate.gov/publications/7311969.pdf.

[20] *See* Opportunities in Home Equity Conversion for the Elderly: Hearing Before the Senate Special Subcommittee on Aging (July 20, 1982) (statement of Kenneth Scholen, National Center for Home Equity Conversion) ("On a simple term product, you could insure the cash flows for the borrower and the encumbered equity for the lender. On a long-term reverse mortgage, by contrast, you are pooling a number of different risks-mortality, mobility, casualty, appreciation- all in one instrument. That is an uncommon combination of risks, and no one knows how it will play out over a period of time."); *id.* (statement of Senator John Heinz) ("What you are saying, in effect, is that the risk associated with a single individual arrangement may be so difficult to figure out that, unless you find a way of pooling the risks into some kind of insurance pool where there is more of an actuarial certainty, that it is difficult or somewhat unlikely that a sufficient number of lenders or investors will come forward."), available at http://aging.senate.gov/publications/ 7201982.pdf.

[21] Anthony DePalma, *Tapping Equity for Retirement Income*, New York Times (Sept. 16, 1984), available at http://www.nytimes.com/1984/09/16/realestate/tapping-equity-for-retirement-income.html?pagewanted=all. [DePalma 1984]

[22] *See* DePalma 1984.

[23] S. 825 (100th Congress) (enacted).

[24] Housing and Community Development Act of 1987, Pub. L. No. 100-242 § 417, 101 Stat. 1815 (codified as 12 U.S.C. §§ 1715z-20(g)).

[25] *See* CFPB Analysis of FHA Loan-Level HECM Data, endnote 2.

[26] Department of Veterans Affairs and Housing and Urban Development, and Independent Agencies Appropriations Act of 1999, Pub. L. No. 105-276 § 593, 112 Stat. 2461 (codified as amended at 12 U.S.C. §§ 1715z-20(g)).

[27] CFPB estimate based on known proprietary loan volumes. There is no comprehensive source of data on proprietary loan volumes, so the estimate is approximate at best.

[28] CFPB interviews with industry experts.

[29] Generation Mortgage, Generation Plus Loan, http://www.generationmortgage.com/jumbo-reverse-mortgage.htm.

[30] Data provided by Generation Mortgage.

[31] Data provided by Generation Mortgage.

[32] FHA Mortgagee Letter 2008-08.

[33] American Recovery and Reinvestment Act of 2009, Pub. L. No. 111-5 § 1204, 123 Stat. 226 (2009).

[34] The HECM Statute and published HECM regulations are silent on the question of whether HECMs may be closed-end or open-end. However, in the first year of the program, HUD issued a Mortgagee Letter stating that

"Because a HUD insured reverse mortgage permits the borrower to use a line of credit, the mortgage is deemed to be "open-end credit" under the Truth-in-Lending Act's Regulation Z (12 C.F.R. § 226) as amended by 54 FR 24670." FHA Mortgagee Letter 1990-17.

[35] FHA Mortgagee Letter 2008-08.

[36] FHA Mortgagee Letter 2007-01.

[37] Housing and Economic Recovery Act of 2008, Pub. L. No. 110-289, 122 Stat. 2654 (2008) (codified at 12 U.S.C. § 1715z-20) (citing Federal Home Loan Mortgage Corporation Act 305(a)(2) (codified at 12 U.S.C. 1452(a)(2)).

[38] American Recovery and Reinvestment Act of 2009, Pub. L. No. 111-5 § 1204, 123 Stat. 226 (2009).

[39] Both Congress and HUD have extended the limit, with the most recent extension implemented by HUD with FHA Mortgagee Letter 2011-39. *See* Department of Interior, Environmental, and Related Agencies Appropriations Act 2010, Pub. L. No. 111-88 § 168, 123 Stat. 2974 (2009) (Congress extending the limit through 2010); Continuing Appropriations Act 2011, Pub. L. No. 111-242 § 144, 124 Stat. 2614 (2010) (Congress extending the limit through fiscal year 2011); FHA Mortgagee Letter 2011-29 (HUD extending the limit through December 31, 2011); FHA Mortgagee Letter 2011-39 (HUD extending the limit through December 31, 2012). HUD has extended the loan size limit pursuant to 255(g) and 255(m) of the National Housing Act. *See* 12 U.S.C. §§ 1715z-20(g) and 1715z-20(m)(2).

[40] *See* CFPB Analysis of SCF 2009 Data, endnote 1.

[41] *See* CFPB Analysis of SCF 2009 Data, endnote 1.

[42] FHA Mortgagee Letter 2010-34 (effective Oct. 4, 2010); FHA Mortgagee Letter 2009-34 (effective Oct. 1, 2009).

[43] HUD Presentation, National Reverse Mortgage Lenders Association Eastern Regional Meeting (Mar. 26, 2012). (Listing both the 2009 and 2010 PLF changes as two of "several policy changes [that] have been introduced to manage risk and strengthen the MMI Fund."); An Actuarial Analysis of FHA Home Equity Conversion Mortgage Loans in the Mutual Mortgage Insurance Fund: Fiscal Year 2011, Prepared for HUD, p. 4 (Oct. 12, 2011) ("[T]he principal limit factors have become more conservative since FY2009... This policy lowers the likelihood and size of claims and reduces FHA's financial risk accordingly, as it reduces the likelihood that the unpaid principal balance will exceed the net proceeds from a house sale.").

[44] FHA Mortgagee Letter 2010-34.

[45] FHA Mortgagee Letter 2010-34.

[46] 24 C.F.R. § 206.33.

[47] 24 C.F.R. § 206.45(a).

[48] 24 C.F.R. § 39.

[49] 24 C.F.R. § 206.32.

[50] 24 C.F.R. § 206.47(a); 24 C.F.R. § 206.47(b).

[51] 24 C.F.R. § 206.27(c)(2).

[52] 24 C.F.R. § 206.205(a).

[53] 24 C.F.R. § 206.27(c)(2). This obligation, and the steps lenders must take before foreclosing on borrowers, is described in more detail in Section 6.6.

[54] 24 C.F.R. § 206.27(b)(5).

[55] 24 C.F.R. § 206.125(a)(2).

[56] 24 C.F.R. § 206.209(a).

[57] 24 C.F.R. § 206.41(a).

[58] *See* 24 C.F.R. § 206.21; 24 C.F.R. § 206.43.

[59] 24 C.F.R. § 206.27(c).

[60] 24 C.F.R. § 206.125(a)(2).

[61] 24 C.F.R. § 206.125(a)(2) (explaining that the borrower can pay the mortgage balance in full, sell the property for at least 95 percent of appraised value, or provide the lender with a deed in lieu of foreclosure).

[62] 24 C.F.R. § 206.125(d). If the lender does not start foreclosure proceedings within the timeframe established by FHA, the lender may not be able to collect on the insurance claim.

[63] *See* CFPB Analysis of FHA Loan-Level HECM Data, endnote 2.

[64] When interest rates are very low, as they are today, FHA uses an interest rate floor such that rates below the floor do not produce any additional proceeds.

[65] Interest rates below 5 percent do not produce any additional proceeds. Interest rates above 10 percent do not produce any proceeds. The minimum age for HECM borrowers is 62, and borrowers over 90 do not receive any additional proceeds. *See* Principal Limit Factor Tables, available at http://portal.hud.gov/hudportal/HUD?src=/program_offices/housing/ sfh/hecm/hecmhomelenders.

[66] Unless they pay off the other loan(s) using another source of funds.

[67] According to interviews with industry participants, secondary market investors do not pay as highly for Saver loans as they do for Standard loans (assuming interest rates are equal) because they are concerned that Saver borrowers might pay their loans off more quickly than Standard borrowers, reducing investor yield. Thus, lenders typically set interest rates on Saver loans a little higher than the rates on Standard loans so as to be able

to earn a similar amount in the secondary market. This pricing difference is reflected in industry rate sheets obtained by the CFPB.

[68] Beginning in 1996, monthly adjustable loans replaced annually adjustable loans as the dominant rate option, though the monthly adjustments were calculated using the same one-year constant maturity treasury (CMT) rate used in calculating annually adjustable HECMs. In October 2007, FHA published a rule allowing monthly adjustable rates to be calculated using the one-month CMT *or* the one-month LIBOR. *See* 72 Fed. Reg. 40048 (amending regulations at 24 C.F.R. § 203.49(b)). The new rule also allowed the use of the one-year LIBOR index to calculate annually adjustable HECMs, though this option did not receive much uptake. Since this policy change in 2007, the monthly adjustable LIBOR has become the dominant adjustable-rate option.

[69] Historically, all HECMs were structured as open-end loans, meaning that lenders wanting to offer a fixed-rate HECM had to be willing to take the interest rate risk of lending new money in the future at an interest rate fixed at origination. Very few lenders were willing to take that risk. The HECM Statute and published HECM regulations are silent on the question of whether HECMs may be closed-end or open-end. However, in the first year of the program, HUD issued a Mortgagee Letter stating that "Because a HUD insured reverse mortgage permits the borrower to use a line of credit, the mortgage is deemed to be "open-end credit" under the Truth-in-Lending Act's Regulation Z (12 CFR 226) as amended by 54 FR 24670." FHA Mortgagee Letter 1990-17. FHA Mortgagee Letter 2008-08, issued on March 28, 2008, clarified that fixed-rate HECMs were permitted to be structured as closed-end credit, opening the door for the market transition to fixed-rate products that happened in 2009.

[70] *See* CFPB Analysis of FHA Loan-Level HECM Data, endnote 2.

[71] Fixed-rate HECMs are currently structured as closed-end, lump-sum loans. Lenders are unwilling to offer an open-end, line-of-credit or monthly payment plan at a fixed rate due to interest rate risk. As with all closed-end loans, borrowers are not permitted to partially pay down the loan and then re-borrow against their authorized loan amount because this would constitute an open-end, line-of-credit structure rather than a closed-end structure.

[72] FHA Mortgagee Letter 2008-08. This letter states that fixed-rate loans may be structured as open-end or closed-end loans. In practice, all or nearly all fixed-rate loans are closed-end loans. CFPB is not aware of any lender offering fixed-rate, open-end HECMs.

[73] 12 U.S.C. § 1715z-20(d)(9); 24 C.F.R. § 206.19.

[74] *See* HUD Handbook, Home Equity Conversion Mortgages, 4235.1 REV-1 § 1-6(B) ("With all payment plans, the lender must be able to make lump sum payments up to the net principal limit at the borrower's request.").

[75] This is not a regulatory requirement, but rather a result of market forces. According to FHA Mortgagee Letter 2008-08, fixed-rate reverse mortgages can be open-end or closed-end. Any lender wanting to offer a fixed-rate, open-end HECM would have to be willing to take the interest rate risk of lending new money in the future at an interest rate fixed at origination. CFPB is not aware of any lenders making open-end, fixed-rate HECMs.

[76] Hui Shan, *Reversing the Trend: The Recent Expansion of the Reverse Mortgage Market*, Federal Reserve Board Working Paper No. 2009-42, Table 2 (Apr. 2009), available at http://www.federalreserve.gov/pubs/feds/2009/200942/200942pap.pdf.

[77] *See* CFPB Analysis of FHA Loan-Level HECM Data, endnote 2.

[78] *See* CFPB Analysis of FHA Loan-Level HECM Data, endnote 2.

[79] Estimates based on industry data obtained by the CFPB.

[80] FHA Mortgagee Letter 2008-33.

[81] FHA Mortgagee Letter 2010-34.

[82] The allowable origination fee was reduced in 2008. *See* Housing and Economic Recovery Act of 2008, Pub. L. No. 110-289, 122 Stat. 2654 (2008) (codified as 12 U.S.C. § 1715z-20(1) (r)(1)). *See also* FHA Mortgagee Letter 2008-34.

[83] FHA Mortgagee Letter 2011-09.

[84] FHA Mortgagee Letter 2010-34. This rate was increased from 0.50 percent on October 4, 2010, as part of a package of reforms (including the introduction of the HECM Saver option and an across-the-board reduction of principal limit factors) designed to improve the financial stability of the FHA insurance fund.

[85] 24 C.F.R. § 206.105 ("Monthly MIP will accrue daily on the mortgage balance at a rate equivalent to one-half of one percent per annum and shall be added to the mortgage balance when paid to the Secretary."); 24 C.F.R. § 206.111 ("Each monthly MIP shall be due to the Secretary on the first business day of each month except the month in which the mortgage is closed.").

[86] This servicing fee margin is mandated by Ginnie Mae for all Ginnie Mae-securitized HECMs, which comprise the majority of HECMs originated today. Lenders wishing to hold loans on balance sheet could, in theory, use a different structure. Also embedded into the interest rate for Ginnie Mae-securitized loans is a 6 basis point (0.06 percent) guarantee fee paid to Ginnie Mae. *See* Ginnie Mae All Participants Memorandum 11-10, Home Equity Conversion Mortgage Mortgage-Backed Securities – Changes to the Servicing Fee Margin (June 10, 2011), available at http://www.ginniemae.gov/apm/apm_pdf/11-10.pdf.

[87] CFPB industry research.

[88] Oversight of the Federal Housing Administration's Reverse Mortgage Program for Seniors: Hearing before the House Subcommittee on Insurance, Housing, and Community Opportunity (May 9, 2012) (statement of Charles Coulter, Deputy Assistant Secretary for Single Family Programs, Office of Housing, Federal Housing Administration), available at http://financialservices.house.gov/UploadedFiles/HHRG-112-BA04-WState-CCoulter-20120509.pdf.

[89] AARP, *Reverse Mortgage Loans: Borrowing Against Your Home* , p.22 (Oct. 2010), available at http://assets.aarp.org/www.aarp.org_/articles/money/financial_pdfs/hmm_hires_nocrops. pdf. [AARP 2010]

[90] For example, the Illinois Department on Aging recently had to cut each Circuit Breaker Tax Grant awarded in half due to budget cuts for fiscal years 2010 and 2011. *See* Illinois Department of Aging Circuit Breaker Tax Grant, available at http://www.cbrx.il.gov/aging/ 1rx/cbrx/taxgrant.htm.

[91] Mass. Gen. Laws 59 § 5.

[92] *See* AARP 2010 at 22, endnote 89.

[93] *See, e.g.,* Wisconsin Deferred Payment Loans, available at http://www.cityofmadison.com/planning/cedu/Documents/HRSPTT.pdf.

[94] *See, e.g.,* Joseph Holstead, OLR Research Report, Government Home Improvement Loans and Grants (Aug. 21, 2006) (discussing Connecticut Home Solutions program), available at http://www.cga.ct.gov/2006/rpt/2006-R-0494.htm.

[95] Additional states, including Georgia, Indiana and Iowa, have the statutory authority to implement reverse mortgage programs but have not done so. *See, e.g.,* Ga. Code § 50-26-17; Ind. Code § 28-15-11-9; Iowa Code § 16.53.

[96] *See* Conn. Gen. Stat. § 8-265(i); Connecticut Housing Finance Authority, Reverse Annuity Mortgage Program Overview, available at http://www.chfa.org/Homeownership/for%20 Homeowners/ReverseAnnuityMortgage Program.aspx.

[97] "'Long -Term Care' describes a wide range of supportive services provided to individuals who have lost some or all capacity to function on their own due to chronic illness, and are expected to require such services for an extended period." State of Connecticut, Aging Servicing Division – State Unit on Aging, Reverse Annuity Mortgages Program, available at http://www.ct.gov/agingservices/cwp/view.asp?a=2515&q=313094.

[98] *See* Mont. Code § 90-6-501 et seq; Montana Department of Commerce, Reverse Annuity Mortgage Program, available at http://housing.mt.gov/About/MF/ram.mcpx; Montana Department of Commerce, Reverse Annuity Mortgage Program Fact Sheet (2011), available at http://housing.mt.gov/content/About/MF/docs/LIHTCRAM/2011RAMfactSheet.pdf.

[99] *See* Website for Homeowner Options for Massachusetts Elders, available at http://elder homeowners.org/.

[100] *See* Program Highlights, Website for Homeowner Options for Massachusetts Elders, available at http://elderhomeowners.org/highlights.htm.

[101] Laura Summer, Commonwealth Fund, *Increasing Participation in Benefits Programs for Low-Income Seniors* (May 2009) (concluding that many eligible low-income seniors do not participate in public benefit programs because they are either not familiar with the program or are discouraged by complex enrollment processes), available at http://www.common wealthfund.org/~/media/Files/Publications/Fund%20Report/2009/May/1266 _Summer_ increasing_particip_benefit_progs_v3.pdf; April Yanyuan Wu, Why Do So Few Elderly Use Food Stamps, University of Chicago Harris School of Public Policy Working Paper No. 10.01, p. 4 (Oct. 2009) (finding that 60% of eligible seniors who were not receiving food stamps were not aware that they were eligible), available at http://harrisschool.uchicago. edu/About/publications/working-papers/pdf/wp_10_01.pdf.

[102] Bonnie Heudorfer, Massachusetts Community and Banking Counsel, Reverse Mortgage Lending Project: An Investigation into the Existing State of Consumer Protections, Issues, and Practices Relative to Reverse Mortgage Lending in the Commonwealth of Massachusetts (May 1, 2011), available at http://www.mcbc.info/files/REVERSE-MORTGAGE-LENDING-PROJECT-REV-B.pdf.

[103] Oversight of the Federal Housing Administration's Reverse Mortgage Program for Seniors: Hearing before the House Financial Services Subcommittee on Insurance, Housing and Community Opportunity (May 9, 2012) (statement of Barbara Stucki) (using National Council on Aging data from the Reverse Mortgage Counseling Toolkit website), available at http://financialservices.house.gov/UploadedFiles/HHRG-112-BA04-WState-BStucki-20120509.pdf.

[104] CFPB estimate derived from 2010 U.S. Census Bureau data, Tables QT-H2 and QT-P2, available at http://factfinder2.census.gov/main.html.

[105] *See* CFPB Analysis of SCF 2009 Data, endnote 1.

[106] NRMLA/Risk Span Reverse Mortgage Market Index, available at http://services.nrmlaonline. org/NRMLA_Documents/RMMI_Third_Quarter_2011.pdf.

[107] There were 582,000 reverse mortgages outstanding as of November 2011. *See* CFPB Analysis of FHA Loan-Level HECM Data, endnote 2.

[108] *See* CFPB Analysis of SCF 2009 Data, endnote 1; MetLife Mature Market Institute, *Changing Attitudes, Changing Motives: The MetLife Study of How Aging Homeowners Use Reverse Mortgages*, pp. 20-22 (Mar. 2012), available at http://www.metlife.com/assets/cao/mmi/ publications/studies/2012/studies/mmi-changing-attitudes-changing-motives.pdf. [Metlife 2012]

[109] *See* CFPB Analysis of FHA Loan-Level HECM Data, endnote 2.

[110] U.S. Census Bureau, Population Division, Table 12: Projections of the Population by Age and Sex for the United States: 2010 to 2050 (Aug. 14, 2008), available at http://www.census. gov/population/www/projections/files/ nation/summary/np2008-t12.xls.

[111] CFPB estimate based on Census population projections, assuming current ratios of population to households and current homeownership rates continue.

[112] As of the 2010 Census, there were about 24 million eligible homeowner households. As of November 2011, there were about 582,000 HECM loans outstanding. Homeowner population: CFPB estimate derived from 2010 U.S. Census Bureau data, Tables QT-H2 and QT-P2, available at http://factfinder2.census.gov/main. html. HECM loans outstanding: *see* CFPB Analysis of FHA Loan-Level HECM Data, endnote 2.

[113] Survey results are weighted to be representative of the underlying population. Donald L. Redfoot et al., AARP, *Reverse Mortgages: Niche Product or Mainstream Solution? Report on the AARP 2006 National Survey of Reverse Mortgage Shoppers*, Appendix D (Dec. 2007), available at http://assets.aarp.org/rgcenter/consume/ 2007_22_revmortgage.pdf. [AARP 2006 Survey]

[114] Survey results are weighted to be representative of the underlying population. *See* AARP 2006 Survey at Appendix D.

[115] Survey results are weighted to be representative of the underlying population. Natalie Jobity, The Harris Poll #70 (July 16, 2007), available at http://www.harrisinteractive.com/vault/Harris-Interactive-Poll-Research-Mortgage-Issues-2007-07.pdf.

[116] Stephanie Rauterkus et al., *The Home Equity Conversion Mortgage: A Study of Attitudes and Awareness*, Journal of Real Estate Portfolio Management 15:3, p. 267 (2009). [Rauterkus 2009]

[117] HUD Presentation, National Reverse Mortgage Association Annual Meeting (Oct. 25, 2011).

[118] Survey results are weighted to be representative of the underlying population. Natalie Jobity, The Harris Poll #70 (July 16, 2007), available at http://www.harrisinteractive.com/vault/ Harris-Interactive-Poll-Research-Mortgage-Issues-2007-07.pdf.

[119] For these low-income homeowners, downsizing was unlikely to yield much savings – their moving options were primarily subsidized or unsubsidized rentals, nursing homes, and moving in with family. This study involved reverse mortgage borrowers in a special program run by a Massachusetts nonprofit rather than the mainstream HECM program. Roberta Leviton, *Reverse Mortgage Decision Making*, Journal of Aging and Social Policy 13:4 (2001).

[120] *See* AARP 2006 Survey at 24, endnote 113.

[121] *See* Rauterkus 2009 at 267, endnote 116.

[122] The borrowers in this study ranged from age 70 to 98 at the time of the study, which was published in 2001. For these low-income homeowners, downsizing was unlikely to yield much savings – their moving options were primarily subsidized or unsubsidized rentals, nursing homes, and moving in with family. This study involved reverse mortgage borrowers in a special program run by a Massachusetts nonprofit rather than the mainstream HECM program. Roberta Leviton, *Reverse Mortgage Decision Making*, Journal of Aging and Social Policy 13:4 (2001).

[123] David Rodda et al., *No Place Like Home: A Report to Congress on FHA's Home Equity Conversion Mortgage Program*, p. 44 (2000), available at http://www.huduser.org/ Publications/pdf/hecmrpt.pdf. [Rodda 2000]

[124] Chris E. Anguelov and Christopher R. Tamborini, *Retiring in Debt? An Update on the 2007 Near-Retiree Cohort*, Social Security Bulletin 70:4, p.70 (2010), available at http://www. ssa.gov/policy/docs/ssb/v70n4/ v70n4p69.pdf. [Anguelov 2010]

[125] Question: Which statement is closer to your own beliefs? A: I hope to leave my children (and heirs) some inheritance to make their future lives easier. B: I want to be able to pay all of my expenses while I am alive so my children (and heirs) do not have to worry about me. Study conducted by Marttila Strategies in October 2010 on behalf of the National Reverse Mortgage Lenders Association, and surveyed 600 seniors without reverse mortgages who own their homes with at least 50 percent equity. Presentation by Marttila Strategies, Survey for the National Reverse Mortgage Lenders Association, National Reverse Mortgage Association Annual Conference (Oct. 24, 2011).

[126] MetLife Mature Market Institute, *Transitioning into Retirement: The MetLife Study of Baby Boomers at 65* (Apr. 2012), available at http://www.metlife.com/assets/cao/mmi/publications/studies/2012/studies/mmi-transitioning-retirement.pdf.

[127] *See* AARP 2006 Survey at 75, endnote 113.

[128] These borrowers gave one of three reasons as the primary reason for not taking out the loan: "The reverse mortgage was not necessary given your financial situation" (10 percent); "The reverse mortgage would make more financial sense in the future than it would now" (9 percent); and "You found another way to meet your financial needs" (9 percent).

[129] *See* AARP 2006 Survey at 75, endnote 113.

[130] *See* Metlife 2012 at 13, endnote 108.

[131] Question: Now that you've had a reverse mortgage for at least two years, do you plan to pay off your reverse mortgage at some point in the future OR do you plan to stay in your home for the rest of your life and use the

proceeds your estate will receive from selling the home to pay off the reverse mortgage? Presentation by Marttila Strategies, Survey for the National Reverse Mortgage Lenders Association, National Reverse Mortgage Association Annual Conference (Oct. 24, 2011).

[132] Question: Which statement is closer to your own view? A) I plan to stay in my home for the rest of my life or B) I plan/ expect to move away from the house in which I currently live.Presentation by Marttila Strategies, Survey for the National Reverse Mortgage Lenders Association, National Reverse Mortgage Association Annual Conference (Oct. 24, 2011).

[133] Presentation by Marttila Strategies, Survey for the National Reverse Mortgage Lenders Association, National Reverse Mortgage Association Annual Conference (Oct. 24, 2011).

[134] *See* CFPB Analysis of FHA Loan-Level HECM Data, endnote 2.

[135] The median age at origination for borrowers taking out loans during the 1990s was 75. The average life expectancy of a 75-year-old in 1995 was 11 years. *See* CFPB Analysis of FHA Loan-Level HECM Data, endnote 2; Centers for Disease Control and Prevention, *Vital Statistics of the United States, Mortality, 2: A,* Table 6-3 (1995), available at http://www. cdc.gov/nchs/data/lifetables/life95_2.pdf.

[136] *See* AARP 2006 Survey at 75, endnote 113.

[137] Presentation by Marttila Strategies, Survey for the National Reverse Mortgage Lenders Association, National Reverse Mortgage Association Annual Conference (Oct. 24, 2011).

[138] *See* CFPB Analysis of FHA Loan-Level HECM Data, endnote 2.

[139] *See* CFPB Analysis of FHA Loan-Level HECM Data, endnote 2.

[140] To facilitate comparisons with the reverse mortgage borrowers in the first three charts, percentages in the fourth chart (2010 Population) are calculated as a percentage of people age 62 and older – not as a percentage of people 60 and older.

[141] These statistics compare averages of 1990-1999 with 2005-2010. 2011 is an anomalous year in which the marital status is unreported on 10% of loans. *See* CFPB Analysis of FHA Loan-Level HECM Data, endnote 2.

[142] *See* Rodda 2000 at 17, endnote 123.

[143] *See* Rodda 2000 at 17, endnote 123.

[144] *See* AARP 2006 Survey, endnote 113.

[145] Notice of Hearings, Federal Reserve Board, Home Mortgage Disclosure Act (June 15, 2010), available at http://www.federalreserve.gov/newsevents/press/bcreg/bcreg20100617a1.pdf.

[146] California Community Groups, Comment Letter to Federal Reserve Board Proposed Rule to Amend Regulation C, Docket No. OP-388, 12 C.F.R Part 203: Home Mortgage Disclosure Act (Aug. 4, 2010) (letter submitted on behalf of 64 nonprofit civil rights and community groups across the State of California), available at http://www.insightcced.org/uploads/ CRWG/LettertoFederalReserve-HMDA.pdf; Woodstock Institute, Comment Letter to Federal Reserve Board Proposed Rule to Amend Regulation C, Docket No. OP-388, 12 C.F.R Part 203: Home Mortgage Disclosure Act (Sept. 2, 2010), available at http://www. federalreserve.gov/ communitydev/files/geoff_smith_remarks.pdf; Neighborhood Economic Development Advocacy Project, Comment Letter to Federal Reserve Board Proposed Rule to Amend Regulation C, Docket No. OP-388, 12 C.F.R Part 203: Home Mortgage Disclosure Act (Aug. 20, 2010), available at http://www.nedap.org/resources/ documents/ HMDANEDAPCommentLetter8-20-10.pdf; Credit Union National Association, Comment Letter to Federal Reserve Board Proposed Rule to Amend Regulation C, Docket No. OP-388, 12 C.F.R Part 203: Home Mortgage Disclosure Act (Aug. 20, 2010), available at http://www.cuna.org/reg_advocacy/comment_ letters/cl_082010.html; National Fair Housing Alliance, Comment Letter to Federal Reserve Board Proposed Rule to Amend Regulation C, Docket No. OP-388, 12 C.F.R Part 203: Home Mortgage Disclosure Act (Sept. 8, 2010), available at http://www.nationalfairhousing.org/Portals/33/NFHA%20 HMDA%20Comments.pdf; New York Banking Department, Comment Letter to Federal Reserve Board Proposed Rule to Amend Regulation C, Docket No. OP-388, 12 C.F.R Part 203: Home Mortgage Disclosure Act (Aug. 6, 2010), available at http://www.federalreserve.gov/SECRS/2010/August/20100810/OP-1388/OP-1388_080610_52157 _586078122944_1.pdf; Federal Trade Commission, Comment Letter to Federal Reserve Board Proposed Rule to Amend Regulation C, Docket No. OP-388, 12 C.F.R Part 203: Home Mortgage Disclosure Act (Dec. 3, 2010), available at http://www.ftc.gov/os/2010/ 12/101217federalreserveregulation.pdf; Lending Schools First Federal Credit Union, Comment Letter to Federal Reserve Board Proposed Rule to Amend Regulation C, Docket No. OP-388, 12 C.F.R Part 203: Home Mortgage Disclosure Act (Aug. 20, 2010), available at http:// www.federalreserve.gov/SECRS/2010/August/20100825/OP-1388/OP-1388_082010_53000_ 543166582938 _1.pdf. But see Independent Alliance Banks, Comment Letter to Federal Reserve Board Proposed Rule to Amend Regulation C, Docket No. OP-388, 12 C.F.R Part 203: Home Mortgage Disclosure Act (Sept. 20, 2010) ("I do not believe the Board should require lenders to report on home-secured loans [such as reverse mortgages] in addition to home purchase, home improvement, and refinancing loans."), available at http:// www.federalreserve.gov/SECRS/2010/September/20100917/OP-1388/OP-1388_091010_53974_542630288 647_1.pdf.

[147] Dodd-Frank Wall Street Reform and Consumer Protection Act, Pub. L. No. 111-203 § 1094, 124 Stat. 2075 (2010) (codified at 12 U.S.C. § 2801).

[148] *See* AARP 2006 Survey at 49, endnote 113.

[149] *See* CFPB Analysis of SCF 2007 Data, endnote 1.

[150] The mortgage debt figures are derived by adding the "Mortgage debt only" and "Both mortgage and other debt" lines in Figure 17. *See* Metlife 2012, endnote 108.

[151] *See* CFPB Analysis of SCF 2009 Data, endnote 1.

[152] Due to data constraints, data on existing mortgages paid off is commingled with data on federal liens or judgments paid off at closing. Some portion of borrowers included in these figures could have owed a federal lien or judgment but not a mortgage, though we assume that portion to be quite small.

[153] *See* Anguelov 2010 at 70, endnote 124.

[154] *See* CFPB Analysis of FHA Loan-Level HECM Data, endnote 2.

[155] "Upfront" is defined to mean funds withdrawn within the first year. *See* CFPB Analysis of FHA Loan-Level HECM Data, endnote 2.

[156] *See* CFPB Analysis of FHA Loan-Level HECM Data, endnote 2.

[157] *See* CFPB Analysis of FHA Loan-Level HECM Data, endnote 2.

[158] CFPB analysis of data obtained from a reverse mortgage lender. This analysis covers the two-year period after the rise in market share of the fixed-rate product from June 2009 through May 2011.

[159] CFPB analysis of data obtained from a reverse mortgage lender. Borrowers who "owned their home free and clear or had only a small existing mortgage balance" are defined as borrowers who did not pay off a lien at closing or who used less than 25 percent of their available proceeds to pay off an existing lien at closing. Existing liens mostly consist of mortgage balances but could include federal liens or judgments. This analysis covers the two-year period after the rise in market share of the fixed-rate product from June 2009 through May 2011.

[160] CFPB analysis of data obtained from a reverse mortgage lender. This analysis covers the two-year period after the rise in market share of the fixed-rate product from June 2009 through May 2011.

[161] *See* CFPB Analysis of FHA Loan-Level HECM Data, endnote 2.

[162] *See* CFPB Analysis of FHA Loan-Level HECM Data, endnote 2.

[163] The median age at origination for borrowers taking out loans during the 1990s was 75. The average life expectancy of a 75-year-old in 1995 was 11 years. Centers for Disease Control and Prevention, *Vital Statistics of the United States, Mortality, 2:A*, Table 6-3 (1995), available at http://www.cdc.gov/nchs/data/lifetables/life95_2.pdf.

[164] Syzmanoski et al., Home Equity Conversion Mortgage Terminations: Information to Enhance the Developing Secondary Market, Cityscape: A Journal of Policy Development and Research 9:1, p.38 (2007).

[165] Housing prices reached their peak in the first quarter of 2006 and remained at similar levels through the first quarter of 2007 before beginning to slide. Case-Shiller National Home Price Index, Seasonally Adjusted Q4 2011, available at http://www.standardandpoors.com/indices/sp-case-shiller-home-price-indices/en/us/?indexId=spusa-cashpidff--p-us----.

[166] *See,* Housing and Community Development Act of 1987, Pub. L. No. 100-242 § 417, 101 Stat. 1815 (codified as 12 U.S.C. §§ 1715z-20(g)) stating that the purpose of the program was "to meet the special needs of elderly homeowners by reducing the effect of the economic hardship caused by the increasing costs of meeting health, housing, and subsistence needs at a time of reduced income, through the insurance of home equity conversion mortgages to permit the conversion of a portion of accumulated home equity into liquid assets." *See also* U.S. Department of Housing and Urban Development, Office of Policy Development and Research, *Preliminary Evaluation of the Home Equity Conversion Mortgage Insurance Demonstration*, pp. 1-8 (Dec. 1992), available at http://www.huduser.org/Publications/pdf/HUD%20-%206094.pdf; Opportunities in Home Equity Conversion for the Elderly: Hearing Before the Senate Special Subcommittee on Aging, p.7 (July 20, 1982), available at http://aging.senate.gov/publications/7201982.pdf.

[167] According to a 2010 industry poll, 81percent of reverse mortgage borrowers and 79 percent of eligible homeowners want to stay in their current home for the rest of their lives. Presentation by Marttila Strategies, Survey for the National Reverse Mortgage Lenders Association, National Reverse Mortgage Association Annual Conference (Oct. 24, 2011). A 2011 survey conducted on behalf of MetLife found that among 65 year olds, 83 percentt had no plans to move. *See* MetLife Mature Market Institute, *Transitioning into Retirement: The MetLife Study of Baby Boomers at 65* (Apr. 2012), available at http://www.metlife.com/ assets/cao/mmi/publications/studies/2012/studies/mmi-transitioning-retirement.pdf.

[168] The 2011 MetLife survey found that among 65-year-olds who moved in the past three years or were planning to move in the future, 52 percent moved or were planning to move to a smaller home. *See* MetLife Mature Market Institute, *Transitioning into Retirement: The MetLife Study of Baby Boomers at 65* (Apr. 2012), available at http://www.metlife.com/ assets/cao/mmi/publications/studies/2012/studies/mmi-transitioning-retirement.pdf.

[169] Department of Veterans Affairs and Housing and Urban Development, and Independent Agencies Appropriations Act of 1999, Pub. L. No. 105-276 § 593(c)(1), 112 Stat. 2461 (codified as amended at 12 U.S.C. §§ 1715z-20(g)).

[170] *See* CFPB Analysis of FHA Loan-Level HECM Data, endnote 2.

[171] Importantly, the maximum claim amount represents the maximum future value of the loan *to the investor* that owns the loan. In reality, some loan balances will exceed the calculated maximum claim amount at repayment if the borrower keeps the loan for a long time and/or interest rates rise significantly (on an adjustable-rate loan). Once the loan value reaches 98 percent or more of the maximum claim amount, the loan servicer can assign (sell) the loan to FHA and receive payment for the actual value of the loan. The FHA insurance fund owns the loan from that point forward and absorbs any losses incurred if the loan balance exceeds the value of the home at repayment. *See* 24 C.F.R. § 206.107(a)(1); 24 C.F.R. § 206.123(a); 24 C.F.R. § 206.129(e)(1).

[172] *See* CFPB Analysis of FHA Loan-Level HECM Data, endnote 2.

[173] The initial principal limit is the maximum amount that a borrower *could* be authorized to borrow. In practice, it is reduced by closing costs, origination fees, mortgage insurance, and/or other costs and fees financed into the loan.

[174] *See* CFPB Analysis of FHA Loan-Level HECM Data, endnote 2.

[175] Over the past 23 years since the HECM program's inception, the secondary market has evolved considerably. Previously, both Fannie Mae and Wall Street securitization houses (e.g., Bank of America Securities, Deutsche Bank, and RBS Greenwich Capital) participated in the HECM secondary market. The evolution of the HECM secondary market is discussed in more detail in Section 4.4.

[176] Darryl Hicks, *Talking Heads: Insights from a Mortgage Trader*, Reverse Mortgage Magazine, National Reverse Mortgage Lenders Association (Jan./Feb. 2012), available at http://services.nrmlaonline.org/NRMLA_Documents/January-February2012.pdf.

[177] As in the traditional mortgage market, reverse mortgage servicers manage all communications (monthly statements, customer service call centers, etc.) with the borrower, including collections and the foreclosure process. In the reverse mortgage market, servicers also disburse future payments to the borrower.

[178] Reverse Market Insight, HECM Trends Report (Feb. 2012), available at http://www.rminsight. net/wp-content/uploads/2012/04/Trends_201202.pdf.

[179] Press Release, Bank of America, *Bank of America Home Loans Shifts Resources to Core Mortgage Operations; Exits Reverse Mortgage Origination Business* (Feb. 4, 2011), available at http://investor.bankofamerica.com/phoenix.zhtml?c=71595&p=irol-newsArticle &ID=1525144&highlight=; Tara Siegel Bernard, *2 Big Banks Exit Reverse Mortgage Business*, New York Times (June 17, 2011), available at http://www.nytimes.com/2011/ 06/18/ your- money/mortgages/18reverse.html.

[180] John Yedinak, *OneWest Exits Reverse Mortgage Business, Shuts Down Financial Freedom*, Reverse Mortgage Daily (Mar. 21, 2011), available at http://reversemortgagedaily.com/ 2011/03/21/onewest-exits-reverse-mortgage-business-shuts-down-financial-freedom/.

[181] Press Release, MetLife, *Metlife Exits Reverse Mortgage Business* (Apr. 26, 2012), available at http://www.metlife.com/about/press-room/index.html?compID=80759.

[182] CFPB interviews with industry participants.

[183] Reverse Market Insight, HECM Originators Report (Feb. 2012), available at http://www.rminsight.net/wp-content/uploads/2012/04/Originators_201202.pdf.

[184] Reverse Market Insight, HECM Trends Report (Feb. 2012), available at http://www.rminsight.net/wp-content/uploads/2012/04/Trends_201202.pdf.

[185] CFPB interviews with industry participants.

[186] A small handful of banks or private investors could be retaining a small number of loans on their balance sheets.

[187] The Ginnie Mae program was created in late 2007, but did not gain appreciable market share until mid-2009. Royal Bank of Scotland MBS Strategy Primer, GNMA HECM Primer and Relative Value (Feb. 28, 2011).

[188] Wells Fargo, Bank of America, MetLife, and One West Bank (the parent company of Financial Freedom) are no longer active originating issuers, though they are continuing to issue new HMBS securities comprised of the "tails" – ongoing servicing fees, mortgage insurance premiums, and ongoing borrower draws (for adjustable-rate loans) – from existing loans. Nationstar Mortgage recently acquired Bank of America's servicing portfolio and has begun issuing "tails" pools from Bank of America's former portfolio, but Nationstar has not yet begun issuing pools based on new originations.

[189] *See* Ginnie Mae All Participants Memorandum 11-01, New Financial Requirements – Home Equity Conversion Mortgage-Backed Securities (Jan. 7, 2011), available at http://www. ginniemae.gov/apm/apm_pdf/11-01.pdf.

[190] Elizabeth Ecker, *After 3 Year Wait, Live Well Gets GNMA HMBS Approval*, Reverse Mortgage Daily (Jan. 31, 2012), available at http://reversemortgagedaily.com/2012/01/31/ after-3-year-wait-live-well-gets-gnma-hmbs-approval/.

[191] John Yedinak, *Bank of America Sells $18 Billion of Reverse Mortgage Servicing to Nationstar*, Reverse Mortgage Daily (Dec. 12, 2011), available at http://reversemortgage daily.com/2011/12/12/bank-of-america-sells-18-billion-of-reverse-mortgage-servicing-to-nationstar/; Press Release, MetLife, *Metlife Exits Reverse Mortgage Business* (Apr. 26, 2012), available at http://www.metlife.com/about/press-room/index.html?compID=80759.

[192] CFPB interviews with industry participants.

[193] LIBOR stands for the London Inter-Bank Offer Rate and is one of the most commonly-used interest rate indices. The new rule also allowed the use of the one-month CMT or the one-year LIBOR index to calculate

adjustable-rate HECMs, though these option did not receive much uptake. *See* 72 Fed. Reg. 40048 (amending regulations at 24 C.F.R. § 203.49(b)).

194 *See* CFPB Analysis of FHA Loan-Level HECM Data, endnote 2. Fannie Mae officially ceased accepting the CMT-based product in September 2009. *See* Fannie Mae Announcement 09-16 (June 1, 2009), available at https://www.efanniemae.com/sf/guides/ssg/annltrs/pdf/ 2009/0916.pdf.

195 FHA Mortgagee Letter 2008-08.

196 In standard mortgage finance terms, the "dollar price" of the fixed-rate pools has ranged between 110 and 112.

197 In standard mortgage finance terms, the "dollar price" of the adjustable-rate pools has ranged between 106 and 109.

198 Pricing for HECM Savers is lower because the product is new and investors are concerned that Saver borrowers may exhibit faster prepayment behavior than HECM Standard borrowers. CFPB interviews with industry experts.

199 CFPB interviews and rate sheets provided by industry participants.

200 CFPB interviews with industry participants.

201 *See* CFPB Analysis of FHA Loan-Level HECM Data, endnote 2; *see also* HECM Single Family Portfolio Snap Shot, public use data, available at http://portal.hud.gov/hudportal/ HUD?src=/program_offices/housing/rmra/ oe/rpts/hecmsfsnap/hecm sfsnap. Note that this data has a lag.

202 CFPB interviews with industry experts.

203 *See* CFPB Analysis of FHA Loan-Level HECM Data, endnote 2.

204 CFPB interviews with industry participants.

205 CFPB interviews with industry experts.

206 Department of Veterans Affairs and Housing and Urban Development and Independent Agencies Appropriations Act of 1999, Pub. L. No. 105-276, § 593, 112 Stat. 2461 (codified as amended at 12 U.S.C. § 1715z-20(g)).

207 *See* CFPB Analysis of FHA Loan-Level HECM Data, endnote 2.

208 Bank of America Securities issued 6 securities: MECA 2006-SFG1, MECA 2006-SFG2, MECA 2006-SFG3, MECA 2007-FF1, MECA 2007-FF2, and MECA 2007-FF3. Deutsche Bank issued 2 securities: REV 2007-1 and REV 2007-2. RBS Greenwich Capital issued 3 securities: RV HECM TRUST 2007-1, RVMLT 2007-3, and RV HECM TRUST 2007-4. RBS Greenwich Capital also issued 2 re-securitizations: RV HECM TRUST 2007-4 and RV HECM TRUST 2008-1. Deutsche Bank's REV 2007-1 was later terminated and the loans repurchased.

209 Moody's recently downgraded these securities, citing possible losses to the trusts due to home price declines and the potential difficulty of selling foreclosed properties at the appraised value in a timely manner. *See*, Rating Action (Mar. 7, 2012), available at http://www.moodys.com/research/Moodys-downgrades-5-billion-of-HECM-reverse-mortgage-bonds--PR_239185.

210 CFPB interviews with industry experts.

211 CFPB estimate using data from industry sources.

212 Ginnie Mae's HMBS program was announced on August 31, 2007 and became effective the following day. *See* Ginnie Mae All Participants Memorandum 07-12, Introducing the Home Equity Conversion Mortgage and Mortgage-Backed Securities (Aug. 31, 2007), available at http://www.ginniemae.gov/apm/apm_pdf/07-12.pdf.

213 Ginnie Mae Mortgage-Backed Securities Handbook 5500.3, Rev.1, Ch. 35-10(B)(1) (July 1, 2011) ("Mandatory Purchase Event: The Issuer is required to purchase all Ginnie Participations related to a HECM loan when the outstanding principal balance of the HECM loan is equal to or greater than 98% of the Maximum Claim Amount.").

214 CFPB interviews with industry participants.

215 24 CFR § 206.107(a)(1)(iv).

216 FHA Mortgagee Letter 2011-01. Specialty servicers are available to provide customer service on a subcontracted basis if the issuer prefers not to service loans itself. However, under Ginnie Mae requirements, the issuer remains the servicer of record and bears financial responsibility for buying the loan out of the pool when it reaches 98 percent of the maximum claim amount. *See* Ginnie Mae Mortgage-Backed Securities Handbook 5500.3, Rev.1, Ch. 35-10(B)(1) (July 1, 2011). Once bought out of the pool, the loan is no longer subject to Ginnie Mae requirements though it remains subject to FHA requirements. If the loan is not assignable to FHA due to a default situation and the issuer-servicer did not want to hold the loan until maturity, the issuer-servicer could conceivably sell the loan to another FHA-approved lender-servicer – if a willing buyer and a mutually agreeable price can be found.

217 The HECM Statute and published HECM regulations are silent on the question of whether HECMs may be closed-end or open-end. However, in the first year of the program, HUD issued a Mortgagee Letter stating that "Because a HUD insured reverse mortgage permits the borrower to use a line of credit, the mortgage is deemed to be 'open-end credit' under the Truth-in-Lending Act's Regulation Z (12 CFR 226) as amended by 54 FR 24670." FHA Mortgagee Letter 1990-17.

218 Fannie Mae Reverse Mortgage Lender Letter 2008-2 (Aug. 1, 2008) ("Introduction of the Fixed-Rate HECM. Effective November 3, 2008, Fannie Mae will accept for purchase closed-end, fully drawn fixed rate HECMs that comply with all relevant Housing and Urban Development regulations and guidance.").

[219] FHA Mortgagee Letter 2008-08.

[220] CFPB interviews with industry participants.

[221] This securitization consisted of adjustable-rate loans and was offered by Goldman Sachs. Goldman was unable to sell the security to investors. Goldman eventually repurchased the loan participations (funded portions) from the securitization trust, terminated the security, and is believed to have re-sold the underlying loans to Fannie Mae. CFPB interviews with industry experts.

[222] Royal Bank of Scotland MBS Strategy Primer, GNMA HECM Primer and Relative Value (Feb. 28, 2011).

[223] Today, all adjustable-rate loans use the one-month LIBOR as the interest rate index and the 10-year LIBOR Swap Rate as the index for the "expected rate." Historically, the one-year Constant Maturity Treasury (CMT) was used as the interest rate index and the 10-year CMT was used as the index for the expected rate. FHA authorized the switch to LIBOR in October 2007 with FHA Mortgagee Letter 2007-13. Adoption of the LIBOR index was slow at first but picked up dramatically in January 2009 and had reached more than 90 percent market share by May 2009 and nearly 100 percent market share by August 2009. *See* CFPB Analysis of FHA Loan-Level HECM Data, endnote 2.

[224] One reason that lower underlying interest rates would lead to higher margins has to do with the FHA underwriting floor, discussed in greater detail in Section 4.5.1. In early 2009, the "expected rate" for underwriting purposes had fallen below this floor, which meant that lenders could increase margins without affecting the proceeds that borrowers received. *See* John Yedinak, *Financial Freedom Eliminates HECM 150, Reverse Mortgage Margins Trend Higher*, Reverse Mortgage Daily (Aug. 12, 2008), available at http://reverse mortgagedaily.com/2008/08/12/financial-freedom-eliminates-hecm-150-reverse-mortgage-margins-trend-higher/; John Yedinak, *New Year Brings Higher Reverse Mortgage Margins*, Reverse Mortgage Daily (Jan. 12, 2009), available at http://reversemortgagedaily.com/2009/01/12/new-year-brings-higher-reverse-mortgage-margins/; Edmund Andrews, *U.S. Details $800 Billion Loan Plan*, New York Times (Nov. 25, 2008), available at http://www.nytimes.com/2008/11/26/business/economy/26fed.html?_r=1&ref= quantitativeeasing.

[225] John Yedinak, *Fannie Mae Pricing Change Brings Higher Margins for Reverse Mortgages*, Reverse Mortgage Daily (Mar. 27, 2009), available at http://reversemortgagedaily.com/ 2009/03/27/fannie-mae-pricing-change-brings-higher-margins-for-reverse-mortgages/.

[226] *See* CFPB Analysis of FHA Loan-Level HECM Data, endnote 2.

[227] CFPB interviews with industry experts.

[228] The re-securitizations are known as H-REMICs and allow for a wider range of cash flow structures and risk profiles to be created from a set of underlying HMBS pools. The first H-REMIC was issued in November 2009, but the program was announced in April 2008. *See* Ginnie Mae All Participants Memorandum 08-06, Inclusion of Home Equity Conversion Mortgage-Backed Securities as Eligible Collateral for the Ginnie Mae Multiclass Securities Program (Apr. 29, 2008), available at http://www.ginniemae.gov/mpm/mpm_pdf/08-06.pdf; Royal Bank of Scotland MBS Strategy Primer, GNMA HECM Primer and Relative Value (Feb. 28, 2011).

[229] Royal Bank of Scotland MBS Strategy Primer, GNMA HECM Primer and Relative Value (Feb. 28, 2011).

[230] Fannie Mae, 10-Q filing with the Securities and Exchange Commission (Nov. 5, 2009).

[231] CFPB interviews with industry participants.

[232] The floor rate is applicable to the interest rate *used to underwrite for proceeds*, not the interest rate on the loan. For fixed-rate loans, these are the same thing. For adjustable-rate loans, the higher "expected" rate is used for proceeds underwriting purposes. *See* Section 4.4.4.

[233] Proceeds are inversely proportional to interest rates, so a floor on interest rates creates a ceiling on proceeds.

[234] FHA Mortgagee Letter 2010-34.

[235] Lenders, counselors, and others interviewed for this study agree that this is true of reverse mortgage borrowers when taken as a whole. As discussed in Section 3.3, certain subgroups, particularly the oldest borrowers and those with higher home values, may be less sensitive to the dollar amount of proceeds than the overall borrower population.

[236] CFPB interviews with industry participants.

[237] CFPB interviews with industry participants.

[238] CFPB interviews with industry participants; *see also* John Yedinak, *Security One Lending Releases New HECM Fixed Product Without SFSA*, Reverse Mortgage Daily (Mar. 17, 2010), available at http://reversemortgage daily.com/2010/03/17/security-one-lending-releases-new-hecm-fixed-product-without-sfsa/; John Yedinak, *Genworth Eliminates Servicing Fee for Fixed Rate Mortgage*, Reverse Mortgage Daily (Mar. 22, 2010), available at http://reversemortgagedaily.com/2010/03/22/genworth-eliminates-servicing-fee-for-fixed -rate-reverse-mortgage/.

[239] *See* CFPB Analysis of FHA Loan-Level HECM Data, endnote 2.

[240] John Yedinak, *Wells Fargo Eliminates Servicing and Origination Fee for Adjustable Rate HECM*, Reverse Mortgage Daily (Apr. 13, 2010), available at http://reversemortgagedaily. com/2010/04/13/wells-fargo-eliminates-servicing-and-origination-fee-for-adjustable-rate-hecm/.

[241] *See* CFPB Analysis of FHA Loan-Level HECM Data, endnote 2; *see also* John Yedinak, *Bank of America Rolls Out No Servicing Fee Adjustable Rate HECM for Wholesale*, Reverse Mortgage Daily (Sept. 7, 2010),

available at http://reversemortgagedaily.com/2010/09/07/ bank-of-america-rolls-out-no-servicing-fee-adjustable-rate-hecm-for-wholesale/.

[242] John Yedinak, *No Reverse Mortgage Origination Fee Trend, Will it Last?*, Reverse Mortgage Daily (Apr. 1, 2010), available at http://reversemortgagedaily.com/2010/04/01/no-reverse-mortgage-origination-fee-trend-will-it-last/.

[243] John Yedinak, *Bank of America Paying Entire Upfront Mortgage MIP on Fixed Rate Reverse Mortgages*, Reverse Mortgage Daily (May 6, 2010), available at http://reversemortgage daily.com/2010/05/06/bank-of-america-paying-entire-upfront-mip-on-fixed-rate-reverse-mortgages/.

[244] The expected rate is the lender's margin plus the 10-year LIBOR swap rate.

[245] *See* Section 2.4.2 and Section 6.9.1 for more discussion.

[246] CFPB interviews with industry participants.

[247] CFPB interviews with industry participants.

[248] As explained in Section 4.5.1, as underlying interest rates have continued to slide, the "expected" rate used to underwrite adjustable-rate securities fell below the floor in late 2011. In response, lenders were able to increase the margin without decreasing proceeds. Higher margins fetch higher premiums in the secondary market.

[249] Royal Bank of Scotland MBS Strategy Primer, GNMA HECM Primer and Relative Value (Feb. 28, 2011).

[250] According to interviews with industry experts, this is one of the reasons given for lower secondary market premiums on adjustable-rate loans. As discussed in Section 3.4.1, there is an emerging segmentation among fixed-rate borrowers and adjustable-rate borrowers, and investors are concerned that today's adjustable-rate borrowers may not exhibit the same prepayment behavior as fixed-rate borrowers.

[251] CFPB interviews with major lender-issuers.

[252] CFPB interviews with industry participants.

[253] As of April 2012, wholesale lenders and aggregator-issuers paid their brokers and correspondent lenders a premium of between 7 percent and 9 percent of the loan balance on fixed-rate loans, and a premium of between 3 percent and 5 percent of the (lower) loan balance on adjustable-rate loans.

[254] CFPB interviews with industry participants.

[255] Unless it becomes a standard market practice to pay brokers and correspondent lenders based on a metric that is less sensitive to loan balance at time of closing, issuers that do so risk becoming the issuer of choice for low-balance loans (because they pay comparatively better than other issuers) and the issuer of last resort for high-balance loans (because they pay comparatively worse than other issuers which reward high loan balances more richly).

[256] CFPB interviews with industry participants.

[257] 12 C.F.R. § 1026.36(d)(2).

[258] CFPB interviews with industry participants; industry rate sheets obtained by the CFPB.

[259] However, steering borrowers based on which type of loan yields greater compensation could implicate the MLO compensation rule. *See* 12 C.F.R. § 1026.36(e). Further, it could implicate the MLO compensation rule for a loan originator to receive or a person to pay a loan originator, directly or indirectly, compensation for originating a closed end reverse mortgage that is based on any of the transaction's terms or conditions. *See* 12 C.F.R. § 1026.36(d)(1).

[260] CFPB interviews with industry participants.

[261] Many reverse mortgage lenders are also subject to enforcement actions by the CFPB under the unfair, deceptive, or abusive acts or practices provision of the Dodd-Frank Act § 1031. Some reverse mortgage lenders may also be subject to enforcement actions by the FTC under the unfair and deceptive acts or practices provision of the Federal Trade Commission Act, 15 U.S.C § 45.

[262] 12 C.F.R. § 1026.19(b)(1).

[263] 12 C.F.R. § 1026.40(e). [264] 12 C.F.R. § 1026.5b(b). [265] 12 C.F.R. § 1026.6.

[266] The HELOC Brochure is available online at http://www.federalreserve.gov/pubs/equity/equity _english.htm.

[267] 15 U.S.C. § 1648 (2011); 12 C.F.R. § 1026.33; 12 C.F.R. § 1026, App K. A sample of the model form in Appendix K to Regulation Z is appended to this report in Appendix II.

[268] 12 C.F.R. § 1026.33.

[269] 75 Fed. Reg. 58544.

[270] 75 Fed. Reg. 58544.

[271] 75 Fed. Reg. 58544.

[272] 75 Fed. Reg. 58509.

[273] 75 Fed. Reg. 58535.

[274] 12 C.F.R. § 1026.36(d)(1)(i).

[275] 12 C.F.R. § 1026.36(d)(1)(ii).

[276] 12 C.F.R. § 1026(d)(2).

[277] However, steering borrowers based on which type of loan yields greater loan originator compensation could implicate the MLO compensation rules *See* 12 C.F.R. § 1026.36(d)(1); 12 C.F.R. § 1026.36(e).

[278] 12 C.F.R. § 1024.7.

[279] 12 C.F.R. § 1024.8.

[280] The RESPA Rule FAQs were last updated January 28, 2010 and are available online at http://www.hud.gov/offices/hsg/ramh/res/resparulefaqs.pdf.

[281] 12 C.F.R. § 1024.2.

[282] 12 C.F.R. § 1024.14.

[283] 12 C.F.R. pt. 1002, Supp. I, § 1002.6, ¶ 6(b)(2)-4 (allows creditors to offer reverse mortgages that require the borrower to be age 62 or older, and to consider age in evaluating a pertinent element of creditworthiness, such as the amount of credit or monthly payments the borrower will receive).

[284] *See* Bennett v. Donovan, No. 11-cv-00498 (ESH), 2011 U.S. Dist. LEXIS 76470 (D.D.C. July 15, 2011) (finding that plaintiffs lacked standing to pursue claims that lenders' failure to comply with the HECM statute (Pub. L. No. 100-242, 101 Stat. 1815 (1988); 12 U.S.C. 1715z-20 subjected the plaintiffs to foreclosure actions that would not have been permissible if the lenders complied with the statute because a decision that HUD did not properly insure the reverse mortgages would not necessarily redress the harm suffered by the plaintiffs); *see also* Gass v. Wells Fargo & Co., No 15713/11, 2012 N.Y. Misc. LEXIS 1335 (Sup. Ct., Queens Cty., Mar. 22, 2012) (dismissing claims brought under the HECM Statute on the basis that the statute does not include language creating a private right of action and provides no basis on which the court can imply a private right of action).

[285] Pub. L. No. 100-242, 101 Stat. 1815 (1988); 12 U.S.C. 1715z-20 (HECM Statute).

[286] Department of Veterans Affairs and Housing and Urban Development, and Independent Agencies Appropriations Act of 1999, Pub. L. No. 105-276 § 593(c)(1), 112 Stat. 2461 (codified as amended at 12 U.S.C. §§ 1715z-20(g)).

[287] Department of Defense Appropriations Act 2007, Pub. L. No. 109-289 §131 (2006).

[288] Consolidated and Future Continuing Appropriations Act 2012, HR 2112 – 147 (Jan. 5, 2011), available at http://www.gpo.gov/fdsys/pkg/BILLS-112hr2112enr/pdf/BILLS-112hr2112enr. pdf.

[289] 12 U.S.C. § 1715z-20; 24 C.F.R. § 206.1, et seq.

[290] 12 U.S.C. § 1715z-20(c).

[291] Housing and Economic Recovery Act of 2008, Pub. L. No. 110-289, 122 Stat. 2654 (2008) (codified at 12 U.S.C. § 1715z-20). [HERA]

[292] *See* HERA (codified at 12 U.S.C. § 1715z-20(o)).

[293] *See* HERA (codified at 12 U.S.C. § 1715z-20(n)).

[294] Cal. Assembly Bill No. 329 (introduced Feb. 18, 2009); La. House Bill 792 (introduced May 4, 2010).

[295] *See* 12 U.S.C. 5101, et seq.; 12 CFR 1008, et seq.

[296] Iowa Code § 528.6.

[297] Mass. Gen. Laws. ch. 167E § 7(d).

[298] Wash. Rev. Code 31.04.525.

[299] Vt. Stat. Ann. tit. 8 § 10704. Allowances for other federal reverse mortgage programs created by the government similar to the HECM program are made.

[300] Texas was the last to allow reverse mortgage lending programs. *See* First Gibraltar Bank, FSB v. Morales, 42 F.3d 895, 897 (5th Cir. 1995).

[301] Massachusetts Division of Banks, *Reverse Mortgage Products: Guidance for Managing Compliance and Reputation Risks*, Regulatory Bulletin 5.1-106 (Dec. 15, 2010), available at http://www.mass.gov/ocabr/government/oca-agencies/dob-lp/division-of-banks-issues-regulatory-bulletin.html; Maryland Commissioner of Financial Regulation Reverse Mortgage Guidance Advisory (Jan. 12, 2010), available at http://www.dllr.maryland.gov/finance/advisories/advisory-jan122010.shtml.

[302] 75 Fed. Reg. 50801. The FFIEC guidance is publicly available online at http://www.ffiec. gov/pdf/FFIEC _Reverse_Mortgages_FR_notice_081610.pdf.

[303] 75 Fed. Reg. 58539.

[304] Copies of the proposed disclosures are appended to this report in Appendix II.

[305] 75 Fed. Reg. 58550.

[306] 75 Fed. Reg. 58645. A copy of the TALC rate table is appended to this report in Appendix II.

[307] Nearly a quarter of Americans aged 71 and over have a mild cognitive impairment. Financial capacity is one of the first abilities to wane as cognitive impairment encroaches – but often goes undetected. Another concern for those with mild cognitive impairment is that the ability to maintain the judgment to act prudently gradually declines. *See* Brenda L. Plassman et al., *Prevalence of Cognitive Impairment without Dementia in the United States*, Archives of Internal Medicine 148: 6 (2008); Eric Widera et al., *Finances in the Older Patient with Cognitive Impairment: He Didn't Want Me to Take Over*, Journal of the American Medical Association 305: 7 (2011); Naomi Karp and Ryan Wilson, *Protecting Older Investors: The Challenge of Diminished Capacity*, AARP Public Policy Institute (Nov. 4, 2011), available at http://www.aarp.org/content/dam/aarp/research/public_policy_ institute/cons_prot/2011/rr2011- 04.pdf.

[308] *See, e.g.*, Tara Twomey and Rick Jurgens, National Consumer Law Center, *Subprime Revisited: How Reverse Mortgage Lenders Put Older Homeowners' Equity at Risk* (Oct. 2009), available at www.nclc.org/images/pdf/pr-reports/report-reverse-mortgages-2009.pdf [NCLC 2009]; Norma Paz Garcia et al., Consumers Union,

Examining Faulty Foundations in Today's Reverse Mortgages (Dec. 7, 2010), available at http://www.consumersunion.org/ pdf/reverse-mortgage-report-2010.pdf.

[309] United States Government Accountability Office, Product Complexity and Consumer Protection Issues Underscore Need for Improved Controls over Counseling for Borrowers, p. 11 (June 2009). [GAO 2009]

[310] *See* AARP 2006 Survey, endnote 113.

[311] *See* GAO 2009 at 11, endnote 309 ("Because HECM borrowers do not make monthly payments to the lender, borrowers are responsible for the total amount of servicing fees, interest charges, and monthly mortgage insurance premiums accrued over the life of the loan, as well as any financed origination fees and up-front insurance premiums, when the loan becomes due.Therefore, the longer the borrower has the loan, the longer the borrower benefits from access to home equity without experiencing any of the costs."); id. at 14 (discussing how some borrowers did not understand monthly servicing charges and that interest rates on the loan was variable and could increase over time).

[312] Oren Bar-Gill, *The Law, Economics and Psychology of Subprime Mortgage Contracts*, Cornell Law Review 94:1073, p. 1079 (2009) (discussing subprime mortgage contracts). [Oren Bar-Gill 2009]

[313] *See* Oren Bar-Gill 2009 ("Imperfectly rational borrowers will not be able to effectively aggregate multiple price and nonprice dimensions and discern from them the true total cost of the mortgage product."); David Laibson, *Golden Eggs and Hyperbolic Discounting*, Quarterly Journal of Economics 112:2, pp. 444-445 (May 1997) (explaining that it is difficult to realize immediate benefits from long-term investments like a home or savings bond); Richard H. Thaler, *Anomolies: Saving, Fungibility, and Mental Accounts*, Journal of Economic Perspectives 4:1 (1990) (explaining that consumers have different marginal propensities to consume for different assets); Shlomo Benartzi and Richard H. Thaler, *Heuristics and Biases in Retirement Savings Behavior*, Journal of Economic Perspectives 21:3(2007) (finding that retirement savings plan consumers with many choices use shortcuts rather than determining the most valuable choice).

[314] High costs appear to be a determining factor in whether an individual decides to take out a reverse mortgage. AARP surveyed potential borrowers who received HECM counseling and decided against taking out a reverse mortgage. They found that the number one reason counseled individuals decided against obtaining a reverse mortgage was the high cost. *See* AARP 2006 Survey at 74, endnote 113.

[315] *See* GAO 2009 at 11, endnote 309.

[316] *See* GAO 2009 at 3, endnote 309.

[317] *See* GAO 2009 at 22-23, endnote 309.

[318] *See, e.g.,* Ark. Code § 23-54-104; Cal. Civ. Code § 1923.2; La. Rev. Stat. § 6:1101.

[319] *See* Ark. Code § 23-54-104; Cal. Civ. Code § 1923.2; Colo. Rev. Stat. § 11-38-109; Minn. Stat. § 47.58; N.C. Gen. Stat. § 53-264; Tenn. Code § 47-30-109.

[320] *See* Mass. Gen. Laws 167E § 7; Mass. Gen. Laws 171 § 65C; Mo. Rev. Stat. § 443.903; SC ST § 29-4-30; SD ST 54-12-21; W. Va. Code § 47-24-4.

[321] Ariz. Rev. Stat. § 6-1703.

[322] Md. Code § 12-1207; Mass. Gen. Laws § 167E § 7; Mont. Code § 90-6-505; N.Y. RPP. Law § 280; Tenn. Code § 47-30-109.

[323] In the Matter of American Advisors Group, Irvine, California, No. 2008-22 (Oct. 21, 2008), Exhibit A, available at http://www.mass.gov/ocabr/docs/dob/aagexhibit1.pdf.

[324] People of Illinois v. Illinois v. American Advisors Groups, Inc., No. 2010-CH-158, Complaint for Injunctive and Other Relief (Feb. 8, 2010).

[325] In the Matter of American Advisors Group, Irvine, California, No. 2008-22 (Oct. 21, 2008), available at http://www.mass.gov/ocabr/business/banking-services/banking-legal-resources/ enforcement-actions/2008-enforcement-actions/american-advisors-group-irvine-ca-.html.

[326] In the Matter of American Advisors Group, Irvine, California, No. 2008-22-CO (Oct. 21, 2008), available at http://www.mass.gov/ocabr/business/banking-services/banking-legal-resources/enforcement-actions/2008-enforcement-actions/american-advisors-group-irvine-ca-consent.html.

[327] People of Illinois v. American Advisors Group, No. 2010-CH-158, Agreed Order and Consent Decree (Feb. 7, 2011).

[328] People of Illinois v. American Advisors Group, No. 2010-CH-158, Agreed Order and Consent Decree (Feb. 7, 2011).

[329] In the Matter of Eldervantage, LLC and Reversemortgagepage.com, Cease Directive (Aug. 23, 2011), available at http://www.mass.gov/ocabr/business/banking-services/banking-legal-resources/enforcement-actions/2011-dob-enforcement-actions/eldervantage-llc-and-reverse mortgagepagecom.html; In the Matter of Lender 411, LLC, Cease Directive (Aug. 23, 2011), available at http://www.mass.gov/ocabr/business/banking-services/ banking-legal-resources/enforcement-actions/2011-dob-enforcement-actions/lender-411-llc-orange-ca-cease-directive.html; In the Matter of Senior Reverse Mortgage Online, Cease Directive (Aug. 23, 2011), available at http://www.mass.gov/ocabr/business/banking-services/banking-legal-resources/enforcement-actions/2011-dob -enforcement-actions/senior-reverse-mortgage-online-houston-tx-.html; In the Matter of Reverse Mortgage Helpdesk, Cease Directive (Aug. 23, 2011), available at http://www.mass.gov/ocabr/business/banking-

services/banking-legal-resources/enforcement-actions/2011-dob-enforcement-actions/reverse-mortgage-helpdesk-las-vegas-nv-.html.

[330] In the Matter of Eldervantage, LLC and Reversemortgagepage.com, Cease Directive (Aug. 23, 2011), available at http://www.mass.gov/ocabr/business/banking-services/banking-legal-resources/enforcement-actions/2011-dob-enforcement-actions/eldervantage-llc-and-reversemortgagepagecom.html;
In the Matter of Lender 411, LLC, Cease Directive (Aug. 23, 2011), available at http://www. mass.gov/ocabr/business/banking-services/banking-legal-resources/enforcement-actions/2011-dob-enforcement-actions/lender-411-llc-orange-ca-cease-directive.html;
In the Matter of Senior Reverse Mortgage Online, Cease Directive (Aug. 23, 2011), available at http://www. mass.gov/ocabr/business/banking-services/banking-legal-resources/enforcement-actions/2011-dob-enforcement-actions/senior-reverse-mortgage-online-houston-tx-.html; In the Matter of Reverse Mortgage Helpdesk, Cease Directive (Aug. 23, 2011), available at http://www.mass.gov/ocabr/business/banking-services/banking-legal-resources/enforcement-actions/2011-dob-enforcement-actions/reverse-mortgage-helpdesk-las-vegas-nv-.html.

[331] In the Matter of Eldervantage, LLC and Reversemortgagepage.com, Cease Directive (Aug. 23, 2011), available at http://www.mass.gov/ocabr/business/banking-services/banking-legal-resources/enforcement-actions/2011-dob-enforcement-actions/eldervantage-llc-and-reversemortgagepagecom.html.

[332] In the Matter of Lender 411, LLC, Cease Directive (Aug. 23, 2011), available at http://www.mass.gov/ocabr/business/banking-services/banking-legal-resources/enforcement-actions/2011-dob-enforcement-actions/lender -411-llc-orange-ca-cease-directive.html.

[333] *See* 950 Mass. Code Regs. § 12.204(2)(i); 950 Mass. Code Regs. § 12.205(9)(c)(15); Administrative Record from the Commonwealth of Massachusetts Securities Division, available at http://www.sec.state.ma.us/sct/sctpropreg/adminrec.pdf (discussing reasons for and objectives of new regulations regarding use of senior designations); NCLC 2009, endnote 308.

[334] *See, e.g.*, 950 Mass. Code Regs. § 12.204(2)(i); 950 Mass. Code Regs. § 12.205(9)(c)(15); N.H. Rev. Stat. § 421-B:6; NCLC 2009, endnote 308.

[335] *See, e.g*, Minn. Stat. § 72A.204; Utah Admin. Code R590-252-1 et. seq. [336] *See* NCLC 2009, endnote 308. [337] Consumer submissions to the CFPB, 2011-2012.

[338] 75 Fed. Reg. 58655. The Board's proposed rule also states that a reverse mortgage advertisement that refers to housing or credit counseling must state a telephone number and website for housing counseling resources maintained by HUD.

[339] Many reverse mortgage lenders are also subject to enforcement actions by the CFPB under the unfair, deceptive, or abusive acts or practices provision of the Dodd-Frank Act § 1031. Some reverse mortgage lenders may also be subject to enforcement actions by the FTC under the unfair and deceptive acts or practices provision of the Federal Trade Commission Act § 5.

[340] *See, e.g.*, NCLC 2009, endnote 308; Reverse Mortgages: Polishing not Tarnishing the Golden, Years Senate: Hearing Before the Senate Special Committee on Aging (Dec. 12, 2007), available at http://aging.senate.gov/publications/12122007.pdf.

[341] For examples of definitions and restrictions on cross-selling, *see* 12 U.S.C. 1715z-20(n)(1); Md. Code § 12-1206(b); R.I. Gen. Laws § 34-25.1-7(7); Vt. Stat. tit. 8 § 10703; Wash. Rev. Code § 31.04.515(7).

[342] Housing and Economic Recovery Act of 2008, Pub. L. 110-289, 122 Stat. 2837 (2008) (codified at 12 U.S.C. § 1715z-20(n)(1)).

[343] *See, e.g.*, Md. Code § 12-1206(b); R.I. Gen. Laws § § 34-25.1-7(7); Vt. Stat. Ann. tit. 8 § 10703; Wash. Rev. Code § 31.04.515(7).

[344] *See, e.g.*, GAO 2009 at 25-29, endnote 309; Reverse Mortgages: Polishing not Tarnishing the Golden Years Senate: Hearing Before the Senate Special Committee on Aging (Dec. 12, 2007), available at http://aging. senate.gov/publications/12122007.pdf; Building Sustainable Homeownership: Responsible Lending and Informed Consumer Choice, Public Hearing on the Home Equity Lending Market before the Federal Reserve Bank of San Francisco (June 2006).

[345] Housing and Economic Recovery Act of 2008, Pub. L. No. 110-289, 122 Stat. 2654 (2008) (codified as 12 U.S.C. § 1715z-20(o)). HERA excludes from the prohibition against requiring the purchase of other products "title insurance, hazard, flood, or other peril insurance, or other such products that are customary and normal[.]"

[346] Housing and Economic Recovery Act of 2008, Pub. L. No. 110-289, 122 Stat. 2654 (2008) (codified as 12 U.S.C. § 1715z-20(n)); FHA Mortgagee Letter 2008-24.

[347] Cal. Civ. Code § 1923.2(i); Cal. Ins. Code § 785.1(a)(1); Massachusetts Division of Banks, *Reverse Mortgage Products: Guidance for Managing Compliance and Reputation Risks*, Regulatory Bulletin 5.1-106 (Dec. 15, 2010), available at http://www.mass.gov/ocabr/government/oca-agencies/dob-lp/division-of-banks-issues-regulatory-bulletin.html.

[348] Md. Code § 12-1206(b); R.I. Gen. Laws § 34-25.1-7(7); Vt. Stat. Ann. tit. 8 § 10703; Wash. Rev. Code § 31.04.515(7).

[349] Subject to certain exception for certain bank products, such as deposits or trust services.

[350] 12 U.S.C. § 1831(x).

[351] 75 Fed. Reg. 58666. The Board's proposed rule excluded from the definition of "financial or insurance product" two types of products and services: "(1) transaction accounts and savings deposit accounts . . . that are established to disburse the reverse mortgage proceeds; and (2) products and services customarily required to protect the creditor's interest in the collateral or otherwise mitigate the creditor's risk of loss" such as appraisals or other property evaluation services, title insurance, flood, homeowner's insurance, and mortgage insurance.

[352] *See* Conference of State Bank Supervisors, American Council of State Savings Supervisors, and American Association of Residential Mortgage Regulators, Comment Letter to Federal Reserve Board Proposed Rule to Amend Regulation Z, Docket No. R-1390, 12 C.F.R. Part 226: Truth in Lending 73 (Dec. 22, 2010) (supporting the safe harbor but purporting that the 10 day period is too short); National Reverse Mortgage Lenders Association, Mortgage Bankers Association, and American Bankers Association, Comment Letter to Federal Reserve Board Proposed Rule to Amend Regulation Z, Docket No. R-1390, 12 C.F.R. Part 226: Truth in Lending 73 (Dec. 22, 2010) (suggesting that in addition to the safe harbor protection, creditors should not have to provide annuity cost disclosures if the borrower indicates that they will not use reverse mortgage proceeds to purchase an annuity).

[353] *See* National Community Reinvestment Coalition, Comment Letter to Federal Reserve Board Proposed Rule to Amend Regulation Z, Docket No. R-1390, 12 C.F.R. Part 226: Truth in Lending 73 (Dec. 21, 2010) ("The safe harbor will completely undermine the ban. It would seem that all an unscrupulous lender has to do is wait for the 11th day and then aggressively cross sell a problematic product."); National Consumer Law Center, Comment Letter to Federal Reserve Board Proposed Rule to Amend Regulation Z, Docket No. R-1390, 12 C.F.R. Part 226: Truth in Lending 73 (Dec. 23, 2010) ("[T]he safe harbor proposed for cross-selling products is unjustified and purports to make some predatory creditor behavior legal when it is already illegal under other law."); AARP, Comment Letter to Federal Reserve Board Proposed Rule to Amend Regulation Z, Docket No. R-1390, 12 C.F.R. Part 226: Truth in Lending 73 (Dec. 23, 2010) ("AARP strongly opposes the inclusion of a 'safe harbor' that would effectively open the door for the 'cross-selling' of any financial or insurance products to a reverse mortgage borrower so long as it is done 10 days after the loan has been made.").

[354] Housing and Community Development Act of 1987, Pub. L. No. 100-242 § 593, 101 Stat. 1815.

[355] FHA Mortgagee Letter 2011-09.

[356] *See* HECM Counseling Protocol, Housing Counseling Handbook, 7610.1 REV-5, Appendix 4, available at http://www.hud.gov/offices/adm/hudclips/handbooks/hsgh/7610.1/76101 HSGH.pdf.

[357] Consumer submissions to the CFPB, 2011-2012.

[358] Consumer submissions to the CFPB, 2011-2012.

[359] *See* GAO 2009, endnote 309.

[360] *See* GAO 2009 at 48, endnote 309.

[361] FHA HECM Counseling Protocol, available at http://portal.hud.gov/hudportal/documents/ huddoc?id=7610-0_COMBINED.PDF.

[362] *See* Shlomo Benartzi and Richard H. Thaler, *Heuristics and Biases in Retirement Savings Behavior*, Journal of Economic Perspectives 21:3 (2007).

[363] Oversight of the Federal Housing Administration's Reverse Mortgage Program for Seniors: Hearing Before the House Subcommittee on Insurance, Housing, and Community Opportunity (May 9, 2012) (statement of Lori Trawinski, Senior Strategic Policy Advisor, AARP Public Policy Institute).

[364] CFPB interviews with HECM counselors and consumer advocates.

[365] FHA Mortgagee Letter 2008-12 ("A client must not be turned away because of an inability to pay.").

[366] FHA Mortgagee Letter 2008-12 ("The cost of HECM counseling can be paid out of a HECM borrower's loan proceeds.").

[367] *See* 74 Fed. Reg. 45311; FHA Mortgagee Letter 2009-47; John Yedinak, *HUD Implements HECM Counseling Roster and Testing Standards*, Reverse Mortgage Daily (Nov. 10, 2009), available at http://reversemortgage daily.com/2009/11/10/hud-implements-hecm-counseling-roster-and-testing-standards/.

[368] These requirements were codified in the HECM regulations. *See* 24 CFR § 206.300 et seq.

[369] Housing Counseling Handbook, HECM Counseling Protocol 7610.1 REV-5, Appendix 4, available at http://www.hud.gov/offices/adm/hudclips/handbooks/hsgh/7610.1/76101 HSGH.pdf; HUD Letter, Mortgage Counseling Toolkit (Aug. 27, 2010), available at http://www.hud.gov/offices/hsg/sfh/hcc/msgs/20100827.txt.

[370] Cal. Civ. Code § 1923.2 and § 1923.5 Form 2; Md. Code § 12-1207.

[371] *See, e.g.*, Ill. Comp. Stat. 205 § 5/6.1; N.Y. Real Prop. § 280-a; S.C. Code § 29-4-60.

[372] Col. Rev. Stat. § 11-38-111.

[373] La. Rev. Stat § 6:1102.

[374] N.C. Gen. Stat. § 53-264; N.C. Gen. Stat. § 53-269; 24 N.C. Admin. Code 1N.0202; Mass. Gen. Laws 167E § 7A; 8 V.S.A. § 10702.

[375] N.C. Gen. Stat. § 53-264; N.C. Gen. Stat. § 53-269; 24 N.C. Admin. Code 1N.0202. [376] 8 V.S.A. § 10702. [377] Mass. Gen. Laws 167E § 7A.

[378] Cal. Assembly Bill No. 2010 (introduced Feb. 23, 2012); Georgia Assembly Bill No. 338 (introduced Feb. 24, 2012).

[379] Housing and Economic Recovery Act of 2008, Pub. L. No. 110-289, 122 Stat. 2654 (2008) (codified at 12 U.S.C. § 1715z-20).

[380] *See* AARP 2010 at 1, endnote 89 ("[D]ue to high upfront costs, reverse mortgages can be especially costly if you sell and move just a few years after taking one out."); Norma Paz Garcia et al., Consumers Union, *Examining Faulty Foundations in Today's Reverse Mortgages*, p. 6 (2010) (citing "reverse mortgages are expensive" as a reverse mortgage drawback), available at http://www.consumersunion.org/pdf/reverse-mortgage-report-2010.pdf; Kenneth Harney, *Proposed Guidelines for Reverse Mortgages Spell Out Potential Pitfalls for Homeowners*, Los Angeles Times (Dec. 27, 2009) (cautioning that "reverse mortgages often entail high upfront fees and substantial insurance and servicing charges"); Jonathan Clements, *The Costly, Restrictive Mortgage That Could Save Your Retirement*, Wall Street Journal (Dec. 17, 2003) ("One glance at these loans, and you will likely suffer severe sticker shock. Reverse mortgages, which allow those aged 62 and up to borrow against their home's value without making any repayments during their lifetime, are pretty darnn expensive."); id. (citing a financial planner's comments that "[t]he fees are just exorbitant. But if you don't have any other choice, you don't have any other choice").

[381] *See* AARP 2006 Survey at 107, endnote 113.

[382] *See* AARP 2006 Survey at 80, endnote 113.

[383] Consumer submissions to the CFPB, 2011-2012.

[384] Housing and Economic Recovery Act of 2008, Pub. L. No. 110-289, 122 Stat. 2838 (2008); FHA Mortgagee Letter 2008-34.

[385] *See* John Yedinak, *Wells Fargo Eliminates Servicing and Origination Fee for Adjustable Rate HECM*, Reverse Mortgage Daily (Apr. 13, 2010), available at http://reversemortgagedaily. com/2010/04/13/wells-fargo-eliminates-servicing-and-origination-fee-for-adjustable-rate-hecm/; John Yedinak, *No Reverse Mortgage Origination Fee Trend, Will it Last?*, Reverse Mortgage Daily (Apr. 1, 2010), available at http://reverse mortgagedaily.com/2010/04/01/noreverse-mortgage-origination-fee-trend-will-it-last/; John Yedinak, *Bank of America Paying Entire Upfront Mortgage MIP on Fixed Rate Reverse Mortgages*, Reverse Mortgage Daily (May 6, 2010), available at http://reversemortgagedaily.com/2010/05/06/bank-of-america-paying-entire-upfrontmip-on-fixed-rate-reverse-mortgages/.

[386] CFPB interviews with industry participants; *see also* John Yedinak, *Security One Lending Releases New HECM Fixed Product Without SFSA*, Reverse Mortgage Daily (Mar. 17, 2010), available at http://reversemortgage daily.com/2010/03/17/security-one-lending-releases-new-hecm-fixed-product-without-sfsa/; John Yedinak, *Genworth Eliminates Servicing Fee for Fixed Rate Mortgage*, Reverse Mortgage Daily (Mar. 22, 2010), available at http://reversemortgagedaily.com/2010/03/22/genworth-eliminates-servicing-fee-for-fixed -rate-reverse-mortgage/.

[387] FHA Mortgagee Letter 2010-34; Press Release, Department of Housing and Urban Development, *HUD Announces New Reverse Mortgage Option* (Sept. 22, 2010) ("Despite the popularity of our HECM loan product, we have noted concerns that some senior citizens find that our fees are too high for them. . . . In response, we created HECM Saver which will provide seniors with a reverse mortgage option that significantly lowers costs by almost eliminating the upfront Mortgage Insurance Premium that is required under the standard HECM option."), available at http://portal.hud.gov/hudportal/HUD?src=/press/press_releases_media_advisories/2010/HUDNo.10-205.

[388] FHA Mortgagee Letter 2010-34.

[389] HECM Savers are subject to lower Principal Limit Factors. *See* discussion in Section 2.4.1 and FHA Mortgagee Letter 2010-34.

[390] FHA Mortgagee Letter 2010-34.

[391] Kelly Green, *Reverse Mortgages Now Look Cheaper*, Wall Street Journal (Apr. 17, 2010) ("Reverse mortgages have long been considered one of the most expensive ways to extract cash from your house. But that is changing as some of the country's biggest reverse-mortgage lenders are slicing closing costs[.]").

[392] HUD Presentation, National Reverse Mortgage Association Annual Meeting (Oct. 25, 2011).

[393] 24 C.F.R. § 206.205(a) ("The mortgagor shall pay all property charges consisting of taxes, ground rents, flood and hazard insurance premiums, and special assessments in a timely manner and shall provide evidence of payment to the mortgagee as required by the mortgage."); 24 C.F.R. § 206.27(b)(5) ("The mortgagor must keep the property in good repair.").

[394] 24 C.F.R. § 206.205(c) ("If the mortgagor fails to pay the property charges in a timely manner, and has not elected to have the mortgagee make the payments, the mortgagee may make the payment for the mortgagor and charge the mortgagor's account.").

[395] HUD Presentation, National Reverse Mortgage Lenders Association Eastern Regional Meeting (Mar. 26, 2012) (estimating that there are now 54,000 HECM loans in default on taxes and/or insurance).

[396] HUD Presentation, National Reverse Mortgage Lenders Association Eastern Regional Meeting (Mar. 26, 2012).

[397] FHA Mortgagee Letter 2011-11 (stating that one of its goals is "to avoid foreclosures as a result of unpaid property charges").

[398] 24 C.F.R. § 206.205(f). According to FHA, lenders sometimes require a set-aside for upcoming property tax or insurance bills when the bill is due shortly after closing, but it is uncommon for borrowers to use, or lenders to require, the use of the property charge set-aside for charges occurring more than one year from the date of closing.

[399] The requirements also do not consider credit history other than delinquent federal debts. *See* HUD Handbook, Home Equity Conversion Mortgages, 4235.1 REV-1 § 4-3(a) ("If the borrower is presently delinquent on any Federal debt…the borrower is not eligible under the delinquent account is brought current, paid or otherwise satisfied[.]").

[400] Consumer submissions to the CFPB, 2011-2012.

[401] FTC Complaints 2011-2012.

[402] FHA Mortgagee Letter 2011-01; 24 C.F.R. § 206.27(c)(2)(iii).

[403] According to FHA, current FHA practice is to reimburse servicers for the corporate advances, so long as the total claim submitted to FHA is not more than the FHA maximum claim amount. Because the claim submitted to FHA is for the *excess* loan balance above and beyond the proceeds from the sale of the home, in most cases the claim amount, including the corporate advances, will fall within the maximum claim amount limit and will be reimbursed to the servicer – so long as the servicer complies with other FHA default servicing requirements. FHA has indicated that further clarification of the treatment of corporate advances will be forthcoming in the future.

[404] Gerald R. Kirkland, HUD Office of Inspector General Audit Report, *HUD Was Not Tracking Almost 13,000 Defaulted HECM Loans With Maximum Claim Amounts of Potentially More Than $2.5 Billion* p.6 (Aug. 25, 2010) ("HUD routinely deferred foreclosure through an informal policy because it indicated that it was unwilling to foreclose on senior citizen borrowers.") [OIG Audit Report]; id. at 6, n. 9 ("HUD's policy was issued via e-mail. HUD was unable to provide a copy.").

[405] OIG Audit Report at 6.

[406] OIG Audit Report at 6.

[407] OIG Audit Report at 6; 24 C.F.R. § 206.125(a)(1) ("The mortgagee shall notify the Secretary whenever the mortgage is due and payable.")

[408] OIG Audit Report at 2. [409] OIG Audit Report at 1. [410] OIG Audit Report at 7. [411] OIG Audit Report at 7. [412] OIG Audit Report at 7.

[413] OIG Audit Report at 7-8. The Audit Report also discusses HUD's evaluation of the property charge issue. This evaluation was based on 11,272 loans. It found that for cases where the amount of loss is significantly greater at the time of loan termination, regardless of whether the loan was called due and payable, the net loss to HUD is $60 million (including 10,865 loans). Id. at 10.

[414] FHA Mortgagee Letter 2011-01.

[415] FHA Mortgagee Letter 2011-01.

[416] These obligations only apply when a borrower has no remaining principal balance. If a borrower has funds remaining, the lender may pay property charges with those funds. The borrower would not be considered in default if their own funds are used to pay the charges. HECM Servicing Frequently Asked Questions, ML 2011-01 (Mar. 30, 2011) ("If the borrower's funds are used to pay property charges, the loan is not considered delinquent."), available at http://portal.hud.gov/hudportal/documents/huddoc?id=ML11-01HECMIndustry FAQ.pdf.

[417] FHA Mortgagee Letter 2011-01.

[418] FHA Mortgagee Letter 2011-01.

[419] FHA Mortgagee Letter 2011-01.

[420] FHA Mortgagee Letter 2011-01.

[421] FHA Mortgagee Letter 2011-01.

[422] The lender then could assign the mortgage under 24 C.F.R. § 206.107, because the borrower would no longer have an unfulfilled obligation. *See* FHA Mortgagee Letter 2011-01 ("When the mortgagor becomes current on all property charges and repays all corporate advances made by the mortgagee to cover property charges, the mortgagor will then be considered in compliance with the terms of the mortgage and if all other FHA requirements have been satisfied, the mortgagee may then request to assign the mortgage to the Department pursuant to 24 C.F.R. § 206.107.").

[423] FHA Mortgagee Letter 2011-01

[424] FHA Mortgagee Letter 2011-01 ("HUD shall require mortgagees to continue loss mitigation efforts when the documentation provided by the mortgagee does not demonstrate an earnest attempt to collaborate with the mortgagor to cure the delinquency."). This guidance denies mortgagees of the option to assign under 24 C.F.R. § 206.107(a)(iv) ("At the mortgagee's option, the mortgagee may forgo assignment of the mortgage and file a claim under any of the circumstances described in §206.123(a)(2)-(5).").

[425] FHA Mortgagee Letter 2011-01 ("Where the mortgagor fails to correct the delinquency and does not proceed to sell the property or execute a deed in lieu of foreclosure, the mortgagee must initiate foreclosure as required under 24 C.F.R. § 206.125(d).").

[426] Oversight of the Federal Housing Administration's Reverse Mortgage Program for Seniors: Hearing before the House Subcommittee on Insurance, Housing, and Community Opportunity (May 9, 2012) (statement of Charles Coulter, Deputy Assistant Secretary for Single Family Programs, Office of Housing, Federal Housing Administration).

[427] Oversight of the Federal Housing Administration's Reverse Mortgage Program for Seniors: Hearing before the House Subcommittee on Insurance, Housing, and Community Opportunity (May 9, 2012) (statement of Charles Coulter, Deputy Assistant Secretary for Single Family Programs, Office of Housing, Federal Housing Administration).

[428] HUD Presentation, National Reverse Mortgage Lenders Association Eastern Regional Meeting (Mar. 26, 2012).

[429] HUD Presentation, National Reverse Mortgage Lenders Association Eastern Regional Meeting (Mar. 26, 2012).

[430] FTC Complaints 2011-2012.

[431] Oversight of the Federal Housing Administration's Reverse Mortgage Program for Seniors: Hearing before the House Subcommittee on Insurance, Housing, and Community Opportunity (May 9, 2012) (statement of Charles Coulter, Deputy Assistant Secretary for Single Family Programs, Office of Housing, Federal Housing Administration), available at http://financialservices.house.gov/UploadedFiles/HHRG-112-BA04-WState-CCoulter-20120509.pdf.

[432] Acting FHA Commissioner Carol Galante, HECM Program Update (Oct. 5, 2011) ("I want to reiterate that HUD's HECM criteria represent the mandatory baseline requirements for approval of a HECM. HUD does not prohibit the inclusion of additional financial capacity and credit assessment criteria and processes in the origination and approval of HECM transactions.").

[433] Elizabeth Ecker, *MetLife Forced to Suspend Financial Assessment as Others Fail to Follow*, Reverse Mortgage Daily (Jan. 25, 2012) (discussing how MetLife suspended financial assessment after brokers brought their business elsewhere), available at http://reverse mortgagedaily.com/2012/01/25/metlife-forced-to-suspend-financial-assessment-as-others-fail-to-follow/.

[434] *See* GAO 2009 at 36-37, endnote 309 (finding that 14 out of 15 housing counselors studied did not explain to borrowers that they could have property charges withheld); FTC Complaints 2011-2012 (some borrowers did not understand that failing to pay property charges could result in loss of their home). The National Reverse Mortgage Lenders Association has been developing a disclosure form that states the borrower's obligations, and how failure to meet those obligations could result in loss of their home.

[435] HUD Presentation, National Reverse Mortgage Lenders Association Annual Meeting (Oct. 25, 2011).

[436] Consumer submissions to the CFPB, 2011-2012.

[437] *See* Bennett v. Donovan, No. 11-cv-00498, 2011 U.S. Dist. LEXIS 76470 (D.D.C. July 15, 2011).

[438] 12 U.S.C. § 1715z-20(j).

[439] 24 C.F.R. § 206.27(c).

[440] Bennett v. Donovan, No. 11-cv-00498, Defendant's Motion to Dismiss Brief, filed April 8, 2011, at 22 - 23.

[441] *See, e.g.,* Ellison v. Wells Fargo Home Mortgage, Inc., No. 09-cv-14175, 2010 U.S. Dist. LEXIS, 108699 (E.D. Mi. Oct. 12, 2010). In *Ellison*, a reverse mortgage applicant's spouse who was below the age threshold transferred all rights to the property to the qualifying spouse, who then obtained a reverse mortgage. The borrowing spouse then attempted to transfer an interest in the premises back to the non-borrower spouse. In an action challenging foreclosure of a reverse mortgage, the court upheld the foreclosure proceedings on the basis that as of the date of the reverse mortgage, the non-borrower spouse had no interest in the property and the later acquired interest was subject to the previously recorded reverse mortgage encumbering the premises. Ellison, 2010 U.S. Dist. LEXIS at **10-11.

[442] *See* Kerrigan v. Bank of America, No. 09-02082, 2011 WL 3565121 (C.D. Cal. Aug. 12, 2011).

[443] Kerrigan v. Bank of America, 2011 WL 3565121 at *5. In *Kerrigan*, the court stated that it finds "particularly significant that the statute which governs HECMs expressly requires that under the terms of the HECM, a 'homeowner's obligation to satisfy the loan obligation is deferred until the homeowner's death' and that the term 'homeowner' 'includes the spouse of a homeowner.'" The court concluded that "[u]nder these circumstances, a misunderstanding on the part of [plaintiff] as to the terms of the HECM and whether "homeowner" included Plaintiff was reasonable."

[444] FHA Mortgagee Letter 2011-31. "Clarification of Signatures on the Certificate: All owners shown on the property deed (or legal representative, in cases involving documented lack of competency) and a non-borrowing spouse must personally receive counseling. The Certificate must be signed and dated by both the counselor, all owners shown on the property deed (or legal representative for cases involving documented lack of competency), and Non-borrowing spouse."

[445] *See* FHA Mortgagee Letter 2011-16.

[446] *See, e.g.,* This section considers fraud as encompassing any criminal misrepresentations in the reverse mortgage context. FBI 2010 Mortgage Fraud Report, p. 5 (Aug. 2011) ("Mortgage fraud is a material misstatement, misrepresentation, or omission relied on by an underwriter or lender to fund, purchase, or insure a loan. This type of fraud is usually defined as loan origination fraud. Mortgage fraud also includes schemes targeting consumers, such as foreclosure rescue, short sale, and loan modification."), available at http://www.fbi.gov/stats -services/publications/mortgage-fraud-2010. Sometimes the term "mortgage fraud"

may be limited to deceiving financial institutions into entering a mortgage contract they may not have otherwise approved.

[447] Consumer submissions to the CFPB, 2011-2012.

[448] Press Release, Kings County District Attorney's Office, *One Defendant Charged with a Hate Crime for Targeting an Elderly Victim* (Mar. 7, 2012), available at http://www.brooklynda. org/press_releases/2012/ Press%20Releases%2003-12.html.

[449] Interview with HUD Inspector General Kenneth Donohue, Reverse Review Magazine (Mar. 3, 2010), available at http://www.reversereview.com/index.php/magazine/features/1897-interview-with-the-hecm-fraud-unit.html.

[450] Press Release, Department of Justice, *Fraudsters Sentenced to Prison for "Reverse Mortgage" Scheme* (Feb. 23, 2011), available at http://www.justice.gov/usao/gan/ press/2012/ 02-23-12b.html.

[451] Press Release, Department of Justice, T*wo Individuals Sentenced in Connection with $2.5 Million Reverse Mortgage and Loan Modification Scheme* (Nov. 4, 2011), available at http://www.justice.gov/opa/pr/2011/ November/11-civ-1457.html.

[452] FinCEN, Advisory to Financial Institutions on Filing Suspicious Activity Reports Regarding Home Equity Conversion Mortgage Fraud Schemes (Apr. 27, 2010), available at http:// www.fincen.gov/statutes_regs/ guidance/pdf/fin-2010-a005.pdf.

[453] Press Release, Wayne County Office of the Prosecuting Attorney, *Prosecutor Worthy Charges in Connection with Reverse Mortgage Fraud Scheme* (June 14, 2006), available at http:// www.co.wayne.mi.us/documents/ 061406-REVISEDWCPChargesinConnectionwith ReverseMortgageFraudScheme.pdf.

[454] The defendant was convicted of six counts of larceny and is currently serving a state prison sentence. *See* Michigan Offender Tracking Information System, www.state.mi.us/mdoc/asp/ otis2profile.asp?mdocNumber= 633246.

[455] FTC Complaints 2011-2012.

[456] 18 USC § 2314. "Whoever transports, transmits, or transfers in interstate or foreign commerce any goods, wares, merchandise, securities or money, of the value of $5,000 or more, knowing the same to have been stolen, converted or taken by fraud; or [w]hoever, having devised or intending to devise any scheme or artifice or defraud, or for obtaining money or property by means of false or fraudulent pretenses, representations, or promises, transports or causes to be transported, or induces any person or persons to travel in, or to be transported in interstate or foreign commerce in the execution or concealment of a scheme or artifice to defraud that person or those persons of money or property having a value of $5,000 or more . . . [s]hall be fined until this title or imprisoned not more than 10 years, or both."

[457] 18 USC § 1344 ("Whoever knowingly executes, or attempts to execute, a scheme or artifice – (1) to defraud a financial institution; or (2) to obtain any of the moneys, funds, credits, assets, securities, or other property owned by, or under the custody or control of, a financial institution, by means of false or fraudulent pretenses, representations, or promises; shall be fined not more than $1,000,000 or imprisoned not more than 30 years, or both.").

[458] "Mortgage lending business" is defined as "an organization which finances or refinances any debt secured by an interest in real estate, including private mortgage companies and any subsidiary of such organization, and whose activities affect interstate or foreign commerce." 18 USC § 27.

[459] Under FERA, convictions for mortgage fraud allow up to a 30-year maximum prison sentence, or a maximum $1 million fine, or both. The statute of limitation is expanded to 10 years, as opposed to the five-year limit for other fraud cases. *See* mail fraud and wire fraud statutes, 18 USC § 1341; 18 USC § 1343.

[460] Ga. Code § 16-8-102 (2010).

[461] Michigan Public Act 205 of 2011; Mich. Comp. Laws § 750.219(d).

[462] Wash. Rev. Code § 43.320.140.

[463] FinCEN, Annual Report (2011).

[464] FinCEN, Advisory to Financial Institutions on Filing Suspicious Activity Reports Regarding Home Equity Conversion Mortgage Fraud Schemes (Apr. 27, 2010), available at http://www.fincen.gov/statutes_regs/ guidance/pdf/fin-2010-a005.pdf.

[465] Anti-Money Laundering Program and Suspicious Activity Report Filing Requirements for Residential Mortgage Lenders and Originators, 77 Fed. Reg. 8148 (finalized Feb. 14, 2012) (to be codified at 31 C.F.R. pts. 1010 and 1029), available at http://www.gpo.gov/fdsys/pkg/ FR-2012-02-14/pdf/2012-3074.pdf.

[466] 12 C.F.R. § 21.11 (requiring banks to file SARs); Bank Secrecy Act of 1970, Pub. L. No. 91-508 (codified at 31 USC § 5318(g)) (giving Secretary of Treasury authority to require financial institutions to file SARs).

[467] Anti-Money Laundering Program and Suspicious Activity Report Filing Requirements for Residential Mortgage Lenders and Originators, 77 Fed. Reg. 8148 (finalized Feb. 14, 2012) (to be codified at 31 C.F.R. pts. 1010 and 1029).

[468] Anti-Money Laundering Program and Suspicious Activity Reporting Requirements for Housing Government Sponsored Enterprises, 76 Fed. Reg. 69205 (proposed Nov. 8, 2011) (to be codified at 31 C.F.R. pts. 1010 and 1030), available at http://www.gpo.gov/fdsys/pkg/ FR-2011-11-08/pdf/2011-28820.pdf.

[469] Press Release, Federal Bureau of Investigation, *Operation Stolen Dreams: Hundreds Arrested in Mortgage Fraud Sweep* (June 17, 2010), available at http://www.fbi.gov/news/stories/ 2010/june/mortgage-fraud-sweep.

470 Presentation by Jason Abend, HUD Office of the Inspector General, National Reverse Mortgage Lender Association Conference (Mar. 28, 2012).

471 Interview with HUD Inspector General Kenneth Donohue, Reverse Review Magazine (Mar. 3, 2010), available at http://www.reversereview.com/index.php/magazine/features/1897-interview-with-the-hecm-fraud-unit.html.

472 Interview with HUD Inspector General Kenneth Donohue, Reverse Review Magazine (Mar. 3, 2010).

473 Presentation by Jason Abend, HUD Office of the Inspector General, National Reverse Mortgage Lender Association Conference (Mar. 28, 2012).

474 *Investigators: Caretaker Stole $18K from Blind, Elderly Houston Woman*, KHOU.com (Dec. 15, 2011), available at http://www.khou.com/news/local/Investigators-Caretaker-stole-18K-from-blind-elderly-Houston-woman-135669233.html. [KHOU.com 2011]

475 KHOU.com 2011.

476 Edward Colby, *Caretaker Stole $35,000 From North Miami Beach Woman Who Spent Life Taking Care of the Elderly*, NBC Miami (Feb. 15, 2012), available at http://www.nbcmiami. com/news/local/Caretaker-Stole-35000-From-North-Miami-Beach-Woman-Who-Spent-Life-Taking-Care-of-Elderly-Police-139403418.html.

477 Reverse Mortgages: Leaving Seniors and Taxpayers on the Hook: Hearing Before the United States Senate Special Committee on Aging (June 29, 2009) (statement of Anthony G. Medici, HUD Office of the Inspector General) ("The HECM counselor could be a valuable first line of defense against fraud. We have asked HUD officials to require that HECM counselors report suspected fraud to FHA and the OIG. We have also recommended that FHA instructs counselors to withhold certificates of counseling in suspected fraud cases that would allow borrowers to proceed with the loan process.").

478 Presentation by Jason Abend, HUD Office of the Inspector General, National Reverse Mortgage Lender Association Conference (Mar. 28, 2012).

479 CFPB analysis of FHA HECM Characteristics Report data, available at http://portal.hud.gov/ hudportal/HUD?src=/program_offices/housing/rmra/oe/rpts/hecm/hecmmenu.

480 National Consumer Law Center, Comment Letter to Federal Reserve Board Proposed Rule to Amend Regulation Z, Docket No. R-1390, 12 C.F.R. Part 226: Truth in Lending 73 (Dec. 23, 2010) [NCLC Comment Letter 2010]; AARP 2006 Survey, endnote 113.

481 *See* NCLC Comment Letter 2010.

482 Richard H. Thaler, *Mental Accounting Matters*, Journal of Behavioral Decision Making 12:3, p.196 (1999) (proposing a behavioral life-cycle model where consumers are more likely to spend current assets, like cash and checking account funds, and less likely to spend i) current wealth like savings accounts, stocks and bonds, and mutual funds, or ii) future income funds such as retirement accounts).

483 CFPB interviews with industry experts; CFPB analysis of data obtained from a reverse mortgage lender.

484 *See* NCLC Comment Letter 2010, endnote 480.

485 *See* NCLC Comment Letter 2010, endnote 480.

486 Darryl Hicks, *Grabbing the Lead: Who You Can Count On for Quality Prospects in a Crowded*, Reverse Mortgage Magazine 2:2, p.16 (Mar./Apr. 2009), available at *Marketplace* http://media.nrmlaonline.org/RMMag/March-April09.pdf. [Hicks 2009]

487 *See* Hicks 2009.

488 In 2010, Genworth Financial purchased ReverseMortgageGuides.org and Reverse.org. *See* John Yedinak, *Genworth Acquires Reverse Mortgage Lead Provider's Websites*, Reverse Mortgage Daily (Nov. 21, 2010), available at http://reversemortgagedaily.com/2010/11/21/genworth-acquires-reverse-mortgage-lead-provider-websites.

489 FTC Complaints 2011-2012. 490 FTC Complaints 2011-2012. 491 16 C.F.R. § 310.

492 12 C.F.R. § 1015.1 et seq; 75 Fed. Reg. 75124 n.373; 75 Fed. Reg. 75124 n.382.

493 *See* Section 5.3.2a.

494 *See e.g.*, FTC v. Dominant Leads, LLC, No. 1:10–cv–0997 (D.D.C. filed Jun. 15, 2010); *see also* United States v. Ryan, No. 09–00173–CJC (C.D. Cal. filed July 14, 2009) (criminal complaint against lead generator named as defendant in FTC action); FTC v. Ryan, No. 1:09–00535 (HHK) (D.D.C. filed Mar. 25, 2009); FTC v.Cantkier, No. 1:09–cv–00894 (D.D.C. Am. Complaint filed July 10, 2009).

495 FTC Complaints 2011-2012.

496 12 U.S.C. § 1061.

497 12 U.S.C. § 1076(b).

498 75 Fed. Reg. 58539 (2010).

499 CFPB estimate based on available data.

500 American Homestead offered this product starting in 1984, with other companies emulating the model in the late 1980s. Total volume for these products was likely around 5,000 loans according to industry experts.

501 Industry experts estimate that volume for the Ever Yours product was likely around 1,000 loans.

502 CFPB interviews with industry experts.

503 Report of the Special Committee on Aging to the United States Senate, Developments in Aging: 2001 and 2002, p. 211, Vol. 1 (Feb. 26, 2003) available at http://www.gpo.gov/fdsys/pkg/CRPT-108srpt265/pdf/CRPT-108srpt265-vol1.pdf.

[504] Fannie Mae Home Keeper Mortgage Lender Fact Sheet (Apr. 2005), available at https://www.efanniemae.com/sf/mortgageproducts/pdf/homekprlenderfactsheet.pdf.

[505] Fannie Mae Home Keeper Mortgage Consumer Fact Sheet (Aug. 2004), available at http:// www.fanniemae.com/global/pdf/homebuyers/homekeeperstriper.pdf.

[506] John Yedinak, *Fannie Mae Discontinues Home Keeper Reverse Mortgage Product*, Reverse Mortgage Daily (Sept. 3, 2008), available at http://reversemortgagedaily.com/2008/09/03/ fannie-mae-discontinues-home-keeper-reverse-mortgage-product/.

[507] Bank of America currently holds $1.1 billion in Independence Plan and other proprietary reverse mortgages.

[508] Generation Mortgage website. http://www.generationmortgage.com/jumbo-reverse-mortgage.htm.

[509] Data provided by Generation Mortgage.

[510] CFPB interviews and rate sheets provided by industry participants.

[511] Data provided by Generation Mortgage.

[512] As an example, the proprietary loans securitized by Lehman Brothers were priced at LIBOR + 5 percent in the early securitizations and LIBOR + 3.5 percent in the later securitizations. HECMs at the time were priced at CMT + 1.5 percent. Proprietary borrowers could expect to receive between 16 and 60 percent of their home value in the early securitizations and between 34 and 55 percent in the later securitizations, depending on age. HECM borrowers could expect to receive between 60 and 90 percent of home value.

[513] Several states have enacted stiff penalties against lenders who fail to make the payments to borrowers as scheduled in a proprietary reverse mortgage product. In North Carolina, Tennessee, and other states, for example, the lender forfeits their right to collect *any* interest on the loan. *See, e.g.,* N.C. Gen. Stat. § 53-266; Colo. Rev. Stat. § 11-38-106; S.C. Code § 29-4-30; Tenn. Code § 47-30- 111; S.D. Codified Laws § 54-12-21; W. Va. Code § 47-24-4. In South Dakota and West Virginia, a lender's failure to make payments not only results a forfeiture of interest but further subjects the lender to administrative penalties. *See* S.D. Codified Laws § 54-12-21; W. Va. Code § 47-24-4. Other states provide that a default may result in damages to the borrower, sometimes triple the amount wrongfully withheld. *See e.g.*, Ark. Code § 23-54-109; Cal. Civ. Code § 1923.2; Wash. Rev. Code § 31.04.535. To date, these regulations have mainly served to provide borrowers with recourse against lender failures to make payments and as a deterrent to prevent undercapitalized lenders from offering proprietary products, as there are no documented instances of a lender failing to make payments to the borrower as agreed.

[514] CFPB interviews with industry experts. CFPB research produced no documented cases of a lender failing to meet payment obligations.

[515] The market share estimate is derived by comparing the securitization issuance of $314.7 million with total HECM production for 1999 of approximately $960 million (on a maximum claim amount basis). These two figures of volume are not strictly comparable, but provide a rough estimate of proprietary market share in the absence of more accurate data. This calculation also ignores non-securitized proprietary products. There is no comprehensive data source of non-securitized, proprietary reverse mortgage originations but industry experts believe the volume contributed by these products to be trivial.

[516] CFPB interviews with industry experts.

[517] CFPB interviews with industry experts.

[518] CFPB analysis of Bank Call Report data (via SNL Financial LC).

In: Reverse Mortgages
Editors: Meghan Galloway and Richard Kantor
ISBN: 978-1-62257-965-5

Chapter 2

REVERSE MORTGAGES: BACKGROUND AND ISSUES*

Bruce E. Foote

SUMMARY

Since the 1970s, parties have sought to create mortgage instruments that would enable elderly homeowners to obtain loans to convert their equity into income, while providing that no repayments would be due for a specified period or, ideally, for the lifetime of the borrower. These instruments have been referred to as reverse mortgages, reverse annuity mortgages, and home equity conversion loans.

Reverse mortgages are the opposite of traditional mortgages in the sense that the borrower receives payments from the lender instead of making such payments to the lender. Reverse mortgages are designed to enable elderly homeowners to remain in their homes while using the equity in their homes as a form of income.

In general, reverse mortgages may take one of two forms: term or tenure. Under a term reverse mortgage, the borrower is provided with income for a specified period. Under a tenure reverse mortgage, the borrower is provided with income for as long as he or she continues to occupy the property.

For borrowers, the most risky reverse mortgage is the term reverse mortgage. Borrowers have been reluctant to enter such mortgages because at the end of the loan term the borrower would likely have to sell the home and move.

For lenders, the most risky reverse mortgage is the tenure reverse mortgage. Lenders have been reluctant to originate such mortgages because the borrower is guaranteed lifetime income and lifetime occupancy of the home. This is risky because the mortgage debt grows over time, and the debt could exceed the value of the home if the borrower lives longer than his or her life expectancy. The use of tenure reverse mortgages has grown in recent years due to the availability of an Federal Housing Administration (FHA)-insured reverse mortgage. Under the FHA program, the risk of the borrower living too long is shifted to the federal government.

* This is an edited, reformatted and augmented version of the Congressional Research Service Publication, CRS Report for Congress RL33843, dated February 22, 2010.

Under prior law, FHA-insured reverse mortgages were subject to the FHA mortgage limit for the area in which a property is located. The Housing and Economic Recovery Act of 2008, P.L. 110-289, established a mortgage limit equal to the conforming loan limit for the Federal Home Loan Mortgage Corporation (Freddie Mac).

Present law limits the aggregate number of FHA-insured reverse mortgages to 275,000 loans, and that limit has been exceeded. Notwithstanding the limit in present law, the Consolidated Appropriations Act, 2010, P.L. 111-117, provided that FHA may continue to insure HECMs through September 30, 2010.

INTRODUCTION

According to the American Housing Survey (AHS), there are about 18.3 million elderly homeowners (age 65 or older) and the median value of their homes is $168,654.[1] About 12.5 million of the elderly homeowners (more than 68%) have no mortgage debt.[2] For many of the elderly homeowners, the equity in their homes represents their largest asset.

Many elderly homeowners find that although inflation has increased the value of their homes, it has also eroded the purchasing power of their fixed incomes. They find it increasingly difficult to maintain their homes while also paying for needed food, medical, and other expenses. Because of their low incomes, many may be unable to qualify for loans to pay for unexpected expenses. "House rich and cash poor" is the phrase often used to describe their dilemma. One option is to sell the home and move to rental housing or purchase a lower-cost home. For a variety of reasons, however, many older Americans prefer to remain in the homes in which they may have spent most of their working years.

Since the 1970s, academics and housing advocates have sought to create mortgage instruments that would enable elderly homeowners to obtain loans to convert their equity into income, while providing that no repayments would be due for a specified period or, ideally, for the lifetime of the borrower. These instruments have been referred to as reverse mortgages, reverse annuity mortgages, and home equity conversion loans.

Generally, when a borrower obtains a mortgage, a lender advances a lump-sum payment to or on behalf of the borrower, and the borrower becomes committed to making a stream of monthly payments to repay the loan. With the reverse mortgage, the lender becomes committed to making a stream of payments to the borrower, and such payments are repaid to the lender in a lump sum at some future date. Thus, reverse mortgages are the opposite of traditional mortgages in that the borrower receives payments from the lender instead of making such payments to the lender. Reverse mortgages are designed to enable elderly homeowners to remain in their homes while using the equity in their homes as a form of income.

Although reverse mortgages are a small part of the total mortgage market, their use has increased substantially in recent years. This report discusses the evolution and history of reverse mortgages, compares reverse mortgage products currently available, discusses the potential use of reverse mortgages as a way to finance long-term care, and raises a number of issues for policymakers and the elderly (aged 65 or older).

THE EVOLUTION OF REVERSE MORTGAGES

Sale-Leaseback Transactions

Under a sale-leaseback transaction a property is sold to a buyer who simultaneously leases the property to the seller. Often, sale-leaseback transactions are used by businesses that seek to raise working capital by selling and leasing back some property that is used in the trade or business. The technique enables firms to raise capital and avoid high borrowing costs. Capital that was formerly frozen in real estate assets can be used to generate a higher rate of return in the business itself. If the business obtained a mortgage against the property, the mortgage would cover only 75 to 80% of the market value of the property. Through the sale-leaseback transaction, the business can obtain cash for 100% of the value of the property (less transaction costs) and still maintain use and possession of the property.

In the 1970s, some advocates suggested sale-leaseback transactions as a way for elderly homeowners to convert the equity in their homes into a source of income. Under this plan, the elderly homeowner would sell the home and lease it back from the new owner. The seller could retain the right of occupancy for life or for a fixed number of years. In either case, the seller would become a renter of the home that he or she formerly owned.

The burden of property taxes, home insurance, and repair and maintenance costs would rest with the new owner. It is argued that these costs make it difficult for elderly homeowners to remain in their homes or cause them to make trade-offs between making home repairs and taking care of necessities such as food and health care. Such trade-offs may result in the elderly having owner-occupied but substandard property. Under a sale-leaseback plan, the owner/investor would be paying the operating costs of the property and be eligible for the associated tax write-offs. Proponents hold that the elderly would remain in well-maintained homes without the financial burden of such maintenance.

The sale-leaseback plan is a complicated form of equity conversion because of the number of variables that must be negotiated between the buyer and seller. The parties must negotiate the sales price, downpayment, loan term, and lease agreement. The items are interrelated and may affect the net benefit of the transaction to the elderly homeowner.

A few programs were initiated. Under the so-called "Grannie Mae" program, a company would arrange for the children or grandchildren to purchase and leaseback the home of the elderly person.[3] Under another plan, the Fouratt Senior Citizen Equity Plan, the leaseback payments took two forms: a promissory note (mortgage) and a deferred annuity.[4] The promissory note would provide for monthly payments to the seller over a term equal to the greater of the seller's life expectancy or 10 years. When the payments from the promissory note ended, the annuity would make the same payments for the lifetime of the seller.

Only three Grannie Mae loans were made. There was interest in the Fouratt program but no loans were ever made. Sale-leaseback transactions are still being suggested as an option for elderly homeowners. Data are not available on whether homeowners are choosing that option.

Reverse Annuity Mortgage

The reverse annuity mortgage is another concept that was suggested in the 1970s by advocates of reverse mortgages. Under a reverse annuity mortgage (RAM), equity in the home is used as security for a loan. An annuity is purchased with the loan proceeds and the borrower receives monthly annuity income, less mortgage interest. The borrower pays only interest on the loan— repayment of the principal is deferred until the death of the owner, the sale of the property, or some prescribed date.

Table 1 shows the net annuity that would be available under a RAM to a female homeowner for a range of ages and interest rates. The age shown is the borrower's age when the loan was taken. It is assumed that a borrower obtains a $200,000 interest-only mortgage on the property and uses the proceeds to purchase an annuity. That means that the loan balance will always be $200,000. Upon the death of the borrower, the sale of the property, or some prescribed date, the borrower or the borrower's heirs would owe the lender $200,000. For a 55-year-old borrower the annuity would be $1,062 monthly. If interest rates are 5%, the lender would deduct $833 from the annuity and forward the borrower a net annuity of $229. If interest rates are 12%, the interest payment would be greater than the annuity payments so the borrower would owe the lender $938 (a net annuity of $-938). This would defeat the purpose of entering into a RAM.

Table 1. Comparison of Monthly Reverse Annuity Mortgage Benefits

	Age of Homeowner					
	55	**60**	**65**	**70**	**75**	**80**
Gross Annuity[a]	$1,062	$1,114	$1,243	$1,380	$1,611	$1,937
Less Interest:[b]						
at 5%	833	833	833	833	833	833
Net Annuity	*229*	*281*	*410*	*547*	*778*	*1,104*
at 6%	1,000	1,000	1,000	1,000	1,000	1,000
Net Annuity	*62*	*114*	*243*	*380*	*611*	*937*
at 7%	1,167	1,167	1,167	1,167	1,167	1,167
Net Annuity	*-105*	*-53*	*76*	*213*	*444*	*770*
at 8%	1,333	1,333	1,333	1,333	1,333	1,333
Net Annuity	*-271*	*-219*	*-90*	*47*	*278*	*604*
at 9%	1,500	1,500	1,500	1,500	1,500	1,500
Net Annuity	*-438*	*-386*	*-257*	*-120*	*111*	*437*
at 10%	1,667	1,667	1,667	1,667	1,667	1,667
Net Annuity	*-605*	*-553*	*-424*	*-287*	*-56*	*270*
at 11%	1,833	1,833	1,833	1,833	1,833	1,833
Net Annuity	*-771*	*-719*	*-590*	*-453*	*-222*	*104*
at 12%	2,000	2,000	2,000	2,000	2,000	2,000
Net Annuity	*-938*	*-886*	*-757*	*-620*	*-389*	*-63*

Source: Calculations by CRS using annuities generated at http://www. immediateannuities.com.

a. Monthly payment to a female on a $200,000 immediate annuity.

b. Monthly interest due on a $200,000 interest-only mortgage.

The table shows that rising interest rates are a risk for homeowners and that the interest rate risk is greater for younger borrowers. For 55 and 60-year-old borrowers, the net annuity would become negative when interest rates are at 7% or higher. The net annuity would become negative at 8% for 65-year-olds, 9% for 70-year-olds, 10% for 75-year-olds, and 12% for 80-year olds. But RAMs may become a bad financial choice long before the net annuity becomes negative. For example, the net annuity becomes negative at 9% for a 70-year old, but would it make economic sense for a 70-year-old to mortgage the home and only receive a net income of $380 monthly when interest rates are 6%?

For the homeowner, another risk of the RAM is that the borrower may die too soon. Suppose a 75-year old female obtained a RAM and died after receiving 12 payments. The estate would owe $200,000, even though the owner only received $19,332 in gross benefits. Of course, the owner could have purchased an annuity with a 10 years certain option or cash refund option. The 10 years certain option provides that if the annuitant lives less than 10 years after the plan is issued, the payments would continue to the beneficiary's estate until the 10 year period is completed. The cash refund option provides that if the total payments to the annuitant are less than the original premium (in this example, $200,000) the beneficiary would receive the balance in a lump sum. These options reduce the monthly annuity payments and thereby reduce the financial viability of the RAM.

Under RAMs, the risks for lenders are that the owner may live too long (mortality risk). The purchase of the annuity shifts the mortality risk to an insurance company.

Though the concept appeared promising, CRS is aware of only one program that offered RAMs, though they were not marketed as such. In the 1990s, Homefirst, a subsidiary of Transamerica Corporation, offered a reverse mortgage plan in many parts of the country. Under the so-called "Lifetime" plan the borrower would receive monthly loan advances for a specified number of years. A deferred annuity was purchased from Metropolitan Life Insurance Company on behalf of the borrower, and it would begin lifetime monthly annuity payments once the borrower received the last loan advance. The borrower would receive lifetime income regardless of whether they continued to occupy the property.

By the late 1990s, there were several complaints regarding the reverse mortgages from Homefirst. An extreme example is illustrated by the case of a New York woman. She took out a reverse mortgage and received loan advances until she died after receiving 32 monthly payments. When her home was sold a few months later, Financial Freedom (Homefirst) demanded more than $765,000 as repayment under the terms of the reverse mortgage. The monthly payments she had received during the life of the loan totaled about $58,000.[5]

As a result of this case and similar cases, three class action lawsuits were filed against Transamerica HomeFirst, Inc., Transamerica Corporation, Metropolitan Life Insurance Company, and Financial Freedom Senior Funding Corporation. The cases were combined and settled before a single judge in the Superior Court of California in San Mateo County under Judicial Council Coordination Proceeding No. 4061.

The above example illustrates the risks to borrowers and lenders of reverse annuity mortgages. Financial Freedom no longer offers the "Lifetime Plan." Instead, it offers the "Cash Account Plan" as a proprietary reverse mortgage product, and that plan is discussed in a section below.

Table 2. Payment Options under a $100,000 Term Reverse Mortgage

Loan Term	Monthly Payments ($)	Cash Advance ($)
10 years	594	52,296
7 years	943	63,523
5 years	1,415	72,316
3 years	2,523	82,327

Source: Calculations by CRS.

Note: This example assumes that the interest rate is fixed at 6.5% and that there are no transaction costs.

Reverse Mortgage

In general, reverse mortgages may take one of two forms—term or tenure. Under term reverse mortgages the borrower is provided with income for a specified period. Under tenure reverse mortgage the borrower is provided with income for as long as they continue to occupy the property.

From the lender's perspective, reverse mortgages are deferred-payment loans. The lender makes a stream of payments (or a lump-sum payment) to the homeowner and expects repayment at some future date. The repayment is predicated upon the sale of the home at some price which exceeds the debt that has accumulated against the home.

The largest risk the lender faces is the risk that over time the outstanding debt may grow to be greater than the property value. This may be referred to as collateral risk. Collateral risk is partly determined by the type of reverse mortgage. The least risky reverse mortgage is the term reverse mortgage under which payments stop after a specified number of years. Payments to the homeowner are calculated so that the loan reaches a target balance at the predetermined period. That target balance is less than 100% of the property value when the loan was originated. As long as the property has not depreciated during the period, the lender is assured that sale of the property will provide sufficient funds to repay the loan.

For lenders, the most risky reverse mortgage is the tenure reverse mortgage because the borrower is guaranteed lifetime income and lifetime occupancy of the home. In this case, the collateral risk may be significant if the age of entry is too low, if property appreciation rates are overestimated, or if occupant survival rates are underestimated.

In general, prior to the 1990s lenders were only willing to make term reverse mortgages. The payment options under these term reverse mortgages are relatively easy to calculate—all that is needed is the interest rate, the term of the loan, and the end-of-term loan balance. With these factors it is a simple matter to calculate the monthly payment that would cause the loan balance to grow to the specified amount over the specified term. As shown in **Table 2** for example, the monthly payment to a homeowner seeking a $100,000 reverse mortgage at a 6.5% interest rate would be $594 for a 10-year term, $943 for a seven-year term, $1,415 for a five-year term, and $2,523 for a three-year term. **Table 2** also shows the maximum cash advance that will grow to a loan balance of $100,000 over the given terms.

The age of the homeowner is not a factor in term reverse mortgages, homeowners would receive the same income regardless of age. If the owner lives longer than the loan term, the home would have to be sold to pay off the debt.

This feature, however, made term reverse mortgages unattractive to homeowners who faced the prospect of having to sell their homes at a specified date, and to lenders who faced the prospect of risking their reputations by forcing such sales. For these reasons there have been few takers for term reverse mortgages.

RECENT REVERSE MORTGAGE PLANS

Over time three major reverse mortgage products became available to consumers in the U.S. They are the Home Equity Conversion Mortgage Program (HECM), the Home Keeper reverse mortgage, and the Cash Account Plan. At present, a relatively new reverse mortgage, the "Senior Equity Reverse Mortgage," is only available in Arizona, California, Delaware, the District of Columbia, Florida, Georgia, Maryland, North Carolina, South Carolina, Texas, and Virginia.

All of the plans provide the borrower with lifetime occupancy of the home—"tenure" reverse mortgages. The availability of tenure reverse mortgages is likely the cause of the dramatic growth of reverse mortgages in the past few years.

These tenure reverse mortgages also provide the borrower with flexibility on how the income from the mortgage is received. A borrower may receive monthly payments as long as the property is occupied by the borrower. The borrower may receive a line of credit which grows at some specified annual rate and upon which the borrower may make draws as needed. The borrower may choose to receive a large up-front cash advance. Or the borrower may choose any combination of the above, such as a smaller cash advance, a line of credit, and monthly income.

The following sections discuss and compare these reverse mortgage products.

The Home Equity Conversion Mortgage Program (HECM)

The Housing and Community Development Act of 1987 (P.L. 100-242) authorized the Home Equity Conversion Mortgage Program (HECM) in the Department of Housing and Urban Development (HUD) as a demonstration program. It was the first nationwide reverse mortgage program which offered the possibility of lifetime occupancy to elderly homeowners.[6] As noted above, such mortgages are referred to as tenure reverse mortgages. The borrowers must be elderly homeowners who own and occupy their homes.[7] The interest rate on the loan may be fixed or adjustable.[8] The homeowner and the lender may agree to share in any future appreciation in the value of the property.[9] The program has been made permanent and the law was amended to permit its use for one-to four-family residences if the owner occupies one of the units. [10]

The borrower can choose from five payment plans:

- Tenure—equal monthly payments as long as at least one borrower lives and continues to occupy the property as a principal residence.
- Term—equal monthly payments for a fixed period of months selected by the borrower.

- Line of Credit—installments at times and in amount of borrower's choosing until the line of credit is exhausted.
- Modified Tenure—combination of line of credit with monthly payments for as long as the borrower remains in the home.
- Modified Term—combination of line of credit with monthly payments for a fixed period of months selected by the borrower.

Prior law provided that the HECM loan may not exceed the Federal Housing Administration (FHA) mortgage limit for the area in which the property is located. The Housing and Economic Recovery Act of 2008, P.L. 110-289, establishes a national HECM limit equal to the conforming loan limit for the Federal Home Loan Mortgage Corporation (Freddie Mac). The mortgage must be a first mortgage, which, in essence, implies that any previous mortgage must be fully repaid either prior to the HECM or from the initial proceeds of the HECM. Prior to obtaining a loan, borrowers must be provided with counseling by third parties who will explain the financial implications of entering into home equity conversion mortgages as well as explain the options, other than home equity conversion mortgages, that may be available to elderly homeowners. To prevent displacement of the elderly homeowners, HECMs must include terms that give the homeowner the option of deferring repayment of the loan until the death of the homeowner, the voluntary sale of the home, or the occurrence of some other events as prescribed by HUD regulations. The borrowers may prepay the loans without penalty.

Borrowers are required to purchase insurance from FHA. The insurance serves two purposes: (1) it protects lenders from suffering losses if the final loan balance exceeds the proceeds from the sale of a home, and (2) it continues monthly payments to the homeowner if the lender defaults on the loan. At loan origination borrowers are required to pay an up-front mortgage insurance premium (MIP) of 2% of the maximum mortgage amount. In addition, borrowers pay an annual insurance premium of 0.5% of the loan balance. Borrowers do not directly pay the insurance premiums. Instead, lenders make the payments to FHA on behalf of the borrowers and the cost of the insurance is added to the borrower's loan balance.

A lender may choose either the assignment option or the coinsurance option when originating the loan. Under the assignment option, HUD will collect all the MIP and the lender may assign the loan to HUD at the point that the loan balance equals the maximum HUD claim amount for the area. Under the coinsurance option, the lender may keep part of the MIP and forfeit the right to assign the case to HUD.

To date, data indicate that all lenders have chosen the assignment option. By choosing this option, effectively, lenders are shifting the collateral risk to HUD.

The American Homeownership and Economic Opportunity Act of 2000 (P.L. 106-569) amended the National Housing Act (12 USC 1715z-20) to waive the up-front insurance premium provided that the HECM proceeds are used to pay for long-term care insurance. The regulations to implement this change have never been finalized. This provision was eliminated by Section 2122 of P.L. 110-289.

When the home is eventually sold, HUD will pay the lender the difference between the loan balance and sales price if the sales price is the lesser of the two. The claim paid to the lender may not exceed the lesser of (1) the appraised value of the property when the loan was originated, or (2) the maximum HUD-insured loan for the area.

The Federal National Mortgage Association (Fannie Mae) has been purchasing the home equity conversion mortgages originated under the program.

The Home Keeper Mortgage

Since November 1996, Fannie Mae had also been offering its own reverse mortgage product: the "Home Keeper Mortgage." This was the only conventional reverse mortgage that was available on a nationwide basis. Private lenders have developed proprietary reverse mortgage products but they are generally only available in a few states.

In September 2008, Fannie Mae announced that, after December 31, 2008, Fannie Mae will no longer purchase Home Keeper mortgages.[11] Fannie Mae noted that it no longer sees a significant role for the Home Keeper mortgage in light of the expansion of HECMs.

The Cash Account Plan

Financial Freedom Senior Funding Corp., of Irvine, CA, offers the "Cash Account Plan" as a proprietary reverse mortgage product. The Cash Account Plan is available to seniors 62 years or older who own homes with a minimum value of $75,000. It differs from the two products above in that it does not offer the borrowers an option of getting monthly payments. It provides an open-end line of credit that is available for as long as the borrower occupies the home. The borrower can draw on the line of credit in full or part at any time; the minimum draw is $500. The unused portion of theline of credit grows by 5% annually.[12] Eligible home types include owner-occupied single-family detached, manufactured, condominium, Planned Unit Development units, or one-to four-unit residences if one unit is owner-occupied. Borrowers are required to obtain counseling from an independent counselor prior to obtaining the loans.

A monthly servicing fee is automatically added to the loan.[13] The interest rate charged to the borrower is equal to the current six-month London Interbank Offered Rate (LIBOR) plus 5 percentage points. The rate is adjusted semi-annually, but the interest rate may never rise more than 6 percentage points above the initial rate.

The Cash Account Plan is available in two forms: the Standard Option and the Zero Point Option. Under the Standard Option, a borrower pays a loan origination fee that is equal to 2% on the first $500,000 of loan balance, 1.5% on the next $500,000, and 1% on the balance in excess of $1 million.

Under the Zero Point Option, the borrower pays no loan origination fee. Closing costs, including third party costs and excluding state and local taxes, will not exceed $3,500. At closing the borrower is required to take a draw on the line of credit, and the minimum draw at closing is 75% of the line of credit. Subsequent draws have a minimum of $500. Full prepayment is permitted and, while there are no prepayment penalties, partial prepayment on the initial draw is not permitted for the first five years. The Zero Point Option is generally marketed to elderly homeowners with homes valued at $450,000 or more.

On June 18, 2008, Financial Freedom announced that it was suspending the Cash Account Plan.[14] This action was taken largely because of liquidity problems of IndyMac, the parent company of Financial Freedom.

The Cash Account Plan was available in the District of Columbia and 24 states: Arizona, California, Colorado, Connecticut, Florida, Georgia, Hawaii, Illinois, Indiana, Maryland, Massachusetts, Michigan, Minnesota, Nevada, New Jersey, New York, Ohio, Oregon, Pennsylvania, Utah, Vermont, Virginia, Washington, and Wyoming.

Senior Equity Reverse Mortgage

In late 2006, Reverse Mortgage of America, a subsidiary of Seattle Mortgage, introduced "The Lifestyle Plan." It was the first new reverse mortgage product to be introduced in nearly a decade. In 2007, Bank of America purchased the reverse mortgage products of Seattle Mortgage. The mortgages are being marketed as the "Senior Equity Reverse Mortgage," and at present are only available in Arizona, California, Delaware, the District of Columbia, Georgia, Maryland, North Carolina, South Carolina, Texas, and Virginia.

Like the Cash Account Plan, the Senior Equity Reverse Mortgage allows homeowners age 62 and older to use some of the equity in their homes while continuing to live there. It is designed for owners of high-value homes, up to $10 million. Borrowers may choose to receive their funds in a single lump sum, in regular monthly installments, as a line of credit, or any combination of these options. So, unlike the Cash Account Plan, the Senior Equity Reverse Mortgage offers a monthly payment to borrowers.

The interest rate on the Senior Equity Reverse Mortgage is the six-month LIBOR Index, plus 2.95 percentage points. The interest rate may vary, but may not exceed 18%. Borrowers pay a loan origination fee of 1% of the home value but not more than $10,000. Borrowers also pay a monthly servicing fee of $25.

The proceeds from a Senior Equity Reverse Mortgage may be used to purchase a primary residence or a second home. The borrower would be responsible for a down payment equal to the difference between the value of the new home and the amount of funds received from the Senior Equity Reverse Mortgage.

Table 3. Payment Options under Reverse Mortgage Programs by Age of Youngest Homeowner

Age	HECM		Home Keeper[a]		Cash Account[a]	
	Monthly Income	Line of Credit	Monthly Income	Line of Credit	Monthly Income	Line of Credit
62	$602	$108,092	$204	$24,244	N/A	$54,650
65	644	113,033	254	32,336	N/A	60,478
70	727	121,331	417	57,675	N/A	71,570
75	839	130,334	633	73,171	N/A	83,602
80	999	139,679	801	90,035	N/A	88,678
85	1,254	149,015	1,053	108,145	N/A	93,378
90	1,749	158,070	1,202	119,864	N/A	98,078

Source: Calculated by CRS using the Reverse Mortgage Calculator on Financial Freedom's website.

Note: Estimates are based on a $200,000 home in Denver, CO. It is assumed that the homeowner had no outstanding loans against the property.

a. These estimates were run before Financial Freedom suspended the program on June 18, 2008 and before Fannie Mae announced the termination of the Home Keeper reverse mortgage.

Table 4. Comparison of Reverse Mortgage Benefits to a Homeowner in Albany, NY

Home Value	HECM		Home Keeper		Cash Account	
	Monthly Income	Line of Credit	Monthly Income[a]	Line of Credit[a]	Monthly Income	Line of Credit[b]
$200,000	$603	$93,461	$413	$57,089	N/A	$75,965
250,000	770	119,392	528	73,082	N/A	96,281
300,000	937	145,324	648	89,074	N/A	116,597
350,000	1,105	171,255	760	105,066	N/A	136,550
400,000	1,272	197,187	875	121,059	N/A	156,457
450,000	1,442	223,619	915	126,491	N/A	176,364
500,000	1,613	250,050	915	126,491	N/A	196,121
550,000	1,783	276,501	915	126,491	N/A	216,023

Source: Calculated by CRS using Reverse Mortgage Calculator on Financial Freedom's website.

Note: Estimates are based on a loan to a 70-year old in Albany, NY. It is assumed that the homeowner had no outstanding loans against the property.

a. The Home Keeper loan limit was $417,000 when these estimates were run, and that determined the maximum payments available under the Home Keeper program.

b. These estimates were run before Financial Freedom suspended the program on June 18, 2008, and before Fannie Mae announced the termination of the Home Keeper reverse mortgage.

CHOOSING AMONG THE PLANS

Table 3 compares the income that may be received under the three major plans for the same valued home. The table shows the monthly income that would be available if the borrower chose only to receive monthly payments, and the largest line of credit that would be available at loan origination if the borrower chose to only have a line of credit. The HECM plan pays the largest monthly payments and has the largest available lines of credit.

Table 5. Comparison of Reverse Mortgage Benefits to a Homeowner in Glendale, CA

Home Value	HECM		Home Keeper		Cash Account	
	Monthly Income	Line of Credit	Monthly Income[a]	Line of Credit[a]	Monthly Income	Line of Credit[b]
$200,000	$609	$94,481	$417	$57,629	N/A	$71,478
250,000	777	120,588	533	73,686	N/A	90,608
300,000	945	146,595	649	89,742	N/A	109,738
350,000	1,114	172,671	765	105,799	N/A	128,696
400,000	1,282	198,748	881	121,856	N/A	147,462
450,000	1,453	225,324	920	127,310	N/A	166,227
500,000	1,629	251,901	920	127,310	N/A	184,992
550,000	1,796	278,477	920	127,310	N/A	203,752

Source: Calculated by CRS using the Reverse Mortgage Calculator on Financial Freedom's website.

Note: Estimates are based on a loan to a 70-year old in Glendale, CA. It is assumed that the homeowner had no outstanding loans against the property.

a. The Home Keeper loan limit was $417,000 when these estimates were run, and that determined the maximum payments available under the Home Keeper program.

b. These estimates were run before Financial Freedom suspended the program on June 18, 2008, and before Fannie Mae announced the termination of the Home Keeper reverse mortgage.

Table 4 compares the benefits available under the reverse mortgage programs for a 70-year-old homeowner in Albany, NY. At all home values, the funds available from the HECM exceed those available from the other plans.

Table 5 has been prepared using the Los Angeles area as a base. As with **Table 4**, it shows that the funds available from the HECM exceed those available from the other plans.

Thus, it is not surprising that reverse mortgages made under HECM account for about 90% of the reverse mortgages made nationwide. The HECM offers better value to most borrowers.

USING REVERSE MORTGAGES FOR LONG-TERM CARE

As indicated previously, the AHS estimates that more than 12.5 million homeowners age 65 older, have homes that are free of mortgage debt. With the growth in the public cost of long-term care for the elderly, there has been research and discussion of ways that elderly homeowners may use reverse mortgages to tap this home equity and fund their own long-term care.

Funding Long-Term Care Directly

One option is for the homeowners to use reverse mortgages to fund long-term care directly. Primarily this would involve paying for home modifications and in-home care that would permit them to "age-in-place." Under its "Use Your Home to Stay at Home" initiative, the National Council for the Aging (NCOA) is encouraging the use of reverse mortgages to fund long-term care. Of the nearly 28 million American households age 62 and older, NCOA has found that about 13.2 million (48%) are good candidates for a reverse mortgage. According to NCOA, an estimated $953 billion could be available from reverse mortgages for immediate long-term care needs and to promote aging in place.[15]

That $953 billion figure, however, appears to have been calculated by assuming that the homeowners would, on average, be eligible for about $72,200 in reverse mortgage loans and then multiplying by the 13.2 million potential reverse mortgage candidates. In effect, that is assuming a 100% participation rate when in fact a much smaller percent of homeowners participate. The percent of elderly homeowners with reverse mortgages has been increasing over the years, and Reverse Mortgage Insight estimates that, as of November 2009, for the first time more than 2% of elderly homeowners have reverse mortgages.[16]

By using reverse mortgages, some of the elderly would be able to fund their long-term care expenses for a number of years, and thereby delay potential entry into the Medicaid program. It is debatable, however, whether and how much savings this approach would provide for the Medicaid program.

The Medicaid program has the ultimate claim on the home equity of program participants. If participants fund their care through reverse mortgages, they may use up most or all of their equity, so there may be little or none left to be claimed by Medicaid. There may be cases where the net cost to the Medicaid program would be less if the participants had entered the Medicaid program earlier instead of consuming their equity through reverse mortgages.

Funding Long-Term Care Insurance

Using the proceeds from reverse mortgages to pay for long-term care insurance (LTCI) is another option for elderly homeowners.

The demographics of reverse mortgages and long-term care insurance do not match for either consumers or the industry. Long-term care insurers want young consumers. Reverse mortgage lenders want old consumers. For consumers, LTCI is best taken at an older age when the benefits are greater, but the premiums are more expensive. For insurers, the major risk is that the purchasers will get sick too soon and need long-term care before they have paid enough premiums into the insurance fund. For reverse mortgage lenders, the major risk is that the borrower will live too long and accumulate debt against the property which exceeds the property value. The different risks result in different outcomes for consumers with the same profile. For example, insurers are reluctant to provide insurance to borrowers with certain health problems, because of the likelihood that the borrowers may need to use the insurance. Lenders, however, will make reverse mortgages to such borrowers, because there is less likelihood that the borrowers will occupy the property too long.

The cost of the insurance is another issue. In recent years, insurers have raised the insurance premiums on current customers. This suggests that a homeowner who used a reverse mortgage to purchase long-term care insurance could face the risk that the cost of the policy could increase at some later date. That would not be a problem if the homeowner could afford the increased cost. But if the increase were unaffordable, the borrower would have to drop the insurance. If this occurred, it might be possible that the borrower would still have some paid-up benefits, but the level of coverage would be less than the borrower had planned when initially purchasing the policy.

Issues for the Elderly

Though there has been growth in use of reverse mortgages in recent years, it is still a relatively little used option for elderly homeowners. Many elderly homeowners do not understand the program and are reluctant to participate. After spending many years paying for their homes, elderly owners may not want to mortgage the property again. There are several options to be considered.[17]

Downsizing

One option is to sell the home and purchase something smaller. Present law permits a seller to exclude from taxation up to $250,000 ($500,000 for a married couple) of the gain from sale of a home. The home must have been used as the principal residence for two out of five years before the sale. Funds not used for the new purchase could be used for investment and as a source of cash to meet future needs.

Selling and Renting

Instead of purchasing another property the homeowner could consider renting an apartment, perhaps in a complex designated for those 55 and older. The proceeds from the sale of the home could be saved and invested and used for income when needed.

Finding Tenants

Rather than sell the home, the homeowner could consider renting part of the home to students, young couples, other retirees. The rental income would help with ongoing expenses. In addition to the economic benefit, a rental might also provide some companionship to the owner.

Reverse Mortgage

The homeowner might consider a reverse mortgage. As mentioned above, a reverse mortgage enables an elderly homeowner to use the equity in the home to receive monthly income, a line of credit, or some combination of the two. Repayments are delayed until the home is no longer occupied as a principal residence. Then the borrower or the heirs must repay the loan. If the home is sold and the sales price exceeds the loan balance, the borrower or the heirs keep any proceeds that remain.[18] If the sales price is less than the loan balance, then the lender suffers the loss. The funds received from the reverse mortgage are tax free because the funds are considered as loan proceeds instead of income. The payments from reverse mortgages do not affect the income or eligibility from Social Security or Medicare. But homeowners who receive Supplemental Security Income (SSI) or Medicaid[19] might have these benefits reduced if the recipients do not spend their entire sum received under the reverse mortgage each month.

When considering a reverse mortgage, several questions should be addressed:

- Participants may be provided with lifetime occupancy, but will borrowers generate sufficient income to meet future health care needs?
- Will they obtain equity conversion loans when they are too "young" and, as a result, have limited resources from which to draw when they are older and more frail and sick?
- Will the "young" elderly spend the extra income on travel and luxury consumer items?
- Should home equity conversion mechanisms be limited as last resort options for elderly homeowners?
- Will some of the home equity be conserved?

- How would an equity conversion loan affect the homeowner's estate planning?
- Does the homeowner have other assets? How large is the home equity relative to the other assets?
- Will the homeowner have any survivors?
- What is the financial position of the heirs apparent?
- Are the children of the elderly homeowner relatively well-off and with no need to inherit the "family home" or the funds that would result from the sale of that home?
- Alternatively, would the ultimate sale of the home result in significant improvement in the financial position of the heirs?
- How healthy is the homeowner? What has been the individual's health history?
- Are large medical expenses pending? At any given age, a healthy borrower will have a longer life expectancy than a borrower in poor health.
- What has been the history of property appreciation in the area?

The above questions are interrelated. Their answers should help determine whether an individual should consider a reverse mortgage, what type of loan to consider, and at what age a reverse mortgage should be considered.

ISSUES FOR CONGRESS

Potential Federal Liability

As revealed in **Table 6**, there has been dramatic growth in the use of HECMs over the past few years. More than 114,300 loans were made in FY2009 compared to little more than 157 in 1990. As of September 30, 2009, the outstanding balance of active HECM loans was $60 billion and the potential HUD liability for these loans was $102.5 billion.[20]

As noted previously, one of the greatest risks for lenders is that the borrower will live too long and that the loan balance will exceed the home value—collateral risk. Under the HECM program this risk falls to HUD because the lender can assign the loan to HUD in those cases. The collateral risk then becomes a potential liability for the FHA insurance fund.

When HUD accepts the assignment of HECM loans, HUD becomes responsible for future borrower advances or fixed payments until termination of the loan due to the death of the homeowner, the refinancing of the loan, or the sale of the home. At the end of FY2009, the value of HECM loans assigned to HUD has grown to $772 million.

HECMs had previously been an obligation of the FHA General Insurance (GI) fund but Section 2118 of the Housing and Economic Recovery Act of 2008 (HERA), P.L. 110-289, made HECMs an obligation of the FHA Mutual Mortgage Insurance fund for all loans obligated in FY2009 and beyond. The HECM activity from FY1992 to FY2008 remains with the GI fund, and the liability for that activity increased from $1.5 billion at the end of FY2008 to $4.8 billion at the end of FY2009.[21] The increase in liability is primarily due to the drop in projections of home price appreciation. Less appreciation in home prices would result in lower recoveries from the sale of homes assigned to HUD in the future.

This will be less of a problem for HECMs made in FY2010 and beyond. Given the interest rate and the age of the prospective borrower, HUD calculates factors which, when multiplied by the appraised value of the property, give the so-called "principal limit" or maximum HECM that initially may be obtained by the borrower. In September 2009, HUD announced new principle limit factors which are 10% lower than the factors used in the past.[22] It will mean that prospective HECM borrowers will be eligible for smaller loans than were otherwise available, and HUD's liability will decrease accordingly.

Table 6. HECM Loans by Fiscal Year

Fiscal Year	Number of HECM Loans	Percent Change (%)
1990	157	
1991	389	148
1992	1,019	162
1993	1,964	93
1994	3,365	71
1995	4,165	24
1996	3,596	-14
1997	5,208	45
1998	7,896	52
1999	7,982	1
2000	6,640[a]	-17
2001	7,781	17
2002	13,049	68
2003	18,097[b]	39
2004	37,829	109
2005	43,131	14
2006	76,351	77
2007	107,558	41
2008	111,661	4
2009	114,316	2

Source: Data from HUD. Year-to-year percentage change calculated by CRS.

a. HECMs could not be made for part of FY2000 (July to early October 2000) because FHA insurance authority had been exhausted temporarily.

b. HUD ran out of insurance authority and could not insure HECMs during the last two weeks of September 2003.

HECM Loan Limit

Some proponents of the HECM program have long suggested that the law should be amended to provide a national HECM mortgage limit instead of having the limit be subject to the area FHA limit. The Housing and Economic Recovery Act of 2008 (HERA), P.L. 110-289, established a HECM mortgage limit equal to the conforming loan limit for Freddie Mac. HERA also provided that, effective January 1, 2009, Freddie Mac will have a general limit and a high-cost limit. The general limit is $417,000. In areas where 115% of median home price exceeds $417,000, the Freddie Mac limit will be the lesser of (1) 115% of the median home price or (2) 150% of the general limit (150% of $417,000 = $625,500). The general limit may be changed on January 1 of each year on the basis of changes in a home price index maintained by the newly created Federal Housing Finance Agency. The nationwide HECM limit is set at the Freddie Mac general limit of $417,000.

The American Recovery and Reinvestment Act of 2009, P.L. 111-5, increased the HECM loan limit to $625,500 for calendar year 2009. The Continuing Appropriations Act, 2010 (Division B of P.L. 111-88), provides a $625,500 national HECM limit during calendar year 2010.

Long-Term Care Insurance

As noted above, prior law provided that a borrower could waive the up front insurance premium for HECMs, provided that the HECM proceeds were used to pay for long-term care insurance.[23]

The law was very restrictive in that it required that all the proceeds of the HECM (after paying off any existing debt on the property) must be used exclusively for long-term care insurance. In exchange for savings on the insurance premium (which would be $4,000 on a $200,000 home), the homeowner would be giving up the option of using future HECM funds to pay for future home repairs, unexpected health costs, or increases in daily living expenses.

This feature made the proposal risky and unattractive to elderly homeowners. This provision has been removed from the law by P.L. 110-289.

Number of HECM Loans

The HECM program was begun as a demonstration program which authorized only 2,500 loans to be made under the program (50 per state).[24] The program has been made permanent and the limit on the aggregate number of HECMs that may be insured has been amended several times. It was raised to 150,000 by P.L. 106-569, to 250,000 by P.L. 109-13, and to 275,000 by P.L. 109-289.

The number of HECM loans now exceeds the 275,000 limit, and technically FHA can no longer insure such loans. Notwithstanding the limit in present law, however, the Consolidated Appropriations Act, 2010, P.L. 111-117, provides that FHA may continue to insure HECMs through September 30, 2010.

Aging in Place

Stephen Golant, a University of Florida professor and former consultant to the Commission on Affordable Housing and Health Facility Needs for Seniors in the 21st Century, suggests that the explosive growth of reverse mortgages may backfire for both elderly homeowners and the nation's cities.[25] He suggests that society should not romanticize the notion of older people aging in place in their homes and be blind to the downside.

According to Golant, the downside is that reverse mortgages encourage the elderly to remain in older housing that may be unsafe because of physical deficiencies. Holders of reverse mortgages are disproportionately poor, they often are in their 70s and 80s, and more likely to live alone. More than half occupy dwellings that are at least 40 years old, which means they are more likely to live in houses with physical deficiencies. They often do not make improvements in their homes that could help them avoid accidents. Golant suggests that we are doing a disservice to elderly homeowners by encouraging them to remain in such homes. Instead, the homes could be sold to younger home buyers who are more likely to make improvements to the homes which would contribute to revitalization of neighborhoods. Golant suggests that, although the elderly may prefer to remain in their own homes, many would be better off in places appropriate for their frailties and close to the support services they may need.

REFERENCES

[1] Ahlstrom, Alexis A, & Anne Tumlinson and Jeanne Lambrew. *Primer: Linking Reverse Mortgages and Long-Term Care Insurance.* The Brookings Institution. The George Washington University.

[2] Case, Bradford & Schnare, Ann B. (1994). "Preliminary Evaluation of the HECM Reverse Mortgage Program." *Journal of the American Real Estate and Urban Economics Association,* Summer.

[3] Cutler, Neal E. (2003). "Homeownership and Retirement Planning: Financial Worries and Reverse Mortgages." *Journal of Financial Services Professionals*, March.

[4] Davodoff, Thomas & Gerd Welke. (2004). *Selection and Moral Hazard in the Reverse Mortgage Market.* Hass School of Business, University of California at Berkeley, October 21.

[5] Eschtruth, Andrew D. & Wie Sun and Anthony Webb. (2006). *Will Reverse Mortgages Save Baby Boomers?* Boston College, Center for Retirement Research, Issue in Brief, No. 54. September.

[6] Gibler, Karen Martin & Joseph Rabianski. (1993). "Elderly Interest in Home Equity Conversion," *Housing Policy Debate*. Vol. *4*, Issue 4.

[7] Golant, Stephan. (1992). *Housing America's Elderly: Many Possibilities/Few Choices.* Sage.

[8] ——. (2004). *Why Urban Mayors Should Dislike Reverse Mortgages*. Paper delivered at the 57th Annual Scientific Meeting of the Gerontological Society of America, Washington, DC, November 20.

[9] Holt, Michael A. (1994). "House Rich but Cash Poor." *The CPA Journal*. Pp. 70-74, February.

[10] Kelly, Tom. (2005). *New Reverse Mortgage Formula: How to Convert Home Equity into Tax-Free Income*. John Wiley & Sons.

[11] Klein, Linda S. & Sirmans, C. F. (1993). "Financial Innovation and the Development of Reverse Mortgage Programs." *Benefits Quarterly*, First Quarter.

[12] Merlis, Mark. (2005). *Home Equity Conversion Mortgages and Long-Term Care.* Health Policy Institute, Long-Term Care Financing Project, Georgetown University, March.

[13] Quinn, Jane Bryant. (2006). "Mortgage Smarts," *Newsweek*, October 23.

[14] Sloan, Katrinka Smith. (1988). "New Developments in Home Equity Conversion." *The Real Estate Finance Journal*. Vol. *3*, Issue 4, March.

[15] Stucki, Barbara R. (2005). *Use Your Home to Stay at Home: Expanding the Use of Reverse Mortgages for Long-Term Care: A Blueprint for Action*, The National Council on the Aging, January.

[16] Symanoski, Edward J. Jr. (1994). "Risk and the Home Equity Conversion Mortgage." *Journal of theAmerican Real Estate and Urban Economics Association,* Summer.

[17] U.S. Bureau of the Census. (2003). *Current Population Reports*. pp. 70-88. *Net Worth and Asset Ownership of Households: 1998 and 2000*. May.

[18] U.S. Department of Health and Human Services, National Center for Health Statistics. (2006). *National Vital Statistics Reports, United States Life Tables, 2003*, Vol. *54*, No 14, April.

[19] U.S. Department of Housing and Urban Development. (2004). *Home Equity Conversion Mortgages: Long Term Care Insurance*; Proposed Rule, 69 F.R. 70344. December 3.

End Notes

[1] U.S. Census Bureau, *American Housing Survey for the United States: 2007*, Current Housing Reports, Series H150/07. Washington, DC, September 2008, p. 474.

[2] U.S. Census Bureau, *American Housing Survey for the United States: 2007*, Current Housing Reports, Series H150/07, Washington, DC, September 2008, p. 478.

[3] "Q and A on Grannie Mae," *Home Equity News*, National Center for Home Equity Conversion, No. 8, June 1984, p. 3

[4] Sloan, Katrinka Smith. "New Developments in Home Equity Conversion." *The Real Estate Finance Journal*, vol. 3, issue 4, March 1988, p 44.

[5] Kenneth R. Harney, "Settlement Shows How Costly Reverse Mortgages Can Be," *Washington Post*, February, 2003, p. H3.

[6] The mortgages were not initially available in Texas because state law prohibited reverse mortgages. Texas law has been subsequently amended to permit reverse mortgages.

[7] If the property has multiple owners, the youngest owner must be at least 62 years of age.

[8] Virtually all of the HECM loans are sold to the Federal National Mortgage Association (Fannie Mae). Since lenders generally make HECM loans with the intention of selling them to Fannie Mae, and since Fannie Mae only buys HECM loans that have adjustable rates, all HECM loans are made with adjustable interest rates.

[9] Fannie Mae will not buy HECM loans that feature equity sharing, so none are made with this feature.

[10] Section 593 of P.L. 105-276.

[11] Announcement to Terminate Home Keeper Reverse Mortgages, Reverse Mortgage Lender Letter 2008-3, Fannie Mae, September 3, 2008.

[12] For example, if a borrower had a $150,000 line of credit and had not drawn on it during the year, the next year the line of credit would be $157,500.

[13] No servicing fee is permitted in Illinois and Maryland.

[14] For details, see http://reversemortgagedaily.com/2008/06/18/financial-freedom-cash-account-discontinued/.

[15] Stucki, Barbara R. *Use Your Home to Stay at Home: Expanding the Use of Reverse Mortgages for Long-Term Care: A Blueprint for Action,* The National Council on the Aging, January 2005, p 9.

[16] Reverse Mortgage Daily, "Reverse Mortgage Industry Reaches 2% Market Penetration," press release, January 27, 2010, http://reversemortgagedaily.com/2010/01/27/reverse-mortgage-industry-reaches-2-market-penetration/ ? utm_source=Reverse+Mortgage+Daily&utm_ medium=email&utm_campaign=cd7758bd23-RMD+Email+RSS.

[17] This list is illustrative rather than exhaustive.

[18] Selling the home is not a requirement. The borrower or the heirs have the option of keeping the home and obtaining a loan or using other funds to repay the reverse mortgage debt.

[19] Medi-Cal in California.

[20] U.S. Department of Housing and Urban Development, *Federal Housing Administration Annual Management Report Fiscal Year 2009*, p. 56.

[21] U.S. Department of Housing and Urban Development, *Federal Housing Administration*, Annual Management Report Fiscal Year 2009, p. 64.

[22] U.S. Department of Housing and Urban Development, *Home Equity Conversion Mortgage (HECM)- Principal Limit Factors*, Mortgagee Letter 2009-34, Washington, DC, September 23, 2009.

[23] 12 U.S.C. 1715z-20(l)

[24] 12 U.S.C. 1715z-20(g)

[25] Stephan M. Golant. *Why Urban Mayors Should Dislike Reverse Mortgages*. Paper delivered at the 57th Annual Scientific Meeting of the Gerontological Society of America, Washington, DC, November 20, 2004.

INDEX

A

B

C

D

E

I

J

L

M

S

T

U

V

W

Y